DATE DUE			

The Old English Elegies

The end of *Soul and Body II* and the beginning of *Deor*, Folio 100a, *The Exeter Book*. Reproduced by permission of the Dean and Chapter of Exeter Cathedral

The Old English Elegies

New Essays in Criticism and Research

Edited by Martin Green

Rutherford • Madison • Teaneck
Fairleigh Dickinson University Press
London and Toronto: Associated University Presses

Associated University Presses, Inc.
440 Forsgate Drive
Cranbury, NJ 08512

Associated University Presses Ltd
25 Sicilian Avenue
London WC1A 2QH, England

Associated University Presses
2133 Royal Windsor Drive
Unit 1
Mississauga, Ontario
Canada L5J 1K5

Library of Congress Cataloging in Publication Data
Main entry under title:

The Old English elegies.

   Includes bibliographical references.
   1. Elegiac poetry, Anglo-Saxon—History and
criticism—Addresses, essays, lectures.   2. Anglo-Saxon
poetry—History and criticism—Addresses, essays,
lectures.   3. Exeter book—Addresses, essays, lectures.
I. Green, Martin, 1940–   .
PR207.04   1983   829'.1   82-48525
ISBN 0-8386-3141-X

Printed in the United States of America

Contents

Preface

This volume derives from two sections on the Old English elegies organized by Tim D. P. Lally at the 1979 Congress on Medieval Studies, Western Michigan University. In addition to the papers by Green, Hollowell, Johnson, Luecke, and Tripp, papers by John Miles Foley, Loren Gruber, and Tim Lally were presented at these sections. The papers by Anderson and Harris were read at other Old English sections at the Congresses in 1979 and 1980. The papers by Leslie, Nelson, Osborn, Raffel, and Renoir were written especially for this volume.

The editor and contributors thank Tim Lally for his efforts in organizing the original sections and for his work in helping to plan this volume.

A Note on Citations and Translations

Unless otherwise indicated, citations of the Old English elegies are from volume 3 of *The Anglo-Saxon Poetic Records, The Exeter Book,* ed. George Phillip Krapp and Elliott Van Kirk Dobbie (New York: Columbia University Press, 1936), and translations are by the authors of the individual essays.

Abbreviations

The standard abbreviations of journal titles adopted by the *MLA International Bibliography* are used throughout the notes to this volume.

Acknowledgments

For permission to quote from or reproduce copyrighted material, grateful acknowledgment is made to the following:

The Dean and Chapter of the Cathedral Church of St. Peter in Exeter (Exeter Cathedral) for permission to reproduce a leaf from the facsimile edition of *The Exeter Book.*

Columbia University Press for quotations from *The Anglo-Saxon Poetic Records,* ed. George Phillip Krapp and Elliott Van Kirk Dobbie. Vol. 3, *The Exeter Book* © 1936; Vol. 6, *The Anglo-Saxon Minor Poems* © 1942.

University of Nebraska Press for quotation from Burton Raffel, trans., *Poems from the Old English* © 1960.

New Directions for quotation from Ezra Pound, *Translations* © 1963 by Ezra Pound.

Faber and Faber for quotation from Richard Hamer, *A Choice of Anglo-Saxon* Verse © 1970; and Ezra Pound, *Translations* © 1963 by Ezra Pound.

Methuen for quotation from T. P. Dunning and A. J. Bliss, eds. *The Wanderer* © 1969 and Ida L. Gordon, ed. *The Seafarer* © 1960.

Oxford University Press for quotation from Charles W. Kennedy, trans., *An Anthology of Old English Poetry* © 1960.

Penguin Books for quotation from Michael Alexander, trans., *The Earliest English Poems* © 1966.

Manchester University Press for quotation from R. F. Leslie, ed., *Three Old English Elegies* © 1961.

University of California Press and Stanley B. Greenfield for quotation from *Old English Poetry: Essays on Style,* ed. Daniel G. Calder © 1979.

Phillimore and Co. and Joseph Harris for permission to reprint "Elegy in Old English and Old Norse: A Problem in Literary History," from *The Vikings,* ed. Robert Farrell © 1982.

Introduction

Martin Green

I

The poems conventionally called the Old English elegies—*The Wan-derer, The Seafarer, The Ruin, The Wife's Lament, Deor, Wulf and Ead-wacer, The Husband's Message, Resignation*—have, individually and as a group, long been the objects of curiosity and intense scrutiny by students of Old English literature. After *Beowulf,* they are the most frequently studied poems in the Old English corpus. Modern readers contemplate the ambiguities of these allusive and elusive products of Anglo-Saxon verbal art, but like Keats's Grecian urn, the poems are silent forms that "tease us out of thought." Like the urn, they seem to resist the most probing of scholarly questions.

What is known about the poems for certain is little enough. They are all found in one codex of the small number of volumes that survive of Old English verse. The Exeter Book, in which they are found, was probably written down sometime toward the end of the tenth century.[1] Beyond that, much is conjectured, speculated, ventured. The date of their initial composition and their authorship are unknown; whether they are one-time compositions or the products of an oral tradition is uncertain. Their relationship to the traditions of primitive Germanic poetry is difficult to determine; their function in a codex donated by an archbishop to his cathedral is puzzling. Several of the poems have suffered from the ravages that time works on ancient manuscripts and are so textually deficient that even the basic facts of how these poems begin and end and what they say cannot be known. Others present their narrative situations in so cryptic a fashion that scholars have to ask their own version of Keats's famous questions to the urn:

> What leaf-fring'd legend haunts about thy shape
> Of deities or mortals, or of both

11

> In Tempe or the dales of Arcady?
> What men or gods are these?

Despite the danger of becoming like Blake's "Idiot questioner who is always questioning/And never capable of answering," readers of the Old English elegies have persevered in addressing the basic genetic and philological problems because they are ultimately fundamental to the larger critical understanding of these poems. And it is understanding that is ultimately elusive but nonetheless sought because the poems, despite (or because of) their mystery, say something that speaks to us across the centuries. As Stanley B. Greenfield commented some years ago, the elegies appeal because they "treat of universal relationships, of those between man and woman . . . and between man and time . . . in a hauntingly beautiful way. . . . They, moreover, call attention in varying degrees to the transitory nature of the pleasures and security of this world."[2]

This concern with the transitory is a central preoccupation of many of the elegies. Its most moving and striking expression, in the final portions of *The Wanderer* and *The Seafarer* and throughout the fragmentary *Ruin,* is the stark imagery of the overthrow of human effort by time and darkness. In *The Wanderer,* ruins dotting the landscape are graphic reminders to the speaker that

> Eall is earfoðlic   eorþan rice,
> onwendeð wyrda gesceaft   weoruld under heofonum.
> Her bið feoh læne,   her bið freond læne. . . .

(All is hardship on earth; Wyrd's power changes
the world under the heavens. Here are possessions
fleeting; here are friends fleeting . . .)

In *The Ruin,* although the perspective may be less cosmic, the presence of what was once a splendid building or city is a reminder that time has swept away its former inhabitants:

> Hryre wong gecrong
> gebrocen to beorgum,   þær iu beorn monig
> glædmod ond goldbeorht   gleoma gefrætwed,
> wlonc ond wingal   wighyrstum scan. . . .

(The place has fallen to ruin . . . where formerly
many a man gladhearted and goldbright, adorned
in splendor, proud and wine-flushed, shone in wararmor. . . .

In *The Seafarer,* even without the physical image of ruin, there is a recognition that all is fleeting:

> Dagas sind gewitene,
> ealle onmedlan   eorþan rices;
> næron nu cyningas   ne caseras
> ne goldgiefan   swylce iu wæron. . . .

(The days are passing away, all the glory of earth;
there aren't kings and princes and goldgivers as
there were once. . . .)

In his fine essay "Image and Meaning in the Elegies," Edward B. Irving, Jr., has noted the connection of these motifs in the Old English elegies to a tradition stretching back to the Babylonian *Gilgamesh,* where Enkidu reports seeing in the "house of dust" "the kings of the earth, their crowns put away for ever; rulers and princes, all those who once wore kingly crowns and ruled the world in days of old."[3] Moreover, the biblical prophet, quoted by J. S. Cunningham, who sees that "All flesh is grass, and all the goodliness thereof is as the flower of the field," would find much to agree with in *Gilgamesh's* and the Old English vision of fallen glory.[4] And the mood and vision of these ancient authors echo in T. S. Eliot's *East Coker,* where "the captains, merchant bankers, eminent men of letters" "all go into the dark/The vacant interstellar spaces."[5]

Not only are the elegies suffused with the imagery of the ruins of fleeting time and the mutability of the world, but they also present evocative portrayals of loneliness and isolation. With the notable exception of *The Ruin,* the speakers of the elegies are in one way or another seeming isolates, cut off from human society. The Wanderer treads weary ways and navigates ice-cold seas without companionship. The Seafarer evokes the pains of winter weather suffered on night watch on a ship sailing perilously close to rocky cliffs; if he has any companions, he does not mention them. The speaker in *Wulf and Eadwacer* is on a fen-bound island, separated from Wulf, usually identified as her husband. Perhaps the most terrifying picture of isolation is in *The Wife's Lament,* whose speaker sits the summer-long day in a cave under an oak tree in a dim valley, aware that elsewhere in the world there are people together while she is *ana* "alone." This solitariness of the elegiac speakers anticipates a major strain of post-Romantic literature with its wanderers, isolates, and alienated individuals, but even the most isolated of figures in modern literature exist in some sort of social world. For the speakers in the Old English elegies, the isolation seems absolute and irrevocable and, as opposed to the voluntary solitude of Wordsworth or Thoreau, theirs is often without consolation and their emotions are far from tranquil.

But the universal resonances and seeming modernity of theme in the Old English poems, which are the grounds for their continued appeal, can also be a barrier to our perceiving their distinctiveness as a group in the canon of Old English poetry and as poems in themselves. It has often been noted that elegy in Old English is not the same as either that of the classical tradition, where the term refers to poems written in a specific meter on a variety of subjects, or that of the post-Renaissance tradition of poems lamenting the death of a friend, acquaintance, or community.[6] C. L. Wrenn, for example, maintains that it is only "the general meditation in solitude of what may be called universal griefs," as in Gray's "Elegy in a Country Church Yard," that is analogous to the Old English poems, and "it is only in the elegiac mood in Gray's sense that lyric expression [in Old English] . . . is usually to be encountered."[7]

Wrenn's is only one recent example of many attempts to define just what elegy is in Old English since the term was first used to describe these poems. The attempts have not always been successful and the debate over the appropriateness of the term has continued unabated. The attempt at a generic classification is nonetheless crucial because even though, as P. L. Henry argued, generic labels are often no more than empty terms serving for "greater convenience in description," they do set up expectations and preconceptions on the reader's part.[8] Early nineteenth-century scholars, for example, thoroughly familiar with pre-Romantic graveyard poetry and poems describing ruins, saw the Old English poems as generic ancestors. The identification of all eight poems as elegies was not immediate or universal, however. John Josias Conybeare, among the first to examine the Exeter Book thoroughly, recognized *The Wife's Lament* (called by him "The Exile's Lament") as "the only specimen approaching to the character of the Elegiac ballad" without specifying that character.[9] Later in the century scholars were still sparing in their use of the term. John Earle, for example, discussed *The Wanderer* and *The Ruin* as examples of "primary poetry" in Old English without using the word elegy,[10] and Richard Wülker, who considered *The Wanderer* and *The Seafarer* as poems of the school of Cynewulf, did not list the term in the index to his *Grundriss*.[11] The use of the term as a generic label to categorize the poems dates from the last quarter of the nineteenth century and the beginning of the twentieth, with articles in Paul's *Grundriss* by Brandl and Koegel and studies by Sieper and Heusler being particularly influential.[12]

Even when elegy became a more common term of description, however, its precise meaning was often elusive. For many scholars at the turn of the century, elegy was an authentic expression of the soul of the Germanic people, a major part of the often idealized and romanticized picture of pre-Christian Germanic life constructed out of evidence from Tacitus's *Germania, Beowulf,* other Old English poems, and the elegies themselves.[13] In that picture the comitatus, the complex structure of relationships of a warrior to his companions and his lord that defined each man's identity, obligations, and responsibilities, was the source of all value and the locus of all positive emotions. Separation from the comitatus—through the death of one's lord or the massacre of one's fellow warriors or through exile—would be the greatest of sufferings, and some of the elegies seem to depict individuals who have experienced such a separation and endured such a suffering. The contrast of the winter landscape of exile and separation with the imagery of the richness, joy, and security of the tribal hall, as in *The Wanderer,* is the central expression of the sense of deprivation, bereavement, and grief. The winter imagery is part of a complex of images comprising ruins, the sea, seabirds, fens, and woodlands that suggested to nineteenth-century scholars an inherent Germanic sensitivity to the natural world and an essentially realistic and melancholy attitude to life.[14]

A consequence of this view of the elegies was the attempt to eliminate from the texts those elements felt to be "inauthentic" intrusions of later tradition—specifically Christianity. The last lines of *The Wanderer* and nearly half of *The Seafarer,* with their homiletic insistence on the joys of heaven as the only true locus of man's happiness, were often singled out for scorn and condemnation. While some scholars acknowledged Christian influence on the elegiac mood and saw no inherent contradiction between Germanic and Christian attitudes, many, because of nationalistic prejudices, were unwilling to accept such influence or maintained that, if anything, Christian influence diminished the vigor and power of the old tradition.[15] They envisaged monkish redactors working over the pure gems of Germanic verse, adding awkward and often contradictory homiletic material to produce the texts that survive. Only *The Wife's Lament* and *Wulf and Eadwacer* seemed to have escaped this tampering. Such views, as Stanley demonstrates, continued well into the twentieth century. But despite the perceptual shortcomings of these scholars, they were right in seeing the mood and imagery of the elegies pervading Old English poetry, informing not only the poems in the Exeter Book, but also central to the atmosphere of *Beowulf,* especially the final third of the poem in which the fortunes of the Geats decline along with those of their king, and the laments of the Last Survivor and the Old Father set the mood and tone against which Beowulf battles the dragon.

Summing up the views of the elegies prevalent in the first part of the twentieth century, B. J. Timmer defined the characteristic elegiac elements as "the personal loss of the lord, the exile, the transitoriness of life, the comparison of former luck to present ill luck. . . ."[16] Timmer, however, questioned whether there was indeed a genre of elegy in Old English. In his view only *The Wife's Lament* and *Wulf and Eadwacer* were elegies "pure and simple," containing all of the characteristic elements; *The Ruin* was too ambiguous in its fragmentary form to determine whether it was or was not an elegy; *Deor* lacked "so many characteristically elegiac elements," particularly the tone of complaint; *The Husband's Message* was "all together different in tone" from the others; and *The Wanderer* and *The Seafarer* were distinctly "religious poems." While Timmer argued that elegy as a generic classification was suspect, he did insist that there was "an elegiac mood" in Old English and that poems such as *The Wanderer* and *The Seafarer* possessed elegiac elements that were "made subservient to religious propaganda." For Timmer, Christian culture prolonged the elegiac mood by adapting it for religious purposes and was not the cause of its decline, as some scholars had argued, nor the cause of its coming into being in the first place as the expression of nostalgia for the lost pagan past.

Timmer's recognition of the positive role played by Christianity in the shaping of the elegiac mood is representative of a shift in the view of the Old English elegies that marks a major portion of the criticism of the poems since the 1930s. In general, that criticism has emphasized the complex intellectual background of the Anglo-Saxon period and called into question some of the more facile generalizations about the relative paganism and Christianity of the Anglo-Saxons that earlier scholars had posited. Several notable studies argued for a link between the Old English elegies and the traditions of early Celtic poetry,[17] but more central has been the research into the Christian literature of the period and the uncovering of Latin homilies and poems that express similar ideas to the elegies in similar terms and images.[18] The work of leading Old English churchmen such as Alcuin reveals the extent to which the mutability of the world was a common topic in Christian writings of the time, and sermons from the earlier patristic period demonstrate how long-standing a theme it was.[19] In Christian tradition, however, the mutability of the world is not the grounds for complaint. St. Augustine's influential *City of God* taught the devout Christian to see this world as a vale of tears that had to be passed through on the way to man's true home—the *civitas Dei*. The central Christian belief in a final judgment of the world at the second coming of Christ assumes a finite world whose mutability and transitoriness are signs of the nearness of the last day.[20]

Against this intellectual background, *The Wanderer* and *The Seafarer* can be seen as poems reflecting the Christian faith in the final reward in heaven and expressing the Christian longing for that final heavenly peace. *The Seafarer* especially has been interpreted as an allegory representing the Christian soul's pilgrimage through the world—a pilgrimage undertaken freely *pro amore Dei.*[21] While the other elegies are even less explicitly Christian than *The Seafarer,* a number of studies have attempted to link them to the Latin-Christian background; *Deor,* for example, has been linked to one of the prime sources for ideas about the mutability of the world in the early Middle Ages, Boethius's *Consolation of Philosophy;* and even *The Wife's Lament* and *The Husband's Message* have been related to, among other things, The Song of Songs.[22]

Seeing the poems against the background of Christian Latin learning has been a corrective to the earlier tendency to dismember the poems into pagan and Christian elements; but seeing them in this way has further complicated the question of genre. A number of critics have proposed that other generic categories are more appropriate for one or another of the poems. The traditions of *planctus, consolatio, penitentia,* and *de exicidio* have been suggested along with such general categories as T. A. Shippey's labeling the group as "wisdom" poems.[23] But such is the force of tradition in scholarship that even though there is some agreement that the label of elegy is only approximate at best, the poems still are conventionally called by this name. A quarter-century after Timmer called the label into question as a generic title, Stanley B. Greenfield yet maintained that despite obvious differences among the poems, there were enough common elements to warrant a single generic rubric. Greenfield's definition is sufficiently general to encompass most—if not all—of the poems in the group; an elegy, in his words, is "a relatively short reflective or dramatic poem embodying a contrasting pattern of loss and consolation, ostensibly based upon a specific personal experience or observation and expressing an attitude toward that experience."[24] But as Greenfield recognized later, in *The Interpretation of Old English Poems,* "If the elegies are a genre in Old English, they are so by force of our present, rather than determinate historical, perspective; that is, by our 'feel' for them as a group possessing certain features in common" (p. 135). It may be, then, that no single definition, no matter how careful and compressed, as Greenfield's obviously is, can begin to encompass the poems as a group or account for their individual complexities and distinctiveness. Nonetheless, this line of examination of the Old English elegies is far from a dead issue.

Generic questions aside, seeing the poems against the Latin-Christian background has had other consequences, particularly the focusing of attention on the poems as individual works of art. The discovery of possible sources and parallels in the Christian tradition stimulated a fresh look at the poems' artistic strategies, and many critics have been able to argue with new evidence for the poems' integrity. The examination of the poems' artistic strategies has been aided in many cases by the application of the analytic methods developed by critics of modern poetry. Attention to imagery, diction, and structure has yielded insights into a number of Old English poetic practices. It has been shown, for example, how key underlying ideas link various images in the poems into complexes of associations;[25] how the temporal perspectives in the poems structure themes;[26] how wordplay and aural/oral effects create patterns;[27] and how syntax is a key instrument in building esthetic effects.[28] The application of modern critical methods to Old English poems, however, is fraught with many difficulties.[29] For one thing, Old English poetry was based on different premises from modern verse. In addition, there are many unresolved—and seemingly unresolvable—philological problems in the texts as they have come down to us.

One notable problem that has occupied a good deal of attention is the question of voice and point of view. Each one of the elegies has presented some problem in this regard. *The Wife's Lament* and *Wulf and Eadwacer,* for example, have traditionally been assigned a female speaker because of certain grammatical forms in the manuscript. While female speakers are not unknown in Germanic traditional poetry, they are not common in Old English, and some scholars have questioned whether in *The Wife's Lament,* at least, the identification of the speaker as a woman is a help or hindrance to our understanding of the poem with its obscure narrative situation.[30] While *The Wanderer* and *The Seafarer* have no such gender ambiguity, their seemingly diverse points of view have troubled many readers despite the many arguments for their unity. In the nineteenth century a number of suggestions were made that the poems were dialogues, even though the manuscript contains few of the modern devices generally used to indicate a shift of speakers. More recently, John C. Pope revived the question.[31] Although Pope later modified his view of *The Seafarer,* a number of subsequent studies continued to follow a similar line of argument.[32] On the other hand, there has been a large body of opinion convinced that the poems can be understood clearly enough without positing multiple voices.[33]

The period between 1940–70 was an active one in the criticism and scholarship of the elegies. Dominated by the work of Cross, Gordon, Pope, Smithers, and Whitelock, it culminated in the appearance of several individual editions of the poems—one of *The Seafarer* (Gordon, 1960), two of *The Wanderer* (Leslie, 1966, and Dunning-Bliss, 1969),[34] and a collective edition of *The Ruin, The Wife's Lament,* and *The Husband's Message* (Leslie, 1961)[35]—and Irving and Greenfield's general treatments of the poems as a group. *The Wanderer* and *The Seafarer,* as the two most complex poems, received a major share of attention, Bolton's "The Dimensions of *The Wanderer*" being perhaps the most comprehensive attempt to explicate that complexity. If there has been no study comparable to Bolton's appearing in the years since 1969, there have nonetheless been a number of excellent essays refining the view of *The Wanderer* and *The Seafarer* on points large and small. Several studies of specific passages in *The Wanderer* and *The Seafarer,* especially the images of the ruin and the seabirds and the motif of the beasts of battle, have filled in aspects of the intellectual background of the poems.[36] Several other studies have indicated new possibilities for understanding the moral and religious ideas of the poems as well as their artistic strategies.[37]

In general, in the period since the mid-1960s, the emphasis of the scholarship and criticism of the elegies has shifted away somewhat from *The Wanderer* and *The Seafarer* to the other poems in the group, *The Wife's Lament, Wulf and Eadwacer,* and *Deor* coming in for most of the scrutiny. As the most problematic of the elegies, these poems have been examined with an eye to unraveling the various narrative conundrums or exploring their dense allusiveness, especially in the case of *Deor.*[38] The number of differing interpretations, however, recalls W. W. Lawrence's comment in 1907 on the critical debate on *The Wife's Lament;* a review of "critical opinion from the beginning," he said, "shows a considerable lack of unanimity all along the line, and confirms the impression that the last word about the poem has not been spoken."[39] With some qualification, much the same could be said about the criticism of the elegies as a group and individually.

II

The essays in this volume do not offer last words either, nor is the volume as a whole intended to be a definitive compilation of all that is known and thought about the elegies. The attempt of each individual essay is to offer a perspective on its subject, and by bringing these essays together, the volume offers an indication of the kinds of critical problems students of the Old English elegies face, the kinds of answers that have been and continue to be given, and, perhaps, some of the future lines of argument.

The question of genre and the related question of cultural background are the subjects of the essays by Joseph Harris, Raymond Tripp, William Johnson, Ida Masters Hollowell, and Janemarie Luecke—all of whom reopen the question of the earlier background of the elegies. Joseph Harris is concerned with the "prehistory" of the elegies—or more precisely, their lack of one. Recent scholarship, he notes, has established "lateral sources and influences that provide more or less probable histories for particular motifs and expressions. . . . But . . . we have no mainstream, no old generic core. . . ." In a manner analogous to the reconstruction of Proto-Germanic words from attested forms in the recorded Germanic languages, Harris examines elements in the Old English poems and the poems in the Old Norse Edda and other sources to construct a "Common Germanic model" of the elegy—"a dramatic monologue spoken by a figure from a known heroic story who told in the first person about the joys and especially the griefs of his [or her] life." Harris's hypothetical reconstruction allows the reconstruction as well of a probable evolution from the common model, in which the story is known and the speaker is identified, to the Old English poems where the details of the story have become generalized, the narrative frame has dwindled away, and there is a "steady growth in the amount of gnomic and homiletic material. . . ." Harris's analysis, though brief, is judicious and challenging. He looks back to a tradition of Germanic scholarship to an extent abandoned in recent years and takes it to new insights.

Harris sees the death-song as a "sub-group of retrospective elegy," and it is to this tradition that Raymond Tripp, Jr., and William Johnson, Jr., call attention. For Tripp, the death-song is related to Old Germanic beliefs in the powers of Odin, among which is his ability, in his role as master of the house of the dead, to cause the dead to arise and tell their stories. Elements of these songs of the dead, Tripp argues, echo in the Old English elegies, especially the autobiographical form and the details of a "wintry eschatology." But Tripp is not positing an either/or choice about the sources of inspiration of the elegies—*either* pagan Germanic *or* Latin-Christian. He argues that "death and the varied responses to it . . . are not the property of any single tradition." Thus Tripp warns of the difficulty and "intricacy of searching out . . . the eschatological tradition buried in the Old English elegies." Johnson's reading of *The Wife's Lament* as death-song is directly influenced by Tripp's thesis. Taking the problematic cruces of the Lament as his starting point, Johnson argues that a narrator who dwells in a "ghostly world somewhere between this life and the next" accounts for the curious narrative situation of why "a woman must dwell in a surreal landscape and be confined to an *eorðscræf* under an oak tree . . . her movement . . . associated with dawn." Like Tripp, Johnson also suggests that the Old Norse tradition of death-song could be transvalued in the Old English Christian tradition to exploit its homiletic possibilities.

Like Harris, Ida Masters Hollowell notes that recent scholarship has emphasized the Latin-Christian background of the Old English elegies to the exclusion of the Germanic elements. Her own attempt to reach new understanding of the Germanic traditions in *The Wanderer* involves her identification of the speaker of the major portion of the poem as a *woðbora,* a seer whose insight into the future results from trances induced by some means—such as meditating on rune staves. The seer is a familiar figure in many ancient traditions—the Irish, for example, had their *fili*—and several Old English poems, such as *The Order of the World,* refer to one who has traveled extensively and has powers to see into the future. In *The Wanderer,* the description of the speaker sitting *sundor æt rune,* the speaker's own description of his travels and of his mind wandering far (lines 51–55), and the vision of the wasting of all things combine to create a circumstantial case to link the central figure in the poem to the tradition of the *woðbora.* Hollowell points out that the word *woðbora* is related etymologically to the name Woden, among whose attributes are wisdom, vision, and the invention of runes.

Janemarie Luecke's approach to the Germanic background of *Wulf and Eadwacer* is through anthropological studies that may help in explicating the social structure underlying this most elusive and difficult of the elegies. Luecke suggests that there are three anthropological ideas that can effect a reading of the poem—matriliny, exogamy, and totemism. Luecke constructs a case for a matrilineal structure in primitive Germanic society, a structure in which the bond between a woman and her blood kin is stronger than that between a woman and her husband's family, and in which the woman's older brother occupies a position of special importance. Such a structure may have left its traces in *Beowulf;* and in *Wulf and Eadwacer,* the *eadwacer* of the title, usually interpreted as the proper name of the speaker's husband, may represent the matrilineal older brother who has intervened in the speaker's marriage to protect his clan's interests. Exogamy is related to matrilineal structures, and the practice leads to divided loyalties, a familiar theme in Germanic saga and epic that could account for the emotional turmoil of the speaker in *Wulf.* Luecke also suggests that the beliefs associated with totemism can account for the notable cruces of the poem—the name *Wulf,* the epithet *hwelp,* and the verbs *apecgan* and *tosliteþ.*

The studies of literary problems in the elegies by Alain Renoir, Roy F. Leslie, Marie Nelson, Marijane Osborn, and Martin Green take the opportunity to examine some basic elements in the respective poems they treat. Based on close examinations of the texts and drawing on the large body of criticism and commentary, they provide detailed consideration of the textual, lexical, structural, and thematic problems in the poems. Their attempt is not always to offer new interpretations but to clear the ground for further interpretations.

In the same way as his essay "Wulf and Eadwacer: A Non-interpretation" brought some fresh perspective to that poem, Alain Renoir's reading of *The Ruin* emphasizes the ways in which the poem can be grasped as poetry even if we do not understand it fully. In the case of *The Ruin,* the barrier to understanding is the fragmentary text of the poem. But Renoir notes that by paying attention to what *is* in the text, we can determine some of its basic premises. Central to his reading are his observations that the poem "has a speaking voice but no speaker" and its "emotional frame of reference is a total vacuum which the modern reader must fill. . . ." The poem does, however, offer a perspective by its use of contrastive structure as the basis for its effect on readers.

Roy F. Leslie returns to the basic problem in *The Seafarer* of how the two halves of the poem work together. Ever since Ida L. Gordon's edition of the poem and Dorothy Whitelock's influential article arguing for it as a depiction of a Christian *perigrinans pro amore Dei,*[40] criticism of the poem has refined our appreciation of the poet's use of the traditional language of elegy and exile for Christian purposes. Leslie, however, sees previous analyses as being essentially either literal or allegorical, and his attempt here is to demonstrate that the poem works on both levels. For such a multilevel interpretation to succeed, he argues, "it must be consistent, that is, each level must be consistent within itself and compatible throughout with the other, and both must be closely related to the text." His careful examination of the text, offered as a kind of "feasibility study," provides analyses of the notorious cruces and ambiguities of the poem and of the structure as a whole. Particularly noteworthy are his discussions of how the first half of the poem prepares for the second and of the famous crux in which the speaker, having described his harsh life at sea, announces that he wishes to undertake a sea voyage, seemingly for the first time.

Resignation has occupied an ambiguous position among the elegies. The poem as we have it may be incomplete and it divides into two parts: a penitential prayer "with an elegy tacked on," as some have characterized it. In a sense the poem is a mirror image of *The Seafarer*, and Marie Nelson's reading of it, like Leslie's reading of *The Seafarer*, is an attempt to see the poem whole and account for the relationship of its parts. Using speech act theory as a means of analyzing the language and emotions of the first part of the poem, Nelson establishes that its single purpose is to "prepare the mind and soul [of the speaker] for death." But that preparation is a difficult one and the speaker does not reach the assurance of mind of the Seafarer; instead, the poem shows a "conflict between faith and fear." The speaker's failure to "express an absolute faith that his soul will find its way to God," Nelson argues, "may well be what makes *Resignation* an elegy."

Careful attention to verbal nuance and emotional overtones is also central to Marijane Osborn's stylistic and contextual analysis of *Wulf and Eadwacer*. Her consideration of the textual evidence in the first half of her essay highlights the enigmatic quality of the speaking voice, vocabulary, and syntax in the poem and sees that enigmatic quality as central to its emotional effect. The poem's emotional dilemma emerges as the poem progresses, and the reader's understanding of the situation emerges along with the speaker's own understanding; "in a sense the primary message of the poem is its strategy of awakening awareness." In the second part of the essay, Osborn offers an interpretation of the relationships that underlie the emotional conflict of the speaker. Rejecting the traditional "romantic" view of the poem as depicting a love triangle, Osborn argues that the conflicting loyalties are those generated within the family. She concludes that the speaker is best seen as the mother rather than the wife or lover of the Wulf figure who is the center of her emotional concern. She hints also that if this identification is right, the poem may also have wider implications.

My own essay on *The Wife's Lament* is a reconsideration of what is perhaps the central preoccupation of the elegies as a group—the problem of man in time. The attitude to time in these poems, however, is, in my view, more complex than that suggested by the definition of the elegies as poems that contrast past joy and present misery. *The Wife's Lament* is a poem that indeed stresses present misery as contrasted to past joy, but that past is so vaguely defined and has been so utterly obliterated by present circumstances that it seems to the speaker as if it never had been. Thus, the weight of the poem is on the present, a weight intensified by the absence of any future consciousness in the poem. How the time sense of the poem is related to and contrasts with the views of time in the ancient and early Christian world and the other elegies is explored to indicate the distinctiveness of *The Wife's Lament* as an artistic expression of great power.

The lexical, grammatical, and manuscript ambiguities of the elegies are only a part of the problem that confronts students of Old English poetry; there is also the question of tone and texture of the poems, and these problems are intensified for those attempting to translate the Old English poems into modern English. Burton Raffel examines a number of attempts—including his own—to translate selected passages from *The Wanderer* and *The Seafarer* and analyzes why he thinks the attempts have not been altogether successful. Raffel's comments are partially in response to Stanley Greenfield's recent essay on translating Old English verse.[41] Greenfield argued that a successful translation needs to "pay closer attention to the fusion of esthetics, lexicon, and syntax in Old English poems," but Raffel argues that it is just these areas that are so much in dispute, and he questions whether Greenfield's efforts at translation are any more successful than others'. For Raffel, translation is inevitably "a movement *away from* [an] original," involving "a series of compromises, of half truths. . . ." The bedrock issue, he concludes, is "[i]f poetry is what is lost in translation, what is it that one chooses to preserve?"

The final essay in this volume, by James Anderson, takes up *Wulf and Eadwacer* again. In Joseph Harris's scheme, *Wulf and Eadwacer* is the most archaic elegy in Old English, "still close to a specific heroic legend and offering little or no generalizing philosophy." The specific legend, however, is not known, and the allusiveness of the poem has frustrated many attempts to unravel it. It is thus not surprising that the three essays on *Wulf* in this volume should offer diverse (although occasionally overlapping) interpretations. The riddling and enigmatic qualities of the poem noted by Osborn are central to Anderson's argument. Like Osborn, he is concerned with textual and contextual evidence, especially the position of the poem in the Exeter Book before the first section of riddles and after *Deor*. In the past *Wulf* has been linked to the riddles—earlier editors identified it as Riddle #1—but it also shares its riddlinglike style with *Deor,* with which it also shares a distinctive structural technique—the use of a refrain—and a similarity of names (Deor/Wulf). Thus Anderson argues for an intimate connection between the poems, which he also links, on the basis of verbal echoes, to the poem that precedes *Deor* in the manuscript, the poem that Krapp and Dobbie label *Soul and Body II*. He sees this latter poem providing thematic underpinnings for the succeeding ones, and the three poems taken as a group form "a long triple riddle which equates heroic abduction with spiritual death and exposes pagan heroism as bitterly unheroic in the end." Even if originally separate poems, these three have been, in the cryptic words of *Wulf and Eadwacer*, "joined together" in the manuscript, and Anderson suggests how the person who did the joining may have left traces of his intentions.

In Ursula LeGuin's fine science fiction novel, *The Left Hand of Darkness*, the hero, an earthling on a distant planet, visits a religious cult whose members can see into the future but whose fundamental principle is the futility of asking questions about the future. If not exactly futile, it is difficult to foretell the future direction of the scholarship and criticism of the Old English elegies. The development of contemporary critical theory by structuralist and poststructuralist schools may offer new approaches to the poems, although the application of these methodologies to Old English poems has not yet been undertaken to any great extent.[42] When it is, it is likely to arouse dissent and objection, as many of the essays in this volume are likely to do, and in the dialectical way in which criticism operates, the attempts to answer basic questions will generate more questions. Nonetheless, in the millennium since the elegies were written down in the *mycel englisc boc* that Archbishop Leofric gave to Exeter Cathedral, it has been the questioning of these poetic foster children of the Anglo-Saxon age that has kept the rich tradition of preconquest English poetry from succumbing completely to "silence and slow time."

NOTES

1. The little that is known of the history of the Exeter Book is outlined by Krapp-Dobbie in *Anglo-Saxon Poetic Records,* and by R. W. Chambers, Max Förster, and Robin Flower in the facsimile edition, *The Exeter Book of Old English Poetry* (London: Lund and Humphries, 1933).

2. Stanley B. Greenfield, "The Old English Elegies," in *Continuations and Beginnings: Studies in Old English Literature* (London: Nelson, 1966), p. 142.

3. Edward B. Irving, Jr., "Image and Meaning in the Elegies," in *Old English Poetry: Fifteen Essays,* ed. Robert P. Creed (Providence, R.I.: Brown University Press, 1967), p. 159.

4. J. S. Cunningham, "'Where Are They?' The After-Life of a Figure of Speech," *Proceedings of the British Academy* 64 (1979):370.

5. T. S. Eliot, *The Complete Poems and Plays: 1909–1950* (New York: Harcourt, Brace and World [1952]), p. 126.

6. See, among others, Herbert Pilch, "The Elegiac Genre in Old English," *Zeitschrift für celtische Philologie* 29 (1964):209–24.

7. C. L. Wrenn, *A Study of Old English Literature* (London: Harrap, 1967), p. 139.

8. P. L. Henry, *The Early English and Celtic Lyric* (London: Allen and Unwin, 1966), p. 20. Cf. Stanley B. Greenfield, *The Interpretation of Old English Poems* (London and Boston: Routledge and Kegan Paul, 1972), pp. 12–13.

9. John Josias Conybeare, *Illustrations of Anglo-Saxon Poetry*, ed. William Daniel Conybeare (London: Harding and Lepard, 1826), p. lxxxi.

10. John Earle, *Anglo-Saxon Literature* (London: Society for Promoting Christian Knowledge, 1884).

11. Richard Wülker, *Grundriss zur Geschichte der angelsächsischen Litteratur* (Leipsig: Verlag Von Veit, 1885).

12. See B. J. Timmer, "The Elegiac Mood in Old English," *English Studies* 24 (1942):33–47, for a summary of early views.

13. For a summary of some characteristic attitudes of nineteenth and early twentieth-century scholars, see E. G. Stanley, *The Search for Anglo-Saxon Paganism* (Cambridge: D. S. Brewer; Totowa, N.J.: Rowman and Littlefield, 1974), pp. 53–64.

14. In addition to the critics quoted by Stanley, a good example of prevailing late nineteenth-century attitudes is provided in C. C. Ferrel, "Old Germanic Life in the Wanderer and Seafarer," *Modern Language Notes* 9 (1894):402–4. Cf. Charles Kennedy, *The Old English Elegies* (Princeton, N.J.: Princeton University Press, 1936), for a slightly modified view.

15. *Search for Anglo-Saxon Paganism*, pp. 53–64.

16. *ES* 24.

17. See Pilch and Henry (cited in nn. 6 and 8 above).

18. Some influential studies are: Bernard F. Huppé, "*The Wanderer:* Theme and Structure," *Journal of English and Germanic Philology* 42 (1943):516–38; Dorothy Whitelock, "The Interpretation of *The Seafarer*," in *The Early Cultures of Northwest Europe*, ed. Sir Cyril Fox and Bruce Dickins (London: Cambridge University Press, 1950), pp. 261–72; G. V. Smithers, "The Meaning of *The Seafarer* and *The Wanderer*," *Medium Ævum* 26 (1957):137–53 and 28 (1959):1–22; and J. E. Cross, "On the Genre of *The Wanderer*," *Neophilologus* 45 (1961):63–75.

19. A convenient compilation of sources and parallels for the OE elegies is provided in Daniel G. Calder and Michael B. Allen, *Sources and Analogues of Old English Poetry: The Major Latin Texts in Translation* (Cambridge: D. S. Brewer; Totowa, N.J.: Rowman and Littlefield, 1976).

20. Smithers, *MÆ* 26 and 28. See also Martin Green, "Man, Time, and Apocalypse in *The Wanderer, The Seafarer*, and *Beowulf*," *JEGP* 74 (1975):502–18.

21. See Whitelock (n. 18 above) and Ida L. Gordon, ed., *The Seafarer* (London: Methuen, 1960), and "Traditional Themes in *The Seafarer*," *Review of English Studies*, n.s. 5 (1954):1–13.

22. See, for example, Murray F. Markland, "Boethius, Alfred and *Deor*," *Modern Philology* 66 (1968):1–4; W. F. Bolton, "Boethius, Alfred, and *Deor* Again," *Modern Philology* 69 (1972):234–35; Michael J. Swanton, "*The Wife's Lament* and *The Husband's Message:* A Reconsideration," *Anglia* 82 (1964):269–90; and W. F. Bolton, "*The Wife's Lament* and *The Husband's Message:* A Reconsideration Revisited," *Archiv* 205 (1969):337–51.

23. See Rosemary Woolf, "*The Wanderer, The Seafarer*, and the Genre of *Planctus*," in *Anglo-Saxon Poetry: Essays in Appreciation*, ed. L. G. Nicholson and D. W. Frese (Notre Dame, Ind.: University of Notre Dame Press, 1975), pp. 192–207; Howell Chickering, Jr., "Thematic Structure and Didactic Purpose in Old English Elegiac Poetry: A Reclassification of Genre," Ph.D. diss., Indiana University, 1967; E. G. Stanley, "Old

English Poetic Diction and the Interpretation of *The Wanderer, The Seafarer,* and *The Penitent's Prayer,*" *Anglia* 73 (1955):413–66; Gareth W. Dunleavy, "A *De Excidio* Tradition in the OE *Ruin?*" *Philological Quarterly* 38 (1959): 112–18; and T. A. Shippey, *Old English Verse* (London: Hutchinson, 1972), pp. 53–79.

24. *Continuations and Beginnings,* p. 142.

25. Irving (see n. 3, above); Thomas C. Rumble, "From *Eardstapa* to *Snottor on Mode:* The Structural Principle of *The Wanderer,*" *Modern Language Quarterly* 19 (1958):225–30; and James L. Rosier, "The Literal-Figurative Identity of *The Wanderer,*" *PMLA* 79 (1964):366–69.

26. Daniel G. Calder, "Perspective and Movement in *The Ruin,*" *Neuphilologische Mitteilungen* 72 (1971):442–45.

27. Roberta Bux Bosse, "Aural Aesthetic and the Unity of *The Seafarer,*" *Papers on Language and Literature* 9 (1973):3–14; Eugene Kintgen, "Wordplay in *The Wanderer, Neophilologus* 59 (1975):119–27.

28. Greenfield, *Interpretation of Old English Poems,* pp. 117–22.

29. Ibid., *passim;* see also, N. F. Blake, *The English Language in Medieval Literature* (London: Dent, 1977).

30. Rudolph C. Bambas, "Another View of *The Wife's Lament,*" *JEGP* 62 (1963):303–9, and Martin Stevens, "The Narrator of *The Wife's Lament,*" *NM* 69 (1968):72–90.

31. John C. Pope, "Dramatic Voices in *The Wanderer* and *The Seafarer,*" in *Franciplegius: Medieval and Linguistic Studies in Honor of Francis Peabody Magoun, Jr.,* ed. Jess B. Bessinger, Jr., and Robert P. Creed (New York: New York University Press, 1965), pp. 164–93.

32. John C. Pope, "Second Thoughts on the Interpretation of *The Seafarer,*" *Anglo-Saxon England* 3 (1974):75–86. Cf. W. F. Bolton, "The Dimensions of *The Wanderer,*" *Leeds Studies in English,* n.s. 3 (1969):7–34, and Earl Anderson, "Voices in *The Husband's Message,*" *NM* 74 (1973):238–46.

33. Stanley B. Greenfield, "*Myn, Sylf,* and Dramatic Voices in *The Wanderer* and *The Seafarer, JEGP* 68 (1969):212–20.

34. R. F. Leslie, ed., *The Wanderer* (Manchester: Manchester University Press, 1966); T. P. Dunning and A. J. Bliss, ed., *The Wanderer* (London: Methuen, 1969).

35. *Three Old English Elegies* (Manchester: Manchester University Press, 1961).

36. Among other examples see: Christopher Dean, "*Weal wundrum heah* and the Narrative Background of *The Wanderer,*" *MP* 63 (1965):141–43; P. J. Frankis, "The Thematic Significance of *enta geweorc* and Related Imagery in *The Wanderer,*" *Anglo-Saxon England* 2 (1973):253–69; Kathryn Hume, "The Concept of the Hall in OE Poetry" *ASE* 3 (1974):63–74, and "The Ruin Motif in OE Poetry," *Anglia* 94 (1976):339–60; Tony Millns, "*The Wanderer* 98: *Weal wundrum heah, wyrmlicum fah,*" *RES* 28 (1977):431–38; Peter Clemoes, "*Mens absentia cogitans* in *The Seafarer* and *The Wanderer,*" in *Medieval Literature and Civilization: Essays in Honor of G. W. Garmonsway,* ed. D. A. Pearsall and R. A. Waldron (London: Athlone, 1969), pp. 62–77; Marijane Osborn, "The Vanishing Seabirds in *The Wanderer,*" *Folklore* 85 (1974):122–27; Niel Hultin, "The External Soul in *The Seafarer* and *The Wanderer,*" *Folklore* 88 (1977):39–45; and George Hardin Brown, "An Iconographic Explanation of *The Wanderer,* lines 81b–82a," *Viator* 9 (1978):31–38.

37. See, for example, Daniel G. Calder, "Setting and Mode in *The Seafarer* and *The Wanderer,*" *NM* 72 (1971):264–75; A. P. Campbell, "*The Seafarer:* Wanderlust and Our Heavenly Home," *Revue de l'Université d'Ottawa* 43 (1973):235–47; F. N. M. Diekstra, "*The Wanderer* 65b–72: The Passions of the Mind and the Cardinal Virtues," *Neophilologus* 55 (1971):73–88; James F. Doubleday, "The Three Faculties of the Soul in *The Wanderer,*" *Neophilologus* 53 (1969):189–93; D. R. Howlett, "The Structures of *The Wanderer* and *The Seafarer,*" *Studia Neophilologica* 47 (1975):313–17; William Klein, "Purpose and the 'Poetic' of *The Wanderer* and *The Seafarer,*" in Nicholson and Frese, pp. 208–23; Lars Malmberg, "Poetic Originality in *The Wanderer* and *The Seafarer,*" *NM* 74 (1973):220–23; Marijane Osborn, "Toward the Contemplative in *The Wanderer,*" *Studia Mystica* 1 (1978):53–69.

38. Extensive references to the problems in *WL* can be found in the notes to the essays by Green and Johnson in this volume. On *Deor* see n. 22 above, and James L. Boren, "The Design of *Deor*," in Nicholson and Frese, pp. 264–76: Norman Eliason, "*Deor*—A Begging Poem?" In Pearsall and Waldron, pp. 55–61; Kevin S. Kiernan, "A Solution to the Mæðhild-Geat Crux in *Deor*," *English Studies* 56 (1975):97–99, and "*Deor*: The Consolation of an Anglo-Saxon Boethius," *Neuphilologische Mitteilungen* 79 (1978):333–40; and Jerome Mandel, "Exemplum and Refrain: The Meaning of *Deor*," *Yearbook of English Studies* 7 (1977):1–9. On *The Ruin* see Calder (n. 26 above); James F. Doubleday, "*The Ruin*: Structure and Theme," *JEGP* 71 (1972):369–81; Arnold Talentino, "Moral Irony in *The Ruin*," *PLL* 14 (1978):3–10; and Karl P. Wentersdorf, "Observations on *The Ruin, MÆ* 46 (1977):171–80. On *Wulf and Eadwacer* see Norman Eliason, in *Old English Studies in Honour of John C. Pope*, ed. Robert B. Burlin and Edward Irving, Jr. (Toronto: University of Toronto Press, 1974), pp. 225–34; and Alain Renoir, "*Wulf and Eadwacer*: A Non-Interpretation," in *Franciplegius*, pp. 147–63. On *The Husband's Message*, see Margaret Goldsmith, "The Enigma of *The Husband's Message*," in Nicholson and Frese, pp. 242–63.

39. *MP* 5 (1907–8):387–405.

40. See nn. 18–20 above.

41. in Daniel G. Calder, ed., *Old English Poetry: Essays on Style* (Berkeley and Los Angeles: University of California Press, 1979).

42. John Miles Foley's paper, "Diction, Audience, and Genre in *The Seafarer*," read at the 1979 Congress on Medieval Studies, is an early attempt to apply reader-response criticism to an Old English poem.

The Old English Elegies

Translating Old English Elegies

Burton Raffel

However we define *elegy*, and for that matter however we define *translation*, I do not think there can be much disagreement about the importance of the elegiac *tone* in Old English poetry generally. As readers of poetry we go to different literatures, written at different times and in different tongues, for distinctly different reasons. Again, without defining what it is one can find, say, in the poetry of seventh-century B.C. Greece, clearly one reads that poetry expecting different things from what one finds in the poetry of T'ang China, or the poetry of Vedic India. Limitations of language, and of culture, and of time are turned to advantage when one recognizes just why certain poems and certain bodies of poetry have unique appeal, and therefore unique utility to their readers. Though there are love poems in the surviving corpus of Old English literature, we do not turn to Old English poetry when love poems are of primary interest. There are witty poems in that surviving corpus too, but they also are not our primary reason for reading. The elegiac, the narrative-heroic, and the lyrical are chief among Old English poetry's tones. For the witty and the erotic, as for the insouciant and the irreverent, or the colloquial and the plain, we must and indeed we do look elsewhere.

Carrying a tone out of one language, and one culture, and one time, and transporting it reasonably intact into a very different language, a very different culture, and a very different time, is patently difficult, risky, and even perhaps impossible. And the translation of Old English poetry, in particular, is even more difficult than is the translation of many other literatures, for the chief tones of Old English verse—again, elegiac, narrative-heroic, and lyrical—include only one even relatively straightforward tone, namely the narrative-heroic. Furthermore, narrative is rarely found in Old English verse without substantial admixtures of both the other dominant tones, elegiac and lyrical, and—still worse for the translator—in Old English poetry

31

these latter are singularly subtle, language- and culture-bound phenomena. It is reasonably easy to find or to invent an equivalent for most forms of wit, and for virtually all forms of eroticism. It is reasonably easy to work out equivalences for the insouciant and the irreverent, for the satirical, for the colloquial and the folksy plain. The lyrical is somewhat more difficult to reproduce, but—despite what the nontranslator may think—usually not fiercely difficult; as I have indicated, however, the high lyricism typical of Old English poetry is in fact more difficult than usual to render properly. But the elegiac tone is, I suspect, normally the most difficult of all to carry over into a new language and a new culture. I do not think it is impossible, given to be sure a high degree of poetic competence and literary understanding. And I should like to devote the bulk of this essay, accordingly, to a discussion of (1) the *specific* difficulties of the Old English elegiac tone, and (2) some of the good, and some of the bad, ways of handling those difficulties in translation.

Stanley B. Greenfield has recently argued that "a closer attention to the fusion of esthetics, lexicon, and syntax in Old English poems can lighten the darkness of even difficult portions of them, and thus help close the gap between us and the heart of the Anglo-Saxon poetic experience."[1] Greenfield's argument, meant in part to introduce his own new translations from Old English poetry, seems to me so pregnantly in error, and his translations so inadequate, that I want to use both argument and translations, here, as a kind of negative touchstone. The argument has three operative terms. He asserts that we must learn to use (1) esthetics, (2) lexicon, and (3) syntax as the *scop* used them, or as close to the *scop's* use as is possible in our time and in our very different language. But as every good linguist should know, Greenfield's second and third categories deal with material that is, in every language on earth, locked irretrievably into its original nexus. No amount of attention to Old English (or to French, or to Latin, or to Chinese) lexicon, or to Old English syntax, will be of very much use *in translating*, no matter how useful in dissecting (as opposed to translating) the original. And as to the first of Greenfield's categories, esthetics, surely one of the basic lessons of both linguistics and history is that the esthetics of the *scop* and his audience are richly worth studying— but in order to come to grips with the *scop's* time, not in order to somehow reproduce his forever-vanished time in our new world. This is indeed why the scholar must know the original language, in order fully to comprehend the mind and the spirit of another place and another time. The scholar cannot study that different time and place in translation: it is hard enough to reorient oneself while working with and through the original language, but it is virtually impossible while working with the inevitably distorting mirror of translation.

In matters of translation, in short, Greenfield displays the scholar's perpetual confusion: even when he is himself translating, the scholar is rarely able to escape the bondage of the original which he has probed and dissected for so many years. In translation, bluntly, the scholar is usually 180 degrees in error. Instead of focusing on the new creation which, willy-nilly, he must produce when he translates, he insists on focusing—determinedly, heavily, almost at times exclusively—on the original. What this ignores, of course, is the inevitable fact that translation is a movement *away from* that original. Equally inevitably, translation is a series of compromises, of half-truths if you will: to insist on the truth whole and unchanged is to deny the possibility of translation. For translation necessarily involves a willingness on all sides—that is, on the part of both translator and reader—to permit and to accept loss as well as change. (Loss and change will inevitably take place, to be sure, whether the translator wishes them to or not, and whether the reader approves of them or not.) The scholar, accordingly, is not actually a translator, even when he translates, so much as he is a kind of "verbal copier"—to borrow a phrase from John Dryden, who knew whereof he spoke. And as Dryden scornfully but accurately concludes, verbal copying is "much like dancing on ropes with fettered legs: a man may shun a fall by using caution, but the gracefulness of motion is not to be expected. . . ."[2] As Dryden had learned from hard and elegant practice, the translator must start from a posture of relative freedom, subservient to both his original and his translation of that original, but with his focus on "gracefulness of motion" *in the translation.*

The stance of the verbal copier is thus a translational fallacy that must forever be combated, for it is an ingrained stance of the scholarly mind. If the war cannot and probably will not ever be won, it must in any event continue to be waged. Rather than choose my own weapons, I shall work with two of the passages chosen by Greenfield, one from *The Seafarer* and one from *The Wanderer;* it is hoped that it will be apparent which warrior is "best for the job of battle, the crashing/ Of standards, the thrust of spears, the cut/ And slash of dagger and sword. . . ."[3] But like Wiglaf on his way to help Beowulf against the dragon, let me pause to make it very clear that it is emphatically not Stanley B. Greenfield, scholar, with whom I propose to wage war. I have immense respect for Greenfield in what I think is clearly his proper role; like everyone concerned with Old English literature I have learned much, and probably appropriated much, from his scholarly writings. But it is Greenfield as a practitioner of, and a theorizer about translation against whom I have no choice but to struggle. And I have reason to think that when he wrote his challenging essay on "Esthetics and Meaning and the Translation of Old English Poetry," Greenfield well knew that he was embarking on an entirely new joust, with strange weapons, and on fields hitherto foreign to him.

> forþon nis þæs modwlonc mon ofer eorþan
> ne his gifena þæs god, ne in geoguþe to þæs hwæt,
> ne in his dædum to þæs deor, ne him his dryhten to
> > þæs hold,
> þæt he a his sæfore sorge næbbe,
> to hwon hine Dryhten gedon wille.[4]

These are the 39th through the 43d lines of *The Seafarer,* one of the two best-known and most frequently translated of Old English elegies. Richard Hamer, whose translation is by design as close to prose as he can make it ("I have tried to give the sense of the texts as closely as possible," he says of his versions[5]), renders these lines:

> Yet no man in the world's so proud of heart,
> So generous of gifts, so bold in youth,
> · In deeds so brave, or with so loyal lord,
> That he can ever venture on the sea
> Without great fears of what the Lord may bring.[6]

What are the specific difficulties of the elegiac tone here? (I assume axiomatically, again, that neither lexicon nor syntax will be of any use whatever in answering this question, for as Hamer accurately declares, "the structure of the language is now fundamentally different." And as for the *scop*'s esthetics, even Hamer concedes readily that "some of the stylistic features of Old English verse are . . . liable to sound absurd in modern English. . . ."[7]) It is of course hard to dissociate the tone of one small passage from the larger tonal reverberations in a poem of 124 lines, but if the passage is doing anything it is "celebrating"—in that odd fashion of mournful yet positive celebration practiced by almost all elegies in almost all literatures—the inevitable discrepancy between creator and created, between God and man. All men are only men; God alone is God; and man must never forget the crucial difference in status between himself and his creator, must never be tempted into hybris. And the sea, the poet assures us, in so huge and powerful and so irrationally motivated that the mere act of sailing out on its surface must remind us of that great gulf between ourselves and God, must and in the event does enforce upon us our necessary humility. The sea is in a sense God's agent, acting in the highest fashion pedagogically. By implication, in the face of a power so great and so manifestly untamable, we mere mortals are forced into a state of comprehension. God himself may perhaps seem unseeable, even unimaginable, but the sea is dreadfully, and therefore magnificently, tangible.

Hamer's translation contains the substantive core, but not the passion, of this passage. I think it could legitimately be argued that, just as an inadequate translation is in a sense no translation at all—since its inadequacy prevents the transference that is at the heart of translation—so too this translation essentially loses the elegiac tone that gives the passage its unique value. This is not the place to detail all the craftsmanlike means employed by the *scop* in creating the elegiac tone he wants. As I have said, the *scop*'s esthetics are pretty much locked into Old English, and into Old English culture and the time in which Old English poetry was composed. But what then is left for the translator, if he cannot rely upon the lexical, syntactical, and esthetic resources of the language and the culture and the time from which he is translating? Plainly, the translator must rely upon the lexical, syntactical, and esthetic features of the language and the culture and the time into which he is translating. His task is to bring those two sets of very different and unmatchable resources into as close a functioning equivalence as he can.

Before we look at what Ezra Pound has done with this passage from *The Seafarer*, let me simply cite Hugh Kenner's considered judgment that Pound's version is a "conspicuous success," and that "underlying conspicuous success of the *Seafarer* order is Pound's conception of what the poet's job is: the rendering, without deformation, of something, within him or without, which he has clearly apprehended and seized in his mind."[8]

> For this there's no mood-lofty man over earth's midst,
> Not though he be given his good, but will have in his
>   youth greed;
> Nor his deed to the daring, nor his king to the faithful
> But shall have his sorrow for sea-fare
> Whatever his lord will.[9]

In simple prose—for Hamer has written his plain translation in blank verse and some deformation can occur even in such limitedly poetic transformation—the passage can be rendered: "For there is no man on earth so proud-spirited (brave), of such excellent endowment, nor so bold a youth, nor so courageous in his actions, nor to whom his lord (or God) has been so gracious, that he feels no anxiety when he puts to sea, no fear of what God will do to him." Pound's version does not square well with this or with Hamer's very similar rendering. In plain fact, it does not square well with the original that both this prose version and Hamer's plain verse rendering attempt to translate. I have argued elsewhere that Pound is primarily interested, in his translation of *The Seafarer,* in presenting some sense of Old English prosody, and not in presenting what is usually called the "meaning" of the poem. Indeed, not only is there a limited sense in which Pound's version of the passage at issue has any meaning at all, but—to quote myself for just a moment—Pound's other, though clearly secondary "purpose is to present the secular harshness, the grey, drizzling, painful old landscape, the groans and aches of the body. The elevation of the soul is no part of that music; Pound extirpates it relentlessly and with admirable consistency."[10] That is not to say, however, that Pound's is either bad translation or in fact no translation at all. To translate the prosody, which I happen to believe Pound has done better than anyone else, is after all to translate something significant. And there clearly is a kind of passion in Pound's rendering. On the other hand, just as clearly it is not really the same passion that motivated the *scop,* and in that respect Pound has largely missed precisely what we are here discussing, namely, the elegiac tone of *The Seafarer.* The "celebration" of man's limitations, his dependency on God, is almost completely absent from his translation.

Greenfield's version, equally clearly, offers us the same sense offered by Hamer's version and by the plain prose rendering I concocted earlier:

> for there's no man on earth so sea-
> soned in spirit, so sure of fortune,
> so graced by youth and a gracious lord,
> that in his sea-faring he has no care
> of what the Lord has in store for him.[11]

And since Greenfield carefully sets this rendering against my own, let me do the same thing here:

> But there isn't a man on earth so proud,
> So born to greatness, so bold with his youth,
> Grown so brave, or so graced by God,
> That he feels no fear as the sails unfurl,
> Wondering what Fate has willed and will do.[12]

The basic sense in both Greenfield's and my translation is much the

same. It is not for me to prejudge readers' reactions, but I think it is
not prejudicial, or even inappropriate, for me to say that there seems
to me to be a lot more of the *scop*'s poetic passion in my own version.
"The English poet . . . does not translate words," says Hugh Kenner,
speaking as before of Ezra Pound's work. "The words have led him
into the thing he expresses . . . [and] he may deviate from the words, if
the words blur or slide, or if his own language fails him."[13] Plainly,
Greenfield has been no more bound by the *words* than I have—though
he seems to think that he has. He mutes the *scop*'s *sorge* into "care,"
which is a downgrading of the emotion involved. "In store for him" is
no more an "exact" rendering of *to hwon hine Dryhten gedon wille* than is
my rendering, "has willed and will do." Indeed, it is arguably rather
less exact, if exactitude is any sort of standard. (Though exactitude is,
at least in theory, an important standard for Greenfield, it is not any
more important to me than, in practice, it turns out to be in his
translations.) The atrocious pun of "sea-/soned in spirit," which vio-
lates not only the sense of decorum of the original but also the orthog-
raphical spirit of Old English verse generally, is curiously defended
by Greenfield in terms that he strongly objects to when employed by
others, notably myself. "And the punning I have *sea*-soned my translation with, while not 'true to' the original passage in all respects, *is* an
esthetic 'equivalent,' taking the poem as a whole."[14] As I have indicated, this is more than dubious; it is in my judgment totally false. No
Old English poem, and no Old English poet, would, could, or, to my
knowledge, ever did do anything even vaguely similar.

Greenfield appears to think that the chief distinction between our
two renderings, and the chief claim to merit of his own, is the translation of *dryhten* in line 41, the third line of the passage at issue here. He
says: "What Raffel has missed here is the deliberate contrast the Old
English poet makes between the earthly *dryhten* whose favor the seafarer (or any-man) may have gained and the heavenly *Dryhten* whose
favor he is concerned about on his sea-voyage; and in omitting this
interplay Raffel has falsified both the esthetic and the meaning of the
poem. Perhaps in this connection we might reverse Keats's lines and
say that *un*heard melodies are sweet, but *heard* ones are sweeter!"[15]
The problem is that the "deliberate contrast" is in fact not so deliberate, and is perhaps nonexistent. To start with, the manuscript does
not make the orthographic distinction employed by Greenfield to
stress and bolster his argument: *dryhten* has no capital in the manuscript in either of the two lines at issue, and indeed no capital is used,
for either line, in the Krapp-Dobbie edition. The capital letter is used
by I. L. Gordon, in her fine little edition, by now pretty much the

standard text of *The Seafarer*. But even Gordon, though she makes the editorial interpretation Greenfield would wish her to make, is very much less certain than is Greenfield. She writes, measuredly, that "*his dryhten* appears to be his earthly lord, distinct from *Dryhten*. . . . The repetition is probably a deliberate play on the word; see Introduction, p.26."[16] When we turn to page 26 of the introduction, interestingly, we find that the scholarly support cited for the use of the capital letter is an article by S. B. Greenfield—and solely that article. The partial circularity of Greenfield's argument becomes still clearer when we recall Krapp-Dobbie's sensible warnings to the effect that "[when] an Anglo-Saxon poem does not fulfill modern expectations with regard to structural unity and coherence," this fact should not be made the basis for serious analysis; both *The Wanderer* and *The Seafarer*, they note correctly, have a good many "minor inconsistencies" and "abrupt transitions," by modern standards.[17] Greenfield may be correct, in short, that the *scop* intended a distinction between one *dryhten* and another *dryhten*, but neither Greenfield nor I have the right, on the evidence available, to be quite so sure as he is of his rectitude, nor quite so enthusiastically condemnatory of others. Again, one can maintain, as Greenfield does, that translating *sæfore* as "sea-faring" "may unfurl no sails, but perhaps it offers more sustenance for the providential contrast between the fortunes *ofer eorþan* and the literal-/symbolic sea which informs the esthetics and meaning of the Old English poem."[18] But one can also urge, just as reasonably, that introducing the basic sense of *Wyrd*, "Fate," offers quite as much intellectual sustenance. What Greenfield does not seem able to perceive, fairly plainly, is that hoisting yourself up by your boot-straps is an intellectual process of singular dubiousness. (Nor does he see the poetic loss involved in choosing something like "sea-faring" for the more evocative "as the sails unfurl." Or if he does see and understand it, he does not seem to perceive its fundamental importance, as I have all along been arguing, for the success and value of any verse translation.)

The Wanderer, which together with *The Seafarer* forms the best-known and arguably the most representative grouping of Old English elegies, is in fact a much different poem. "The simiarity of style, thought, and emotion, between *The Wanderer* and *The Seafarer* is such that they are usually taken together, even though two poems separate them in the Exeter Book," says Bruce Mitchell.[19] This is surely a defensible position, though I am not myself entirely confortable with it: in my *Poems From the Old English* there are nine, and not just two poems, separating these two primary elegies. *The Wanderer* seems to me a more secular poem, and markedly less celebratory. The *scop* who produced *The Seafarer* seems to me much more positive about heaven and its reward; his focus seems to me less strongly on the things of this world than on the rewards of the next. The diction and thus the tone of *The Wanderer,* accordingly, seem to me more hard-edged; the movement of the verse, too, strikes me as somewhat shorter-breathed, less sweeping, less soaring—though these are definitely impressionistic reactions, founded less on analytical study than on poetic intuition, and though I of course recognize that any evaluation of Old English verse movement is tentative, given our continuing uncertainty about how the *scops* themselves sounded their poetry.

> Wat se þe cunnað
> hu sliþen bið sorg to geferan
> þam þe him lyt hafað leofra geholena:
> warað hine wræclast, nales wunden gold;
> ferðloca freorig, nalæs foldan blæd;
> gemon he selesecgas ond sincþege,
> hu hine on geoguðe his goldwine
> wenede to wiste—wyn eal gedreas![20]

Hamer's translation of this passage, lines 29b–36 of a 115-line poem, is once again a good starting point, in substitute for a plain prose version: note that seven-and-a-half lines of Old English here expand to nine-and-a-half lines of modern English:

> He knows who has experienced it how bitter
> Is sorrow as a comrade to the man
> Who lacks dear human friends; fair twisted gold
> Is not for him, but rather paths of exile,
> Coldness of heart for the gay countryside.
> He calls to mind receiving gifts of treasure
> And former hall-retainers, and remembers
> How in his younger years his lordly patron
> Was wont to entertain him at the feast.
> Now all that joy has gone.[21]

Critics are apt to comment, in comparing *The Wanderer* and *The Seafarer,* on the tighter, more logical structure of the former. From the translator's point of view, however, it seems to me that *The Wanderer* is a great deal more difficult to bring over into modern terms. Its very specificities lock it that much more firmly into Old rather than New English culture. The *geholena* ("confidants, friends, protectors") of the original have no strict modern counterpart; *wunden gold* ("twisted, worked gold"—i.e., rings, the medium of exchange, as it were, of the *comitatus*) has no modern counterpart whatever, nor does *sincþege* ("the receiving of treasure"). That is, the *concepts* of the *scop*'s poem are more alien to us, today, than are by and large the concepts of *The Seafarer*. Good translation is inevitably very much more difficult under such circumstances, and is equally inevitably bound to be distinctly freer. To repeat Hugh Kenner's words, in this very different context: the translator "may deviate from the words, if the words blur or slide, or if his own language fails him." Lacking a Poundian version, here is the self-assertedly Poundian rendering of Michael Alexander:

> He knows who makes trial
> how harsh and bitter is care for the companion
> to him who hath few friends to shield him.
> Track ever taketh him, never the torqued gold,
> not earthly glory, but cold heart's cave.
> He minds him of hall-men, of treasure-giving,
> how in his youth his gold-friend
> gave him to feast. Fallen all this joy.[22]

It would be hard to turn out a more confused rendering, I am afraid, and most especially in the all-important matter of tone. Alexander jumbles together pseudo-King James, and a kind of invented medieval pidgin ("He minds him of hall-men"), and his own brand of Poundian obscurity ("Track ever taketh him"), and veers in general between the lofty ("never the torqued gold") and the more or less low ("Fallen all this joy"). But then, earlier in the poem, he turns *Swa cwæð eardstapa*, "So (or thus) spoke (or said) the wanderer," into the literally atrocious "Thus spoke such a 'grasshopper'"—and the fashionable use of single quotation marks cannot save so awful a rendering. Whatever the problems of the original, this is no way to escape them. It is one thing to argue, as Robert Lowell does in his much misunderstood book, *Imitations,* that "I have been reckless with literal meaning, and labored hard to get the tone."[23] Alexander—here and throughout his translations from Old and Middle English—has been consistently reckless, feckless, and unsuccessful.

A much more responsible translator, Kevin Crossley-Holland, struggles doggedly—much too doggedly, in the event—with these lines:

> He who has experienced it
> Knows what a cruel companion sorrow can be
> To any man who has few loyal friends.
> For him are the ways of exile, in no wise twisted gold!

For him is a frozen body, in no wise the fruits of the earth!
He remembers hall-retainers and how in his youth
He had taken treasure from the hands of his gold-friends
After the feast. Those joys have all vanished.[24]

The tone is at least consistent. But it is not so much elevated as, again, dogged: the Old English elegiac is never so confused or so frequently low as Alexander makes it, but neither is it so clotted and heavy as Crossley-Holland here presents it. The Old English may seem to have similar breath-markers, but the translator cannot escape, nor in my judgment should he try to escape, from the impossibility of sound-transference. Says the *scop,* pungently, *gemon he selesecgas ond sinc-þege,/hu hine on geoguðe his goldwine/wenede to wiste,* and the staccato movement of the Old English propels the verse forward, keeps it taut and swift. It is almost impossible to read Crossley-Holland's rendering of these lines straight through to the end of the syntactical unit: "He remembers hall-retainers and how in his youth/He had taken treasure from the hands of his gold-friends/After the feast." To put it differently, Old English only *seems* agglutinative: its piled-up syntax, like its piled-up metaphors, reverberates far more like crashing cymbals than like a pounding bass drum. The translator cannot ape the formal patterns of his original; the best he can do is tap his own and his own language's resources to find or to construct (or even to fake) some sort of equivalent. In Hugh Kenner's extraordinarily well-chosen words, "what [the translator] writes is a poem of his own following the contours of the poem before him."[25] Crossley-Holland has unfortunately not written any sort of poem here; to some degree he has been trapped by the scholarly mis-focus I spoke of earlier and, seeing the original so terribly clearly, he has failed to look hard enough at the translation.

There was an older imitative fallacy, perhaps best exemplified by the translations of Charles W. Kennedy, which ought to be mentioned at this point. Analysis of Kennedy's rendering does not seem to me necessary, after all that has been said already. The lines speak, or do not speak, for themselves:

Who bears it, knows what a bitter companion,
Shoulder to shoulder, sorrow can be,
When friends are no more. His fortune is exile,
Not gifts of fine gold; a heart that is frozen,
Earth's winsomeness is dead. And he dreams of the hall-men,
The dealing of treasure, the days of his youth,
When his lord bade welcome to wassail and feast.
But gone is that gladness.[26]

Rudyard Kipling might have liked Kennedy's version—most especially that "shoulder to shoulder" heartiness, which has no reference to anything in the Old English. But though more fluent than either Alexander's or Crossley-Holland's renderings, Kennedy's is heavily dated by now, hopefully the last gasp of the so-called "lift-dip" school. All the same, Kennedy's version helps underline the point I made earlier: translators are of necessity forced to struggle and to produce freer translations, when the original is as difficult as *The Wanderer*. Crossley-Holland, once again, sticks too closely to his last, and turns out an extremely pedestrian likeness of the original. Kennedy does not, I think, do well here, but because he allows himself more freedom he does better.

Greenfield falls, I think, somewhere between Kennedy and Crossley-Holland:

> He knows who him-
> Self has sorrow as his sole friend
> How cruel a lot such a comrade is:
> His the dark of exile, not bright gold,
> Cold heart, not warmth-enfolding glory:
> He recalls the warriors in the hall,
> Fair treasure given, how bright feasts were
> Before his lord when young—lost now, all.[27]

Greenfield's freedoms do not, I suspect, need enumeration by this point, though a few that are peculiar to his version are worth noting. Says the *scop*, "*lyt . . . leofra geholena*," "few . . . beloved friends/confidants/protectors," and Greenfield turns this into "sole friend." The wanderer has *sorg to geferan*, "sorrow as a comrade," the *scop* tells us, and that *sliþen biδ*, "is cruel." Greenfield expands the phrase to "How cruel a lot such a comrade is," there being of course no textual authority for "a lot." *Waraδ hine wræclast, nales wunden gold*, the *scop* reports: "It is the path of exile which holds/preoccupies him, not at all the wound/twisted/worked gold." Greenfield adds that the exile is "dark," which is not in the original, and turns the gold into something "bright" rather than something twisted or worked. Again, I point out these freedoms not to condemn the version Greenfield has produced, but only to indicate both that freedoms are necessary with a text like this, and also that Greenfield's forthright claim to greater *authority* than previous translators—because, that is, he sees his versions as closer to the true esthetic of the original, as well as closer to the lexicon and to the syntax of the original—is to say the least doubtful.

On another level Greenfield's version strikes me as unusually clumpy, from the awkward inversion of "He knows who himself has sorrow had," to the strained and obscure syntax of "how bright feasts were before his lord when young." This heavy, soggy verse no more matches, or translates, the crisp Old English original than does Greenfield's almost Poundian ending, "lost now, all!" The *scop* says, with beautiful (but not truncated) simplicity, *wyn eal gedreas,* "That joy/delight is all/entirely fallen/vanished/perished." Even Hamer's plain rendering, "Now all that joy has gone," is clearly infinitely closer to the esthetic, to the lexicon, and to the syntax of the *scop*.

In my own version, finally, I struggled quite as hard as have all the other translators. Indeed, I began my career as a translator of Old English with this poem, and my first attempt, consigned to the trash bin almost thirty years since, began on the thoroughly mistaken assumption that Old English prosody and syntax should and could be carried over into our modern language. The patent failure of the attempt—which I can recall as sounding rather like brisk hail on a flat tin roof—is surely in part responsible for the freedom of my translation, perhaps even as much responsible as is the difficult nature of the original. My translations's strategy—and as I have been pointing out repeatedly, all translators of *The Wanderer* are obliged, willy-nilly, to have a strategy: they cannot simply and blindly translate the Old English words of this poem if they are to produce anything worth reading—is to personalize the *scop*'s third-person elegiacs. Not that the *scop* does not himself personalize in much of the poem: *oft ic sceolde,* he writes, and *mine ceare, ic to sope wat ic hean ponan,* and so on. That is, my personalization is by no means without warrant in the original; it is however clearly an extension of the *scop*'s poem and not a mirror-image transference:

> How cruel a journey
> I've travelled, sharing my bread with sorrow
> Alone, an exile in every land,
> Could only be told by telling my footsteps.
> For who can hear: "friendless and poor,"
> And know what I've known since the long cheerful nights
> When, young and yearning, with my lord I yet feasted
> Most welcome of all. That warmth is dead.[28]

As Robert P. Creed assured me twenty years ago, "This is the most 'impressionistic' of all your translations. . . ."[29] I would not translate it the same way were I to tackle it now; to be perfectly honest I am not even sure that, in passages like this, I even like my version as much as once I clearly did. On the other hand, Creed's prediction that this version would "arouse the most controversy" of any of the renderings in *Poems From the Old English* has proved to be wrong, and I can only think that the reason for his error lies in the nature of the Old English original rather than in the nature of my translation. I find it hard to defend this passage, though I have no great desire to attack it. And for all my doubts I find it, still, a good deal better than Greenfield's—for what the M.B.A.'s of America like to call "the bottom line" remains, to quote myself for the last time, that "Only the original is the original. . . . If poetry is what is lost in translation, what is it that one chooses to preserve?"[30] This is the bedrock issue in "Translating Old English Elegies," to my mind: it is a task for the poet, not for the scholar, and I have not the slightest doubt that the poet's hesitations are vastly preferable to the scholar's certainties. In the end it is talent and not knowledge, it is ability and not speculative insight, it is music and not philosophy which lift and carry any and all translations of any poetry, Old English elegies included.

NOTES

1. Stanley B. Greenfield, "Esthetics and Meaning and the Translation of Old English Poetry," in *Old English Poetry: Essays on Style*, ed. Daniel G. Calder (Berkeley: University of California, 1979), pp. 109–10.

2. John Dryden, *Of Dramatic Poesy and Other Cricital Essays*, ed. G. Watson (London: Everyman's Library, 1962), 1:273.

3. "The Battle of Brunanburh," trans. Burton Raffel, *Poems from the Old English*, 2d ed. (Lincoln: University of Nebraska, 1964), p. 25.

4. *The Seafarer*, ed. I. L. Gordon (London: Methuen, 1960), pp. 38–39.

5. Richard Hamer, *A Choice of Anglo Saxon Verse* (London: Faber, 1970), p. 22.

6. Ibid., p. 189.

7. Ibid., p. 22.

8. Hugh Kenner, "Introduction," in Ezra Pound, *Translations* (New York: New Directions, 1963), p. 10.

9. Pound, *Translations*, p. 208.

10. "The Translator's Responsibility," Vanier Lecture Series, 1978, École de Traduction, University of Ottawa (to be published by University of Ottawa Press).

11. Greenfield, "Esthetics and Meaning," p. 96.

12. *Poems from the Old English*, p. 32.

13. Kenner, "Introduction," p. 11.

14. Greenfield, "Esthetics and Meaning," p. 97.

15. Ibid., p. 96.

16. I. L. Gordon, *The Seafarer*, p. 38n.

17. *The Exeter Book*, ed. G. P. Krapp and E. v. K. Dobbie (New York: Columbia, 1936), p. xxxix.

18. Greenfield, "Esthetics and Meaning," p. 97.

19. *The Battle of Maldon and Other Old English Poems*, ed. Bruce Mitchell, trans. Kevin Crossley-Holland (London: Macmillan, 1967), p. 114.

20. *The Wanderer*, ed. T. P. Dunning and A. J. Bliss (London: Methuen, 1969), pp. 110–11.

21. Hamer, *A Choice*, p. 177.

22. *The Earliest English Poems,* trans. Michael Alexander (Baltimore, Md.: Penguin, 1966), pp. 70–71.

23. Robert Lowell, *Imitations* (New York: Noonday, 1962), p. xi. See my "Robert Lowell's *Imitations,*" *Translation Review* (Summer 1980), pp. 20–27; reprinted in altered form in Burton Raffel, *Robert Lowell* (New York: Ungar, 1982), pp. 99–122.

25. Kenner, "Introduction," p. 11.

26. *An Anthology of Old English Poetry,* trans. Charles W. Kennedy (New York: Oxford, 1960), pp. 5–6.

27. Greenfield, "Esthetics and Meaning," p. 106.

28. *Poems from the Old English,* pp. 59–60.

29. Burton Raffel, *The Forked Tongue: A Study of the Translation Process* (The Hague: Mouton, 1971), p. 131.

30. Ibid., p. 19.

Elegy in Old English and Old Norse: A Problem in Literary History

Joseph Harris

Recent Anglo-American scholarship seems to have given up the effort to write a real literary history that includes Old English poetry, and this is especially true of the elegies, which we appreciate, analyze, and edit but are content to see as a genre without a history. Stanley B. Greenfield seems even to have taken the next logical step: "If the elegies are a genre in Old English, they are so by force of our present, rather than determinate historical, perspective; that is, by our 'feel' for them as a group possessing certain features in common."[1] The caveat is well taken, but for me the "feel" is strong enough still to demand the construction of a common literary history for as many as possible of the texts embraced by this "feel." So far no literary history has succeeded.[2] For example, Herbert Pilch's straightforward derivation from Welsh is not persuasive, and the Ovidian and Vergilian origins argued in a confusing fashion by Rudolf Imelmann and more simply by Helga Reuschel are no more convincing than P. L. Henry's claims for the milieu of Celtic Christianity and specifically its penitential aspects.[3] What *has* been accomplished for the Old English elegies is the establishment of lateral sources and influences that provide more or less probable histories for particular motifs and expressions, and especially for many important ideas. Thus the *ubi sunt* topoi and the *sum* catalogues are understood as having a firm home in Latin-Christian thought, while the ruined hall and cuckoo are somewhat less securely considered Celtic-Classical or purely Celtic borrowings.[4] But among all these plausible "influences" we sense no mainstream, no old generic core to be developed and absorb the lateral contributions; we need to remind ourselves that the Old English genre consists predominantly of dramatic monologue in which a human speaks in the first person about the past, mostly his own past life, and (in

46

Greenfield's phrase) "expresses an attitude toward experience."[5] The past may have been happy or unhappy or both, but the contrast with the speaker's present, a contrast invested with sadness, is constant.

The most successful literary histories of this genre stem from German-language scholarship and connect the Old English poems with a pre-invasion Common Germanic literary culture and with the rich evidence for various kinds of poetry associated with the dead. Rudolf Koegel's basic discussion (1894) was expanded and refined by L. L. Schücking in 1908 and by Georg Baesecke and Gustav Ehrismann in the interwar years.[6] However, Andreas Heusler's *Die altgermanische Dichtung,* the proper starting point for every consideration of the history of Old English secular poetry, fails us here, and Heusler leaves the Old English elegy hovering on the very edge of his great map of old Germanic verse.[7] He is uncertain about the connection to native funeral lament and to memorial poetry and seems surer of the outside influence from Ovid—but influence on what?

I believe that Schücking was on the right path and that the several kinds of funeral verse form the true ultimate origin, though many links will remain missing. However, the immediate predecessor of Old English elegy would have been a Common Germanic heroic elegy. Heusler shied away from postulating such a genre because of his convictions, discussed below, about elegy in Old Norse and, more generally, because he was writing in a tradition that trusts too rigidly in a development from heroic to "novelistic" plots and from honor to sentiment as motives. I want to argue that the features common to elegy in Old English and Old Norse can be ascribed to a Common Germanic elegiac genre just as we use comparative reconstruction in linguistics; such reasoning is universally accepted when it leads to the idea of the Common Germanic alliterative line and to the Common Germanic form of the heroic lay, though it has rarely been suggested for elegy. Ernst Sieper's 1915 book on Old English elegy seems to be the only major work to embrace the derivation from ritual lament and to discuss Old Norse elegy in the same context.[8]

Elegy in Old Norse can be divided into two groups of texts. First there are skaldic *erfikvæði* or memorial poems like Egill Skalla-grímsson's *Sonatorrek.* I do not intend to discuss these memorial poems by historical poets in praise of the dead, but they are regarded by Heusler, Sieper, and others as having Common Germanic roots in laments for the dead. The second group includes six heroic elegies in the *Poetic Edda* and seven similar poems in sagas of ancient times found in Icelandic and in Saxo Grammaticus's Latin paraphrases.[9] In addition there are a number of passages in other Eddic heroic poems that can be considered more or less elegiac.[10] The generalizations of the present paper have been tested in detail only against the Eddic elegies proper but should also hold for the elegiac passages and the non-Eddic poems listed. Like the Old English poems, the Eddic elegies are in large part retrospective narratives in the first person. the major difference is that all these poems are firmly tied to particular heroic legends and replete with proper names—in Old English there are only four comparable names.[11] The chronology of events is stricter in the Old Norse poems, probably because they are still so firmly rooted in a story, and the burden of ideas is proportionally greater in the Old English, as if progressive loss of story has made room for the lateral sources and influences from Latin and Celtic literatures. Triangulating backward, then, from the surviving examples of Old Germanic elegy in Old English and Old Norse, we can imagine the general form of the Common Germanic elegy.

It was a dramatic monologue spoken by a figure from a known heroic story who told in the first person about the joys and especially the griefs of his life. If the speaker was a woman, and it often was, she might be in the midst of her life like Guðrún in the first Guðrún poem or at its end like Guðrún in *Guðrúnarhvǫt*. If the speaker was a man, he was most likely to be an old retainer, like the Wanderer or Starkaðr, who had outlived his lord and comrades; but *Deor* and the *Seafarer* suggest that this characterization may be too narrow. In any case, he has been through a great deal, and his speech may come close to the end of his life. In fact, so insistent is the association with the death of a male speaker that the well-documented death-song type must be considered a subgroup of retrospective elegy in general.[12] The intellectual content consisted in a contrast of Once and Now, a sense of the *lacrimae rerum*, loss, and sometimes, it seems, of consolation. There may have been room for some conventional wisdom or at least generalization, especially near the beginning and end. It is not clear whether our model should provide for the possibility of a narrative frame; *Wulf and Eadwacer,* the *Wife's Lament,* the second Guðrún poem, and most of the extra-Eddic poems like *Víkarsbálkr* are pure monologues, but *Guðrúnarhvǫt,* the first Guðrún poem, and *Oddrúnargrátr* have developed frames, while the *Wanderer,* the "Lament of the Last Survivor," and the "Father's Lament" in *Beowulf* have more or less brief frames. One solution is to assume that informal introductory and concluding prose originally formed a sagalike matrix for a monologue and that the two elegy traditions have independently shared a development toward framing the speech in narrative verse.

This model of a Common Germanic heroic elegy is, of course, a hypothetical construct that could not seriously be compared in degree of certainty with the proto-Germanic form of a word reconstructed from attested forms in North and West Germanic and supported by the entire apparatus of comparative Germanic grammar. However, both are unreal constructs that serve the purpose of establishing a history for the real reflexes, and the poetic development of elegy in Old English can be clarified as a progression toward generalization and finally allegory. *Wulf and Eadwacer* would, then, be our most archaic text, still close to a specific heroic legend and offering little or no generalizing philosophy. The development from *Wulf and Eadwacer* to the *Wife's Lament* preserves the basic generic form and remains based on a certain—if not quite ascertainable—story, but loss of all proper names and an increase in the gnomic content makes this second stage of Old English elegy perhaps the most characteristic for the genre in its English development. To the latter part of this stage belong also the "Father's Lament" and the "Lament of the Last Survivor"; in addition both of these elegies included in *Beowulf* have developed a narrative framework that was lacking or lost in the stage or stages represented by *Wulf and Eadwacer* and the *Wife's Lament*. In the *Wanderer,* a third stage, only those elements of an underlying autobiography are retained which allow themselves to be interpreted in terms of human life in general; the poem progresses from the life of an individual to the life of man, to man the microcosm, and finally to the macrocosm itself; the framing narrative, already quite general in the *Beowulf* passages, is also reduced to a few general remarks, and of course there is a quantum leap in philosophical content. Finally, in a fourth stage the elements of individual autobiography are further reduced and revised to accord with the larger symbolic purpose; this can be seen in an early phase in the *Riming Poem* and in a late phase in the *Seafarer.* In these poems the vestigial narrative setting of the *Wanderer* is gone, and all the information we need is conveyed by the monologue itself. The development from heroic autobiography to allegory of the life of man is accompanied by a steady growth in the amount of gnomic and homiletic material, in "ideas," until at the end of the *Seafarer* every trace is lost of the old generic core—that original fictional human voice complaining about the situation of experience in time.

In North Germanic the starting point was the same Common Germanic form, but the development was quite different. Briefly and tentatively, I see three stages. The most primitive poem of the group is *Guðrúnarkviða in forna.* There is no poetic frame, although the introductory prose of Codex Regius tells us Guðrún is speaking to Þjóðrekkr (Dietrich, Theodorich)—a setting that almost all scholars consider to be an invention of the literary man responsible for the arrangement of the manuscript.[13] The first-person speaker looks back over the disasters and the few joys of her life from a point after her forced marriage with Atli. The wandering mind and combination of passionate ferocity and passive suffering bear close comparison with *Wulf and Eadwacer* and the *Wife's Lament*, but the underlying story is realized in a much clearer form, and the story is more complicated here than we must imagine for the original type; however, this complication is not an aspect of the history of the literary form itself but of the growth of the story complex *(Sagengeschichte)*. In this first Norse stage, the Common Germanic model has evolved toward narrative complexity and perhaps toward specificity, and certain motifs from later sources have been added; but the old generic core is intact. In a second stage we find four poems that have developed a situation framing the elegiac monologue proper. *Guðrúnarhvǫt,* for example, opens with Guðrún "whetting" her last remaining sons, sending them out to meet certain death in an attempt to avenge their sister; then the tragic mother settles down to a long elegiac rehersal of her life experiences that agrees in every way with our model. To this stage, then, belong also *Helreið Brynhildar, Guðrúnarkviða I,* and *Oddrúnargrátr,* which provide more and more developed frames for the heroine's elegiac retrospective. Finally, in *Guðrúnarkviða III* the narrative-dramatic frame has won out over the elegiac monologue, which is here reduced to one or two stanzas. We could see the old genre pass into verse homily in the *Seafarer;* here in *Guðrúnarkviða III* it passes into medieval novelistic narrative. In English the development was from heroic story to psychology and general life patterns and on to allegory and homily, in other words from experienced events to experience itself and thence to ideas little connected with experience; while in Old Norse the old core of traditional experienced events becomes surrounded with a second growth of pure story and finally overgrown with new events, not now filtered through an experiencer.

Admittedly a more elaborate plan is required to fit in all the relevant Old Norse texts, but I want to make it clear that in all this I am speaking of a typological development and not of the dates of surviving texts or even their actual relative chronology. For the Norse poems are all considered by consensus to have originated in a time later than even the manuscripts of the Old English poems, and I must now turn to this problem. Heusler had no faith in a Common Germanic heroic elegy because he believed the Old Norse poems to be the product of an Icelandic *Nachblüte* or poetic renaissance of the later eleventh through twelfth centuries; and not only were the extant texts composed there, but the genre of heroic elegy itself was invented in Iceland. He made this argument in very brief form in a paper of 1906 and then enshrined his view in both editions of *Die altgermanische Dichtung.*[14] But this view of the Eddic elegies is unconvincing because Heusler, while elaborating on the milieu and on the materials, failed to provide any models or to show how this completely new poetic type came into existence *ex nihilo.* Most of the early paper is concerned not with the elegies but with other poetry of the Icelandic *Nachblüte,* and I think a close look at his argument concerning one of these poetic types, the heroic catalogue or *þula,* would show that Heusler was confusing the date and provenance of a particular text or group of texts with its generic provenance and history. For he rightly claims the majority of the preserved *þulur* as learned codifications of the Icelandic renaissance; but when his overall presentation implies that the genre itself is a product of this milieu, the results contradict the well-known Common Germanic origin that Heusler himself affirms in *Die altgermanische Dichtung.*

Despite such potential objections, Heusler's view of the elegies held the field until Wolfgang Mohr's two learned, diffuse, and difficult monographs of 1938 and 1939.[15] Mohr's starting point is a comparison of the language, motifs, and spirit of the Eddic elegies with the much later Danish ballads. The rich hoard of coincidences leads him to derive the Icelandic texts from lost eleventh- and twelfth-century predecessors of the ballads. These were heroic elegies that themselves derive from a revitalization of heroic poetry through the international wave of novelistic fictions of ultimately southern origin. The milieu of these lost heroic elegies was Danish and North German, and the Icelandic poets of the twelfth and thirteenth centuries find their roles severely limited in Mohr's theory. Mohr's lead has been followed with modifications by other recent scholars, including especially Jan de Vries, Hanns Midderhoff, and Robert J. Glendinning.[16] Mohr's investigations were, I believe, on the right track, but a large number of problems in his method, some noted by de Vries, remain. I cannot give these problems the full airing they deserve here, but one group of difficulties is raised by the reconstructed oral sources. The novelistic poems that provided the model for the Danish heroic elegies are deductively arrived at; none survive. Presumably their content was international tales and not Germanic heroic material; yet contemporary ballad scholars keep pushing the date of the origin of ballads as a genre later into the High Middle Ages, while Mohr's theory requires at least proto-ballads in the eleventh and certainly by the twelfth century.[17] Above all I find it contradictory that Mohr, while making free use of early West Germanic material from the *Heliand* and Old English poetry for his linguistic comparisons, nevertheless excludes the very similar elegies in Old English from his derivation of the proto-forms of the Old Norse poems. Mohr himself looked this objection in the eye in the last brilliant pages of his second article, where he cites some of the evidence for an old, Common Germanic elegy, especially evidence from *Beowulf* and the *Heliand,* but fails to recognize or at least to conclude that this earlier evidence for the same basic generic structure demands to be integrated into the overall evolution. My suggested modification of Mohr's theory would project the old generic core and some of the language and motifs that flesh it out (but of course no individual poem now extant) back into the continental period before the Anglo-Saxon invasions. From that starting point the novelistic influences Mohr has demonstrated from proto-ballad poetry can be absorbed in the same way that the Old English elegiac genre absorbed lateral influences. For as literary history, Mohr's plan is liable to objections similar to those that met studies of the Old English elegies: an accumulation of influences is accounted for, but his model for the creation of the genre itself is either implausible or omits similar and related documents.

Mohr collected his coincidences of motif and language by a systematic comparison with the much larger corpus of ballads. I have emphasized instead more general considerations of literary history and generic structure, but I believe a systematic comparison between the heroic elegies in Old Norse and Old English will support the general theory with agreements also at the level of plot-type, theme, motif, and language. Such a catalogue is a major undertaking for another occasion, but I will conclude with a concrete example that is peculiar enough, I think, to demand a genetic, rather than a typological, explanation—we might call it elegiac exaggeration.

This takes the form of extravagant numbers of sad examples in *Deor* and *Guðrúnarkviða I* (which have been compared by F. P. Magoun)[18] or the list of superlative griefs in *Guðrúnarhvǫt,* stanzas 16–17. In *Hamðismál,* st. 4–5, Guðrún exaggerates her isolation when, in fact, she has her two sons remaining—if only she would not send them out to die. Tones of a similar exaggerated isolation may be audible in the *Wife's Lament* and the *Wanderer,* and Egill in *Sonatorrek,* st. 4, is certainly exaggerating with ". . . my line is at its end like the withered stump of the forest maple."[19] For Egill had a surviving son as well as daughters and grandchildren.

But truly striking examples of a conventional "plural of grief" are found in *Beowulf* and *Guðrúnarkviða II*. In the "Lament of the Last Survivor" the shift from singular to plural is not illogical but nevertheless arresting:

> Nah, hwa sweord wege
> oððe fe(o)r(mie)   fæted wæge
> . . . .
> feormynd swefað (2252b–56b).[20]

(I have no one to bear the sword or to polish the decorated cup. . . . The polishers are sleeping [in death].)

Note the repetition of the verb as plural verbal noun. In the "Father's Lament" the one son "rides" on the gallows (" . . . þæt his byre ride/giong on galgan," 2445b–46a), but eleven lines later in the paraphrased "sorrowful song" the father declares: "ridend swefað,/hæleð in hoðman" ("the riders are sleeping, heroes in the grave," 2457b–58a). Whether these are gallows-riders or equestrians or a bit of both,[21] the shift to the plural is probably not a scribal error but an elegiac convention parallel to *feormynd swefað*. Finally, in the second Guðrún poem, the one called "the old," the heroine meets the horse of the slain Sigurðr; Grani has returned home with an empty saddle stained with blood: "Weeping and wet-cheeked I went to talk with Grani, I asked the steed the news; Grani then drooped, hung his head to the grass. The steed knew this: his owners were not living."[22] This closing plural in *eigendr né lifðot* is distinctly illogical but also effective if we know the convention.[23] Grani, of course, had only one owner, and in this context only Sigurðr's death can be referred to, but the plural carried conventional tones of elegiac ruin like the *waldend licgað* ("the rulers are lying [dead]") of the *Wanderer* (1. 78b) and the *betend crungon,/hergas to hrusan* ("the rebuilders have fallen, [whole] armies have fallen to the earth") in the *Ruin* (11. 28b–29a).

The similarity between a line like *gedroren is þeos duguð eal* ("fallen is all this company") in the *Seafarer* (1. 86a) and the sublime exaggeration of Henry Vaughan's "They are all gone into the world of light" (from *Silex scintillans* [1655]) must, of course, be due to a typological, not a historical, association; but in genetically related literatures— closely related traditional literatures such as Old English and Old Norse secular poetry—a shared minor feature such as the convention of elegiac exaggeration and the subordinate form I called the plural of grief seems to be based on a common heritage. Like the common structural core of the elegiac genre in these sister literatures, the major feature by which the genre is defined, this minor motif is not a literary universal or even linked to a common story; instead it seems to be genre-bound, likely to be produced by the genre even when in violation of logic, and the prevalence of present-participial nouns here seems to point to a common dictional ancestor as surely as the common structural features do. It will be a formidable task to excavate and evaluate the many similar coincidences on all levels between the two bodies of elegy, and Mohr's work requires a much more extended critical scrutiny than I have been able to give it here, but I believe that this is the way to a better literary-historical understanding of the elegy in Old English and Old Norse.

NOTES

1. *The Interpretation of Old English Poems* (London and Boston: Routledge, 1972), p. 135.

2. For reasons that will become plain, *The Ruin* and probably *The Husband's Message* must be omitted from the usual inventory of elegies in standard treatments such as Stanley B. Greenfield's "The Old English Elegies," pp. 142–75, in *Continuations and Beginnings: Studies in Old English Literature*, ed. Eric Gerald Stanley (London: Nelson, 1966). *The Ruin* is imbued with *elegiac sentiments* but is not, according to the structural definition offered in this paper, itself an *elegy*. *The Husband's Message* contains some elegiac retrospective, but the best contemporary opinion is that it belongs structurally (and therefore generically) to the poetry of speaking objects (prosopopoeia), in this case a cross; cf. R. E. Kaske, "A Poem of the Cross in the Exeter Book," *Traditio* 23 (1967):41–71 and Margaret E. Goldsmith, "The Enigma of *The Husband's Message*," pp. 242–63 in *Anglo-Saxon Poetry: Essays in Appreciation*, ed. Lewis E. Nicholson and Dolores Warwick Frese (Notre Dame and London: University of Notre Dame Press, 1975).

3. Herbert Pilch, "The Elegiac Genre in Old English and Early Welsh Poetry," *Zeitschrift für celtische Philologie* 29 (1964):209–24; Imelmann, *Forschungen zur altenglishchen Poesie* (Berlin: Weidmann, 1920), esp. pp. 187–238; Helga Reuschel, "Ovid und die ags. Elegien," *Beiträge zur Geschichte der deutsche Sprache und Literatur* 62 (1938):132–42; P. L. Henry, *The Early English and Celtic Lyric* (London: Allen and Unwin, 1966).

4. J. E. Cross, "'Ubi Sunt' Passages in Old English—Sources and Relationships," *Vetenskaps-societeten i Lund, Årsbok*, 1956, pp. 25–44 and "On The Wanderer lines 80–84, a Study of a Figure and a Theme," *Vetenskaps-Societeten i Lund, Årsbok*, 1958–59, pp. 77–110 and "On the Genre of *The Wanderer*," *Neophilologus* 45 (1961):63–72, esp. 68–72; Ernst Sieper, *Die altenglishche Elegie* (Strassburg: Trübner, 1915), pp. 70–77. For further references and a complete review, R. F. Leslie, ed., *The Wanderer* (Manchester: Manchester University Press, 1966), pp. 25–37 and *Three Old English Elegies* (Manchester: Manchester University Press, 1961), p. 61. Gerhard Dietrich, "Ursprünge des Elegischen in der altenglishchen Literatur," in *Literatur-Kultur-Gesellschaft in England und Amerika: Aspecte und Forschungsbeiträge Friedrich Schubel zum 60. Geburtstag*, ed. G. Müller-Schwefe und K. Tuzinski (Frankfurt: Diesterweg, 1966), pp. 20–22, offers still further caveats (beyond those of Leslie) to the Celtic cuckoo.

5. Greenfield, "Old English Elegies," p. 143.

6. Koegel, *Geschichte der deutschen Litteratur bis zum Ausgange des Mittelalters*, 1, 1. Teil: Die stabreimende Dichtung und die gotische Prosa (Strassburg: Trübner, 1894); the

discussion of *Totenlieder* is pp. 47–55, but Koegel's derivation of the extant Old English elegies is different and independent, pp. 62–63; Schücking, "Das angelsächsische Totenklagelied," *Englische Studien* 39 (1908):1–13;Baesecke, *Vor- und Frühgeschichte des deutschen Schriftums*, 1: Vorgeschichte (Halle: Niemeyer, 1940), pp. 358–65; Ehrismann, *Geschichte der deutschen Literatur bis zum Ausgang des Mittelalters*, 1. Teil: Die althochdeutsche Literatur, 2d ed. rev. (Munich: Beck, 1932), pp. 35–44.

7. 2d ed. rev. (Potsdam, 1941; 1st ed., 1926; reprint ed., 1957), esp. pp. 143–50; for a thorough review of origin theories and a further development of Heusler's views, see Dietrich; another recent survey, Karl Heinz Göller, "Die angelsächsischen Elegien," *Germanisch-romanische Monatsschrift* 44, n.s. 13 (1963):225–41, is more general.

8. Sieper, pp. 3–31 and 78–106; cf. Gustav Neckel, "Anhang: die altgermanische Heldenklage," pp. 495–96 in his *Beiträge zur Eddaforschung, mit Exkursen zur Heldensage* (Dortmund: Ruhfus, 1908) (partly contradicting his discussion of "Egil und der angelsächsische Einfluss," pp. 367–89). Stray comments touching this subject may be found in: N. Kershaw (Chadwick), ed., *Anglo-Saxon and Norse Poems* (Cambridge: Cambridge University Press, 1922), e.g., p. 6 and in notes; Bertha S. Phillpotts, *Edda and Saga* (New York: H. Holt; London: Butterworth, 1931), pp. 66–67; and Ursula Dronke, ed., *The Poetic Edda*, 1: Heroic Poems (Oxford: Oxford University Press, 1969), p. 184.

9. *Edda: Die Lieder des Codex Regius, nebst verwandten Denkmälern*, ed. Gustav Neckel, 4th ed. rev. Hans Kuhn, 1: Text (Heidelberg: Winter, 1962): *Guðrúnarkviða I, Guðrúnarkviða II (in forna), Guðrúnarkviða III, Helreið Brynhildar, Oddrúnargrátr*, and *Guðrúnarhvǫt. Eddica minora: Dichtungen eddischer Art aus den fornaldarsǫgur und andern Prosawerken*, ed. Andreas Heusler and Wilhelm Ranisch (Dortmund: Ruhfus, 1903): *Víkarsbálkr, Hrókslied, Hiálmars Sterbelied, Hildibrands Sterbelied*, and *Qrvar-Odds Sterbelied*. From Saxo Grammaticus, *Gesta Danorum* (ed. Alfred Holder [Strassburg: Trübner, 1886]): *Starkads Jugendlied* (parts of pp. 182–88 and the fragment in *Eddica minora*, XI, D) and *Starkads Sterbelied* (pp. 269–73). (For the exact contents of *Starkads Jugendlied*, the Latin prose resolution of a lost [Icelandic?] poem, cf. *Eddica minora*, pp. xxxi–xxxii, and Paul Herrmann, *Erläuterungen zu den ersten neun Büchern der dänischen Geschichte des Saxo Grammaticus*, 2. Teil: Kommentar [Leipzig: Englemann, 1922], pp. 424–42 and references there; for *Starkads Sterbelied*, cf. *Eddica minora*, p. xxxi, and Herrmann, pp. 557–67.) This list of Old Norse elegies is taken over, along with their titles, from Heusler, *Altgermanische Dichtung*, pp. 183–86.

10. Parts of *Helgakviða Hundingsbana II, Grípisspá, Sigurðarkviða in skamma, Atlamál*, and *Hamðismál* in the *Poetic Edda* and of the *Innsteinslied* and *Qrvar-Odds Männervergleich* in the *Eddica minora*.

11. "Wulf," "Eadwacer," "Deor," "Heorrenda."

12. Lars Lönnroth, "Hjálmar's Death Song and the Delivery of Eddic Poetry," *Speculum* 46 (1971):1–20.

13. The prose passage represents the "collector's" hypothesis about the occasion of *Guðrúnarkviða II* and is based on his reading of *Guðrúnarkviða III*, but R. J. Glendinning, "*Guðrúnarqviða forna*: a Reconstruction and Interpretation" in *Edda: A Collection of Essays*, ed. R. J. Glendinning and Haraldur Bessason, University of Manitoba Icelandic Studies 4 (Winnipeg, 1981), reverses these relationships, taking the prose as integral to *Guðrúnarkviða II* and *Guðrúnarkviða III* as a further development of the prose-verse complex. However, when *Vǫlsunga saga* introduces *Gkv II*, it is as a soliloquy spoken in the lady's bower (chap. 32), and *Norna-Gests þáttr*, which alludes to the poem, knows nothing of þjóðrekkr.

14. Heusler, *Altgermanische Dichtung*, pp. 183–89, and "Heimat und Alter der eddischen Gedichte: das isländische Sondergut," *Archiv für das Studium der neueren Sprachen und Literaturen* 116 (1906):249–81 (reprinted in *Kleine Schriften* [Berlin: de Gruyter, 1969]:165–94, esp. 168–69).

15. "Entstehungsgeschichte und Heimat der jüngeren Eddalieder südgermanischen Stoffes," *Zeitschrift für deutsches Altertum* 75 (1938–39):217–80, and "Wortschatz und Motive der jüngeren Eddalieder mit südgermanischem Stoff," *Zeitschrift für deutsches Altertum* 76 (1939–40):149–217.

16. Jan De Vries, "Das zweite Guðrúnlied," *Zeitschrift für deutsche Philologie* 77 (1958):196–99; Midderhoff, "Zur Verbindung des ersten und zweiten Teils des Nibelungenstoffes in der Lieder-Edda," *Zeitschrift für deutsches Altertum* 95 (1966):243–58 and "Übereinstimmungen und Ahnlichkeiten in den liedereddischen und epischen Nibelungen," *Zeitschrift für deutsches Altertum* 97 (1968–69):241–78.

17. For a recent review, cf. *The European Medieval Ballad: a Symposium,* ed. Otto Holzapfel, Julia McGrew, and Iørn Piø (Odense, Denmark: Odense University Press, 1978).

18. "Deors Klage und Guðrúnarkviða I," *Englische Studien* 75 (1942–43):1–15; cf. Phillpotts, p. 66.

19. "Þvíat ætt mín/á enda stendr,/sem 'hræbarnar/hlinnar marka'" (text of E. O. G. Turville-Petre, *Scaldic Poetry* [Oxford: Clarendon, 1976], p. 31).

20. *Beowulf and the Fight at Finnsburg,* ed. Fr. Klaeber, 3d ed. rev. (Boston: Heath, 1950).

21. Cf. Klaeber's note and Schücking, "Das angelsächsische Totenklagelied," pp. 10–11, where, however, the convention cited is different from the one I propose.

22. *Guðrúnarkviða II,* st. 5: "Gecc ec grátandi við Grana rœða,/úrughlýra, ió frá ec spialla;/hnipnaði Grani þá, drap í gras hǫfði;/iór þat vissi: eigendr né lifðot."

23. Most commentators pass over this plural in silence; Karl-Hampus Dahlstedt, "Gudruns sorg: Stilstudier över ett Eddamotiv," *Scripta Islandica* 13 (1962):40 refers it to Sigurðr and his slayer, who in some versions is slain by the dying hero; F. Detter and R. Heinzel, edd., *Sæmundar Edda,* II: Anmerkungen (Leipzig: Wigand, 1903), notes to Vǫluspá 6:5 and esp. to Hávamál 28:5, cite many instances of plural forms for singular concepts, not all convincingly explained; Sophus Bugge, ed., *Norrœn fornkvæði* . . . (Christiania, 1867; reprint ed. Oslo: Universitetsforlaget, 1965), p. 423, thought of Sigurðr and his son Sigmundr; de Vries, p. 186, n. 25: "Die Redensart ist etwas verschwommen, vielleicht soll der Plural die harte Realität, dass es hier nur Sigurd betrifft, verschleiern."

Odin's Powers and the Old English Elegies

Raymond P. Tripp, Jr.

The one area of agreement about the Old English elegies is most likely to center on their complexity.[1] This has generated a multitude of interpretations and a formidable bibliography.[2] A few years ago I suggested that some progress had been made in reading the elegies as something else beside romantic monologues.[3] My object then was to draw attention to the possibility that the main speaker, particularly in *The Wife's Lament,* might be dead—a pagan or apostate *revenant,* serving Christian homiletic purposes by relating his *post mortem* sufferings.[4] I should like now to carry these ideas of death and autobiographical utterance a step or two farther, in the direction of the "death-song" proper and the idea, shared by pagan and Christian alike, that the dead live on in death and may be awakened by God— whether Odin or Christ.[5]

This approach revives the general question of the relative importance of pagan and Christian traditions touching death and dying as these appear in the elegies. Recently, greater influence has been attributed to Christian sources in general. Death and dying, that is, "doomsday as a suitable and instructive theme," has not been connected to "any specific heathen notions which might be profitably christianized."[6] Death and varied responses to it, however, are not the property of any single tradition. The desire to escape or somehow to accommodate death seems universal; and for this reason, the beliefs of any age or nation are unlikely to derive from a single or a primarily literary source, especially when, as in the case of Old English poetry, an epochal shift between two cultures is involved. The paganism one finds in the elegies depends in part upon how and where one looks.

Recent mythography has outlined the general development from lunar to solar myths.[7] It has shown, in particular, how these differ in

57

their conception of death and man's fate after death. A literal under-world, a Hell, Hades, or Gehenna, gives way to more abstract concep-tions of the afterlife. Before the "good news" of solar religion, most people followed the way of the fathers through the immemorial vegetative cycle of life and death. Only a few, the heroes, escaped, to such places as Valhalla or Elysium. The survival of such universal ideas is very likely to have qualified any poetry touching on the subject of doomsday. On these subjects, death, dying, and judgment, as well as upon the question of sources for specific eschatological notions in Old English poetry, older criticism acknowledged the difficulty in specifying "just how far the poets relied in this case upon any direct and immediate originals or how far they drew upon their own imagi-nation or upon current tradition. . . ."[8] Such general opinions—on either side of the question—can, however, be only as sound as the reading behind them is subtle. Each generation of rereading the elegies, though failing of any consensus regarding their provenance, has brought to light a world of detail, rich enough to warrant careful reconsideration of our most trusted convictions. A recent reading of *The Fates of Men,* for an immediate example, has convincingly demon-strated the presence of shamanistic practices, and thus of northern influence.[9] The well-known and problematic passage (21–26) where a man "falls featherless" from a tree reflects Odin's sacrifice of himself to himself by hanging upon a tree.[10] The Christian cross and the pagan gallows are specifically contrasted in *The Dream of the Rood.*[11]

Beyond such well-acknowledged parallels, however, certain specific powers that Odin acquires by hanging himself upon a tree bear a special relation to the elegies, and to *The Exeter Book* as an early reli-gious anthology. For among Odin's specific achievements is the ability to make the dead rise and tell their stories. In the *Hávamál* he reports:

> I know a twelfth charm: if I see up in a tree a dead man hanging and I cut and darken runes, then the man comes and talks with me.[12]

In another instance, *Baldrs Draumar,* Odin rides to a witch's grave and uses this power to force her to rise and to answer his questions:

> Then Odin rode on up to the eastern door where he knew a witch slept in her grave; skilled in magic he took to speaking charms until she was forced to rise and speak: "What man is this, unknown to me, who has made me come this terrible way? I was buried in snow and beaten by rain, overdrifted with dew: dead have I long been."[13]

The witch's words are very similar to those of the "seafarer," who is also harassed by ice and snow (8b–19a), and the "wanderer" too (45–

48). The dead witch rises and talks with Odin. Examples of such raising of the dead are easily multiplied.[14]

That these powers of Odin are not exceptions, but something taken for granted, may be seen from the *Hárdbarðzljóð*, where they are the subject of a casual reference. In this poem, Odin, posing as a ferryman, a role he often plays, refuses to transport Thor across a river. An argument ensues, and insults are exchanged. Thor asks where his interlocutor ever learned such insulting language. To this Odin replies:

> "I find such words among the old men who live in the woods at home."

Thor's reply to this remark is:

> "Indeed you give a good name to graves, when you call them the woods at home."

Odin cryptically returns:

> "That is what I call such things."[15]

That Odin has graves in mind seems clear from the MS variants of *haugom* and *hauga* for *scógom* and *scóga*.[16] Odin is without doubt in the habit of chatting with the dead, whose tales include insults as well as the details of their lives. The "wife" of *The Wife's Lament* also, it should be recalled, dwells in the woods, specifically in an "earth-cave" "under an oak tree" (27–32a).[17] This ominous detail of the residence of the dead appears again in the "walking of Angantyr" from the *Hervarar saga ok Heiðreks konungs,* where Hervor cries out, "Wake up, all of you underneath the tree roots."[18]

In both pagan and Christian traditions the dead live on under the ground and can be made to tell their stories. In the representative judgment day section of the Old English *Christ,* the dead are also commanded, if collectively, to rise out of the ground:

> [Then] wake from the dead the sons of man, all of the race of men, by God's decree, through his majestic power, [He] commands each man, all the speech-bearers, to rise out of the graves of earth. . . . Then swiftly all of Adam's race receive their flesh, the earth-rest of the grave comes to an end.[19]

Mankind are called up as "speech-bearers," and each human being will tell his own story, for better or worse:

Then will the Lord Himself hear of his deeds from the speech of each man's mouth a retribution for sin.[20]

The theological provenance of Odin's calling up individuals and the Christian God's calling up mankind collectively, to be judged individually, is, to be sure, different. But at the same time in either situation each man confesses and tells his story individually, and, further, both styles of resurrection are grounded in a literal belief that the dead live on and are not obliterated. The various developments of this archaic conception are, thus, by no means as alien or antithetical as their several later uses and adaptation might at first indicate. As the Old English riddler cryptically puts it: *Nemað hȳ selfe,* "They name themselves"—or "Name them yourself."[21]

God and Odin can call up the dead and compel them to tell their stories. The parallel traditions, as it were, of local resuscitation and confession provide the earlier Christian apologist with an ideal means to speak in terms northern pagans would understand, and in a way at once suited to his new message while compatible with those native values he would first transform and ultimately supplant. The universal belief that the dead can be summoned to tell their stories needs only a new occasion and a new God to hear them. And the new religion could hardly have found a better spokesman to testify to the futility of pagan ways than the example of a pitiful revenant with his tale of unmitigated *post mortem* suffering.

These eschatological coincidences point to a common ground as suggested by Deering long ago.[22] The tradition of the death-song proper provides us with a common literary form, one used by Bede himself.[23]

> Before the necessary journey [of death] no one becomes
> Wiser in thought   than there be need for him
> To ponder   before his going hence
> What to his soul   of good or evil
> After the day of death   will be adjudged.

This is a common enough homiletic thought, but "there is," as Greenfield comments, "an enigmatic quality to this one-sentence poem. . . . The 'day of death' seems to have reference both to the individual's dying and to the Day of Judgment."[24] What the death-song and confession have significantly in common is, of course, the attempt to secure a better after-death existence. Some time ago Nora K. Chadwick, in her long essay upon Norse ghosts, surveyed ample evidence for the connection between confession and the death-song and raised the question:

> Is it possible that the death-song originally constituted the claim of the hero who dies a violent death to a place in Valhöl, and the reference to the circumstances of this death, or the allusions to his past adventures, are calculated to make valid his appeal for the favour of the god of poetry and battle?[25]

The death-song, to be sure, is more of a positive claim or assertion, and less of an apology or supplication than confession, but both are first aimed at establishing the true worth and, thus, the deserts of the dying or dead speaker.

Once this connection is acknowledged, numerous similarities between death-songs and after-death pronouncements and those poems in the *Exeter Book* loosely classified as elegies present themselves.[26] Bede's death-warning, for example, is very much like what the so-called seafarer says:

> Therefore is no man on earth that proud of mind, that good of his gifts, that active in his youth, that bold of his deeds, nor that loyal to his lord, that he should not always have sorrow about his "sea-journey," about what the Lord will do to him.[27]

This wintry eschatology of death and its locus have already been noted. The "seafarer's" clinging icicles and flying showers of hail, and even the "wanderer's" rime and snow mixed with hail, remind us of Odin's long-dead witch "buried in snow and beaten by rain." The likeness extends to the "wife's" departed "friend," who

> sits under a rocky cliff, covered with frost from storms, my friend weary in spirit, overflowed with water in a dreary hall. (47–50a)[28]

Even the dying—and clearly allegorical—Phoenix, when he "relinquishes court and homeland," "departs weary in spirit, harassed by winter," and heads for the "woods," where he builds a new "nest," exhibits characteristics common to both genres.[29]

The most pronounced of these, of course, and that which most intimately links the death-song and the confessional elegy is the autobiographical perspective. As Heusler puts is, "Germeinsam ist der ich-bericht."[30] The "wife" begins her "lament" with:

> I this story relate about myself full sadly, about my own life. (1–2a)[31]

This sounds very much like another dead woman, Brunhildr, who, as she is being carried to her funeral pyre, replies to the witch who taunts her:

> I can tell you
> The true story,
> You false creature,
> If you care to listen,
> Of how I was treated
> By Gjuki's offspring
> With lack of love
> And broken oaths.[32]

The strength of this first-person perspective as a link between the death-song and the confessional poem becomes readily apparent when its better-known examples are gathered from *The Exeter Book.* We have heard from the "wife," but then there are similar personas from (1) *The Wanderer:*

Often I alone had each morning to speak my cares (8–9a);

(2) from *The Seafarer:*

I can about myself relate a true story, tell of my life (1–2a);

(3) from *Widsith:*

I have heard of many men ruling nations (10);

(4) from *Maxims I:*

Ask me with wise words. Do not let your spirit be hidden, or secret what you most deeply know. Nor will I to you tell my secrets if you hide your mind-craft from me and your heart's thought (1–3);

(5) from *The Riming Poem:*

Glad was I in mirth, adorned with colors, with the hues of bliss, and the colors of blossoms (2–3).
Bold was I in adornments, free along the ways; my joy was noble, my way of life hopeful (38–39).
Now my heart is disturbed, fearful on account of sorrowful journeys, near to distress; that departs at night in flight which was beloved during the day (43–45a).

(6) from *Soul and Body II:*

I dwelled with you inside. Nor was I able to get out, contained by flesh (30–31a);

(7) from *Deor:*

This I will say about myself, that I was once the poet of the Heodenings, dear to my lord. Deor was my name. For many winters I had a good life, a kind lord (35–40a);[33]

(8) and from *Resignation:*

I about myself mostly speak this sorry history, and tell about my life, anxiously eager, and think about the sea. (96b–98a)[34]

Not all of these passages deal directly with personal experience; those which do not, however, such as *Widsith* and *Maxims I*, still touch on areas closely related to confessional, death-song matters. Widsith, who lives too long to be an ordinary person, reveals more than ordinary knowledge; and the narrator in *Maxims I* also trades in secrets.[35] All deal with mysterious matters, immediate and vicarious, which T. A. Shippey has recently described as a group in terms of "wisdom and learning."[36]

Death and confession are never far from the surface of these *Exeter Book* pieces we are accustomed to call elegies, and these two themes hark back to pagan ideas of the divine (and shamanistic) power of calling up the dead and making them tell their stories. The critical problem does not turn on this obvious connection, nor even the difference between collective and individual resuscitation; Christ raises Lazarus, and Aelfric had John raising a variety of individual people.[37] The question turns upon the degree of internalization and euhemerization. Are we dealing with poems in which, as R. Harvey has remarked, "the tendency to rationalize by effacing supernatural features wherever they occur" has resulted in a loss or confusion of "original revenant elements"?[38] Since E. G. Stanley's *The Search for Anglo-Saxon Paganism*, it has become the habit to look exclusively toward Rome for the content of Old English poetry.[39] This historical narrowness, however, needs to be broadened with a fresh awareness of euhemerized native traditions. The eastern door or direction, for example, as the entrance to the other world appears to Bede, again in Aelfric, as well as in pagan pieces like *Baldrs Draumar* and *Hjalmars Death-Song*.[40] It is a fair question to ask if Anglo-Saxon churchmen were consciously aware of the perennial source and implications of their image. Such a question, though clearly beyond the scope of this present inquiry, does point up the intricacy of searching out—or calling up—the eschatological traditions buried in the doubtless tangled roots of the pieces we call the Old English elegies. But Odin, we must recall, is the god also of poetry; his power extends over the dead because it extends first over the magic of words. In this respect the "tremendous assertiveness" of the Old English poet, who often invented "a sage or a prophet to give authority to his own opinions," retains Odin's power, figuratively if no longer literally.[41] Odin, "the ancient one-eyed god, crafty and skilled in magic lore, a great shape-changer, and an expert in the consultation of the dead," summoned them and made them speak.[42] The poet of the elegies summons his personas in the same way. His formulas still command the past to speak.

NOTES

1. Those poems traditionally considered as elegies are: *The Wanderer, The Seafarer, Deor, Wulf and Eadwacer, The Wife's Lament, The Husband's Message,* and *The Ruin.* This list varies, of course. In this essay I extend this classification to other short religious poems in *The Exeter Book.*

2. William Bruce Knapp, "Bibliography of the Criticism on the Old English Elegies," *Comitatus* 2 (1971):71–90, covers the period from the nineteenth century through mid-1970, listing in the order of the poems in n. 1 above, 78, 66, 54, 29, 40, 22, and 22 items respectively, for a total of 291; and the pace has not slackened since.

3. "The Narrator as Revenant: A Reconsideration of Three Old English Elegies," *PLL* 8 (1972):339–61.

4. I have expanded upon related ideas in "The Effect of the Occult and the Supernatural upon the Way We Read Old English Poetry," in Luanne Frank, ed., *Literature and the Occult: Essays in Comparative Literature* (Arlington, Tex.: University of Texas at Arlington Press, 1977), pp. 255–68.

5. Rosemary Woolf, "*The Wanderer, The Seafarer,* and the Genre of Planctus," in L. E. Nicholson and D. W. Frese, eds., *Anglo-Saxon Poetry: Essays in Appreciation, For John C. McGalliard* (Notre Dame, Ind.: University of Notre Dame Press, 1975), pp. 192–207, has refined and extended the belletristic approach to the elegies (excluding *The Ruin, Deor,* and *Resignation*) in this direction, in asserting that the elegies are properly complaints.

6. L. Whitbread, "The Descent into Hell Theme in Old English Poetry," *Beiträge zur Geschichte der deutschen Sprache und Literatur* Tübingen (1967):452–81. Passage cited, p. 453. R. T. Farrell, "*Beowulf:* B. The Scandinavian Backgrounds of B[eowulf]," *Reallexikon der germanischen Altertumskunde,* ed. Johannes Hoops, 2d ed., 2:2–3, 241–44, sees no general influence between Old Norse and Old English. Conrad H. Noordby, *The Influence of Old Norse Literature upon English Literature* (New York: Columbia University Press, 1901: reprint ed. AMS Press, 1966), begins his study with Thomas Gray. By *influence* he means revival rather than survival of Old Norse ideas. His book is, significantly, reissued without revision or reservation. Noordby cites Sir William Temple as the primary source for Gray and, like Temple, sees attitudes toward corporeal life after death as the main difference between pagan and Christian times.

7. See, for a convenient example, Joseph Campbell, *The Masks of God: Oriental Mythology*, (New York: The Viking Press, 1962).

8. Waller Deering, *The Anglo-Saxon Poets on the Judgment Day* (Halle: Ehrhardt Karras, 1890), p. 60. See also pp. 28, 57, 82, and 84, for similar judgments. In particular, Deering saw "the specific Ags. or Germanic features" of descriptions of the dead and the other-world to lie in the "awful magnificence of their coloring" (p. 82). Graham D. Caie, *The Judgment Day Theme in Old English Poetry* (Copenhagen: Nova, 1976), stresses over and over again that scriptural accuracy is not the poet's intention, but immediate conversion through the impact of doomsday scenes; see, for example, pp. 98–113, *et passim*.

9. Neil D. Isaacs, "Up a Tree: To See *The Fates of Men*," in *Anglo-Saxon Poetry*, pp. 363–75. There is considerable shamanism scattered throughout Old English poetry, as in *Christ*, ll. 720 ff., where Christ "leaps" into and out of material reality to save mankind. Clearly Christ is wearing "seven-league boots" and "steps" over reality like the Hindu God Vishnu. See H. H. Wilson, trans. *The Vishnu Purana, A System of Hindu Mythology and Tradition* (Calcutta: Punthi Pustak, 1972), p. 214: "In the present Manvantara, Vishnu was again born as Vamana, the son of Kaśyapa by Aditi. With three paces he subdued the worlds, and gave them, freed from all embarrassment, to Purandara." This story of Vishnu's "leaping" occurs in many works; see the *Bhagavata Purana*, bk. 8, chaps. 15–23. Caie, p. 165, n. 8, writes: "The central image in *Christ II* is that of the 'leaps of Christ' which has its ultimate source in the *Song of Songs*, 2, 8 and 9: 'he cometh leaping upon the mountains, skipping upon the hills. My beloved is like a roe or a young hart,' and is a common theme in patristic works such as those by Gregory, Ambrose, Cassiodorus and Alcuin." This is not, perhaps, untrue, but seems too particular a source for a universal image.

10. Isaacs, "Up a Tree," pp. 366 ff.

11. *ASPR* 2:61, 10b.

12. Translations are my own. The Old Norse is:

> 157 þat kann ec iþ tólpta,   ef ec sé á tré uppi
>   váfa virgiliná:
>   svá ec ríst   oc í rúnom fác,
>   at sá gengr gumi
>   oc maelir við mic.

Cited from Hans Kuhn, ed., *Edda, Die Lieder des Codex Regius nebts verwandten Denkmälern, herausgegeben von Gustav Neckel*, 4th ed. (Heidelberg: Carl Winter Universitätsverlag, 1962), p. 43.

13. Ibid., p. 277. The Old Norse reads:

> 4   þá reið Óðinn   fyr austan dyrr,
>   þar er hann vissi   vǫlo leiði;
>   nam han vittugri   valgaldr qveða,
>   unz nauðig reis,   nás ord um qvað:
>
> 5   "Hvat er manna þat,   mér ókunnra,
>   er mér hefir aukit   erfit sinni?
>   var ec snivin snióvi   oc slegin regni
>   oc drifin dǫggo,   dauð var ec lengi."

14. See Inger M. Boberg, *Motif-Index of Early Icelandic Literature* (Copenhagen: Munksgaard, 1966). Bibliotheca Arnamagnaeana, vol. 27.

15. Kuhn, *Edda*, p. 85. The pertinent verses for this exchange are 43–46. The verses cited are:

> 44 Nam ec at mǫnnom þeim inom aldrœnom, er búa í heimis scógom.
> 45 þó gefr þu gott nafn dysiom, er þú kallar þat heimis scóga.
> 46 Svá dœmi ec um slíct far.

16. Kuhn, *Edda*, notes to verses 44 and 45.

17. Joseph Harris, "A Note on *eorðscræf*/*eorðsele* and Current Interpretations of *The Wife's Lament*," *ES* 58 (1977): 204–8, rejects the "revenant reading of E. Lench and R. P. Tripp" on the grounds that these two words do not necessarily imply an actual grave. His semantic argument, however, neglects context and the preponderance of occurrences in Old English poetry where *eorðscræf* clearly indicates a grave.

18. Since the original text is not available to me, I have cited Patricia Terry, trans., *Poems of the Vikings: The Elder Edda* (New York: Bobbs-Merrill, 1969), p. 251.

19. *ASPR* 3, lines 886–88, 1027–9a; the Old English runs:

> Weccað of deaðe   dryhtgumena bearn,
> eall monna cynn,   to meotudsceafte
> egeslic of þære ealdan moldan,   hatað hy upp astandan.
>
> Þonne eall hraðe   Adames cynn
> onfehð flæsce,   weorþed foldræste
> eardes æt ende.

20. *Ibid.*, *Soul and Body II*, lines 86–88a:

> ðonne wile dryhten sylf   dæda gehyran
> æt ealra monna gehwam   muþes reorde
> wunde wiþerlean.

21. Frederick Tupper, Jr., *The Riddles of the Exeter Book* (reprint ed. Darmstadt: Wissenschaftliche Buchgesellschaft, 1968), *Riddle* 57, 6b. See Gregory K. Jember, *An Interpretive Translation of the Exeter Book Riddles*, Ph.D. diss., University of Denver, 1975, pp. 151–52, who suggests the solution "Souls of the Damned."

22. See n. 8 above.

23. *ASPR* 6:108. The West Saxon version runs:

> For þam nedfere   næni wyrþeþ
> þances snotera,   þonne him þearf sy
> to gehisgenne   ær his heonengange
> hwæt his gaste   godes oþþe yfeles
> æfter deaþe heonon   demed weorþe.

24. Stanley B. Greenfield, *A Critical History of Old English Literature* (New York: New York University Press, 1965), p. 201.

25. "Old Norse Ghosts," *Folklore* 57 (1946): 50–65, 106–27. On this note, Beowulf's so-called digressions on his past exploits and just behavior as king of the Geats represent a more archaic form of the death-song than those which appear later in the sagas. On the romantic transformation even among these see Jan de Vries *Altnordische Literaturgeschichte* 2, *Grundriss der germanischen Philologie* 16 (Berlin: Walter De Gruyter, 1967), pp. 171–72: "Vielleicht ist Hildebrands Klage nur eine schwächere, blassere Nachahmung von Hjalmars Sterbelied: jedenfalls ist Heusler darin zuzustimmen, dass Hildebrandr, mit der kraftvollen Erhabenheit des deutschen Doppelgängers nicht viel mehr als das Adjektiv *sváss* gemein' hat. . . . solcher Lieder . . . sind nur das Resultat einer Modesucht, die dazu geführt hat, dass die Verfasser von romantischen Sagas *(fornaldarsǫgur)* das Interesse für ihre phantasievollen Geschichten durch die Einschaltung eddisch anmutender Lieder haben steigern wollen."

26. Lars Lönnroth, "Hjalmar's Death Song and the Delivery of Eddic Poetry," *Speculum* 46 (1971): 1–21, has recently restated the connection between the Old English elegies and the death-song. Referring to such poems as *Brynhild's Ride to Hel*, he comments: "Within this large group of elegiac *Ruckblicksgedichte*, which are obviously related to the Old English elegies, the death-songs may be said to constitute a special sub-genre or perhaps a 'theme' in the sense introduced by Parry and Lord" (p. 11, n. 32). See Andreas Heusler, *Die altgermanische Dichtung* (Darmstadt: Wissenschaftliche Buch-

gesellschaft, 1957), p. 188, "Mit den altenglischen Elegien . . . hat unsre eddische Gruppe eine oft bemerkte Verwandtschaft in der Stimmung, im menschlichen Baustoff."

27. *The Seafarer*, in G. P. Krapp and E. V. K. Dobbie, eds. *The Exeter Book* (New York: Columbia University Press, 1936), *ASPR*, 3:144, ll. 39–43.

28. Ibid., l. 17, and *The Wanderer*, *ASPR* 3:135, l. 48. See n. 17 above and the article there cited for previous arguments that the "wife's" friend is indeed dead.

29. *The Phoenix*, *ASPR* 3:106, ll. 428–32a.

30. Heusler, *Die altgermanische Dichtung*, p. 146.

31. Alain Renoir, "A Reading of *The Wife's Lament*," *ES* 58 (1977):4–19, discusses this question of *ic*, pointing out that it is most common in *The Exeter Book* (8–10). He restricts his attention, however, to poems that begin with *ic*, rather than all "statements directly involving the author" (9).

32. I cite the version in the *Nornagests-thattr*, from Ernst Wilken, ed., *Die prosaische Edda im Auszuge nebst Volsunga-saga und Nornagests-thattr* (Paderborn: Ferdinand Schoningh, 1877). The Old Norse runs (Wilken, p. 255):

(Helr. Br. 5) Ek mun segja þér
sanna roeðu.
velgjarnt hofuð,
ef þik vita lystir,
hvé gerðu mik
Gjúka arfar
ástalausa
ok eiðrofa!

33. See Chadwick, n. 25 above, who, p. 61, relates how the dead poet Thorliefr comes out of the barrow in *Thorliefs Thattr Farlsskjalds* (*Flateyarbok*, 1:207 ff.) to teach Hallbjorn how to compose a panegyric on him. Chadwick also discusses how Ögvaldr in the *Halfs Saga*, chap. 2, comes out of the barrow and chants his life story.

34. Since it is the presence of the "I" here that encompasses the point in hand, it is not necessary for argumentative purposes to cite the Old English. The passages are to be found, respectively, in *ASPR*, 3: (1), p. 134, (2), p. 143, (3), p. 149, (4), pp. 156–57, (5), pp. 166, 167, 168, (6), p. 175, (7), p. 179, (8), p. 218. It is interesting to note that, just as Noordby begins his book on the influence of Old Norse upon English literature with Thomas Gray (n. 6 above), Alan Sinfield begins his recent book, *Dramatic Monologue* (New York: Barnes & Noble, 1977) well into modern times. His chapter "Before The Victorians" (pp. 42–52) does not mention anything from the Old English.

35. My present research involves an essay comparing "Widsith" to the transmigratory manifestations of God in Irish and Hindu literature.

36. T. A. Shippey, *Poems of Wisdom and Learning in Old English* (Cambridge: D. S. Brewer, 1976).

37. See Benjamin Thorpe, ed., *The Homilies of the Anglo-Saxon Church* (London: The Aelfric Society, 1844), "VI. Kal. Jan., Assumptio Scī Iohannis Apostoli," 1:58–76, in which John raises Drusiana (p. 60) and Stacteus (p. 68), and later two thieves (p. 74). Clearly, power over death is a sign of divinity.

38. In "The Unquiet Grave," *Journal of English Folkdance and Song Society* (1940):99. For a similar argument, see my "Narrator as Revenant," n. 3 above, especially pp. 360–61. For the later medieval history of poems dealing with death, raising of the (speaking) dead, and judgment, see Rosemary Woolf, *The Religious Lyric in the Middle Ages* (Oxford: The Clarendon Press, 1968), pp. 312–36, especially; and Phillippa Tristram, *Figures of Life and Death in Medieval English Literature* (London: Paul Elek, 1976), pp. 152–83. On the question of "primitive analogues" for beliefs about death, such as "the sentient corpse," Tristram argues that these "are more immediately explained by the materialist tendencies of a faltering faith" (p. 156). I have not seen Reidar Christiansen, *The Dead and the Living*, *Studia Norvegica* 2 (Oslo, 1946).

39. (Cambridge: D. S. Brewer, 1975). Those people who tend toward classical-

Christian sources also tend to avoid the semantics of individual words and phrases and cite their sources on a peculiarly abstract or literal level. For the opposite emphasis, see William Whallon, *Formula, Character, and Context* (Washington, D.C.: Center for Hellenic Studies, 1969), who refers to Old English as "reformed but not converted," p. 116.

40. See *The Old English Version of Bede's Ecclesiastical History of the English People*, Book V, chapt. 13, ed. Thomas Miller, Early English Text Society, o.s. 95,96 (London: N. Trubner, 1890), p. 424, line 20. The OE Bede's *ongen norð east rodor* becomes in Aelfric *to east-dæle* (*Homilies*, 2:350, 352) as both relate the vision of Dryhthelm. For *Baldrs Draumar, austan dyrr,* see n. 13 above; and for *Hjalmars Deathsong,* see Andreas Heusler and Wilhelm Ranisch, eds., *Eddica Minora* (Dortmund; Wilh. Ruhfus, 1903), "Hiálmars Sterbelied," pp. 49–53 (two versions), from the *Hervararsaga,* l. 8, *Hrafn flygr austan.* For the distribution of the idea that the "door" to the underworld lies to the "East," see James Hastings, ed., *Encyclopedia of Religion and Ethics,* s.v. "Door," 4:446–52, and "Points of the Compass," 10:73–88.

41. Shippey, *Poems of Wisdom,* pp. 3 and 25. J. R. R. Tolkien, *Tree and Leaf* (Boston: Houghton Mifflin, 1965), has, like Sidney and Shelley before him, reasserted the divine power of the poet as "sub-creator" and "real maker" to generate a truly independent "secondary world," p. 70.

42. H. R. Ellis Davidson, *Gods and Myths of Northern Europe* (Harmondsworth, Middlesex, England: Penguin Books, 1964), p. 140.

The Wife's Lament as Death-Song

William C. Johnson, Jr.

> There was an old woman
> Lived under a hill—
> And if she's not gone,
> She lives there still.
>
> Mother Goose

The critical history of *The Wife's Lament* illustrates a number of problems facing readers of the Old English lyric.[1] A valid interpretation must encompass several stumbling blocks: an indefinite narrative situation; unclear identities of the participants; and some obscure words and unusual constructions. Such problems, furthermore, may result as much from the very age of the text as from any inherent obscurity, for even in the putatively universal "love-lament" we cannot expect close coincidence between medieval England and the twentieth century. Contexts of implication often vary widely within a contemporaneous audience, let alone between audiences separated by centuries. This meeting of archaic text and modern reader has already resulted in a number of interpretive compromises. The most frequently encountered generalization about the poem, for example, is that it constitutes a woman's lament over her separation or estrangement from her lord or husband. The narrator is taken to be an ordinary human being comprehensible in terms of a modern sociobiological model. The poem is held to express, in a psychological manner, her reactions to emotional strife.[2] Even this seemingly self-evident assumption, however, can be questioned. The most obvious difficulty, which has given rise to some ingenious extrapolation, is the question of why a woman must dwell in a surreal landscape and be confined to an *eorðscræf* under an oak tree, apparently without sustenance, in a place in which her movement is mysteriously associated with dawn.[3] The simplest explanation of this situation—that the woman dwells in the world of the grave and is perhaps dead herself—

accounts for these and other difficulties and provides new insights into elegiac poetic strategies.

Two recent interpretations propose that the wife is actually dead. Elinor Lench argues that the narrator has been murdered by her husband and speaks from the grave as one of the "living dead," a prominent group in Norse literature and folklore.[4] Raymond P. Tripp, Jr., sees the narrator as the *revenant* of ballad tradition, forced to return to its grave at dawn and yearning for reunion with its lord, who is viewed as a circumlocution for the rational soul.[5] These views have generated controversy insofar as they rely on Northern instead of Latinate traditions and because they deal with attitudes alien to modern culture.[6] These and similar lines of thought, however, offer the most useful context for interpreting the otherwise unusual narrative situation and poetic force of *The Wife's Lament*. The present essay looks at three kinds of evidence—lexical, literary, and homiletic—that suggest that the poet is adapting the Germanic death-song for religious purposes.

Whatever the precise situation of the narrator, it is difficult to avoid the fact that she dwells in a ghostly world somewhere between this life and the next.[7] The poetic evocation of deathlike status appears in a combination of nuance and detail. The stark singularity of her condition—*minre sylfre sið* (2a)—itself provides a context of isolation from humanity that permeates and frames the poem. Her plight, furthermore, is worse than the troubles of either youth or old age (*niwes oþþe ealdes,* 4b). She refers to an unspecified murder or violent death (*morþor,* 20b) committed, contemplated, or suffered by her lord, or perhaps referring to her own demise. The language of the poem likewise stresses the permanence of her suffering. Robert Stevick notes that many of the verbs "present a constant feeling of long-lasting or repeated action (or circumstance) which anticipates no end."[8] The clearest evidence that the narrator dwells in the grave world, however, appears in the poet's verbal expansion of characteristics of her dwelling. Associations of nature, the earth, and of a dreary dwelling-place combine:

> Heht mec mon wunian   on wuda bearwe   (27)
> under actreo   in þam eorðscræf;
> eald is þes eorðsele,   eal ic eom oflangað.
> Sindon dena dimme,   duna uphea,
> bitre burgtunas   brerum beweaxne,
> wic wynna leas;   ful oft mec her wraþe begeat
> fromsiþ frean.   Frynd sind on eorþan,
> leofe lifgende   leger weardiað,

þonne ic on uhtan   ana gonge
under actreo   geond þas eorðscrafu.

(One commanded me to dwell   in a woody grove
Under an oak-tree   in the *eorðscræf;*
Old is this earth-hall;   I am wholly possessed by longing.
The valleys are dim,   the hills raised up,
Bitter enclosures   overgrown with briars,
A joyless dwelling;   often it took me grievously,
My lord's departure.   Friends on the earth
Live happily   and take to their beds
When I go at dawn   alone
Under the oak-tree   throughout this *eorðscræf.*)

The use of the definitive *þam* (28b) and the echoic variation of *eorðscræf* and *eorðsele* suggest that the *eorðscræf* is, in Leslie's words, "an outstanding feature of the landscape" (p. 56). The contrast between friends alive on the earth and the narrator alone in an extraordinary setting suggests that she, like the dragon in *Beowulf*, whose barrow is also called *eorðsele* (2515a) and *eorðscræf* (3064a), is mysteriously earth-bound, perhaps by a spell, but more obviously by death itself. The emphasis on enforced confinement defines her isolation as a spatial entombment, especially through words and phrases such as *wunian/ on wuda bearwe* "dwell in a woody grove" (27), *wic wynna leas* "joyless dwelling" (32a), *eorðscræf* "earth-cave" (28b, 36b), *eorðsele* "earth-hall" (29a), *dena dimme* "valleys are dim" (30a), and *bitre burg-tunas* "bitter enclosures" (31a). Such language reveals an interpenetration of the grave world, perpetual confinement, and emotive despair, creating a symbolism of *dwelling as living death*. The narrator's voice is decidedly "human," but it speaks through archaic parameters of consciousness and being, which, as the OE riddles and cognate Old Icelandic works reveal, often transcends the limits of a modern, biologically determined psychology.

The word *eorðscræf* itself may be a key to interpretation of the poem. Elsewhere in OE poetry it usually signifies "grave." T. P. Dunning and A. J. Bliss comment:

> This not uncommon compound is often translated "earth-cave," a rendering which is not wholly perspicuous. Though the simplex *scræf* normally means "cave," the compound *eorðscræf* often means "grave." In *Psalm* 67:7 *on eorðscræfum* glosses *in sepulchris . . .* in *Andreas* 802–3 *moldern* "sepulchres" is expanded as *open eorðscræfu.*[9]

Of the twelve occurrences of the compound in the poetic corpus, two appear in the *WL*. Of the other ten instances, six unambiguously refer to the grave and a seventh to the dragon's barrow in *Beowulf,* which is most likely a chambered tomb.[10] Leslie translates the word in the *WL* as "chambered barrow" (p. 56). The interpretive problems introduced by the conventional translations "earth-cave" or "earth-dwelling" make the alternative—"grave"—even more attractive, for such a reading answers the vexing question of the nature of the narrator's surroundings, which as a place for merely mortal punishment would be strange in the extreme. As Lench argues: "Even if one assumes . . . that the husband is responsible for her exile, the strangeness of the wife's residence forces the invention of reasons for this extraordinary mode of handling domestic difficulties" (p. 12).

The poet's expansion of symbolism of a grave-dwelling also sheds light on the nature of the *wudu bearwe* (27b) or "forest grove" in which the *eorðscræf* is located. The grave, as we recall, is under an oak tree (28). The oak, as several critics have noted, is the "holy tree of the Germanic peoples" and represents the powers of life and death.[11] If Malone is correct in emending the manuscript reading *hearheard* (15b) to *hereard* "grove-dwelling," then it becomes possible to view the narrator as one condemned by an unspecified but oak-related spell to dwell in a sacred grove surrounding a burial place.[12] She can move throughout (*geond,* 36b) the *eorðscræf* itself, but never beyond the *eard* (15–16, 35–37). Within the barrow she suffers her anguish; the sacred enclosure itself surrounds and contains the barrow. Such spell-binding, moreover, could have resulted in or itself represent death, in which case the poem expresses a defunct narrator's complaint over its postmortem condition—as ghost, *draugr,* or *revenant.* As L. C. Wymberly describes the ballad *revenant:* "The ghost of folksong does not remain near or hover about the corpse. It is the corpse."[13] Whether the narrator is literally dead or has entered the grave-setting or barrow alive as do other figures in the Norse sagas, may never be determined. What seems clear, however, is that the poet takes pains to dramatize the narrator's situation as a condition of death. The *eorðscræf* is certainly a grave of some kind, and the grove, its *bitre burgtunas* perhaps suggesting a group of burial mounds, evokes an atmosphere of chthonic mystery. In this context the oak tree may reflect archaic associations of spellbinding, oath-making and breaking, death and the grave.[14] That the grave itself is a dwelling-place is, of course, a prominent motif in folklore universally.[15]

These associations may derive from a poetic use of the Germanic death-song. Nora Chadwick presents a detailed summary of skaldic, Eddic, and saga death-songs and points out that they were known to the Anglo-Saxons.[16] The death-song or chant is a lament expressed by the hero or heroine at the point of death, but in several cases the principle sings after death, as a *draugr* within the barrow. Chadwick notes that "the death-chant is an ancient Teutonic institution, and . . . is closely associated with the barrow already in ancient times" (115). She explains further the connection between the chant and the gift of poetry attributed to the *haugbui* or barrow-dweller:

> It would seem to be something in the nature of the hero's introduction to the spirit world. If such were, indeed, the traditional idea associated with the death-song, and as these songs may have been chanted within the tomb in the case of those who entered the tomb alive, it would be by a natural transition that poetry and song should come to be associated with the barrow, and the power to inspire with similar gifts those who came to visit them. (116)

Death-songs are sung by women as well as by men. Specific parallels between the *WL* and several Eddic chants support the argument that the OE poet adopted and adapted this genre.

The Eddic death-songs of Sigrun, Guðrun, and Brynhildr occur in contexts of ritual suttee, through which they seek reunion with their dead lords.[17] In *Helgakviða Hundingsbana* II, Sigrun meets the dead Helgi in a burial mound *(haugr)*, sleeps with him, and dies of grief when he departs to seek the house of the dead *(draughusa)*. Her death-chant reveals both longing for her departed husband and gloom over the prospects of perpetual separation:

> Kominn væri nú, ef koma hygði, (st. 50)
> Sigmundar burr frá sǫlom Oðins;
> qveð ec grams þinig grænaz vanir,
> er á asclimom ernir sitia
> oc drífr drótt oll draumþinga til.

> (Now were he come, if he intends to come,
> Sigmund's son, from Odin's hall;
> I talk of the hero's return, turning gray with hope,
> When on the ash-limbs eagles sit
> And all men seek out the meeting of dreams.)

Here there is no explicit mention of suttee, but the context is similar to that of *Guðrunarhvat* and *Helreið Brynhildar*. A maiden tells Sigrun that she would be mad to seek the house of the dead at night, because at that time the ghosts are strongest (st. 51). Similarly, in *Guðrunarhvat* the living heroine appeals to the dead Sigurðr to ride back to earth to meet her. She asks, in this case, that the funeral pyre be piled with oak:

Hlaðit ér, iarlar,   eikikǫstinn,   (st. 20)
látið þann und hilmi   hæstan verða!
megi brenna brióst   bǫlvafult eldr,
. . . . um hiarta   þiðni sorgir!

(Pile up, jarls,   the pyre of oak;
Make it for a hero   the highest ever;
Let it burn my breast   grief-filled, the fire,
. . . about the heart   until my sorrows melt.)

As in the *WL*, the oak is associated with death, and the narrator's grief seems unbearable. In *Helreið Brynhildar*, the heroine, after exercising her duty of suttee, departs on a death-ride. She is confronted by a *gygr* or giantess, who accuses her of having brought disaster on Gjuki's house. In a proud reply, she recalls her life as a young valkyrie, when she and her sisters were captured by a king who placed their skin-shapes *(hami)* under an oak tree *(under eic borit)*. Parallel verses in the *Flateyjarbók* give a reading even closer to that of the *WL:*

Lét mic af harmi,   hugfullr konungr,   (Neckel-Kuhn
Atla systor,   under eic búa.   st. 6, n.)

(He commanded/placed me from harm,   the proud king,
Sister of Atli,   to dwell under an oak.)

The precise meaning of these variants remains obscure. Perhaps the power of the sacred oak allows the king to capture or possibly to protect the young Brynhildr by means of a spell.[18] The apparent confusion between these two versions (*hami* "skin shapes" or *harmi* "from harm"?) suggests an archaic tradition of shape-shifting imperfectly understood or perhaps disbelieved. Nonetheless, there remains a close parallel between the *Flateyjarbók* version and lines 26–27 of the *WL*. Brynhildr speaks after death about having been commanded to dwell under an oak tree. Despite the differences in perspective, the generic likenesses seem significant: in confinement, a woman speaks a lament from the world of the dead.

The absence of specific identities and definite narrative circumstances in the *WL* makes point-for-point parallels with these Eddic poems impossible. There are enough similarities, however, to warrant the possibility that the poet is adapting a death-song. These parallels, furthermore, may shed new light on several long-disputed passages in the *WL*. Each of the Eddic poems, for example, records a lament in death about love that had been damaged by blood feuds. Sigrun's brother is driven by family revenge to slay his brother-in-law, Helgi; Brynhildr incites Gunnar to slay his brother-in-law, Sigurðr, Gud-

run's husband. In more general terms, the wife voices a similar kind
of complaint:

> S[c]eal ic feor ge neah   (25)
> mines felaleofan   fæðu dreogan.

> (Both near and far I must
> With respect to my beloved   suffer a feud.)

OE *fæðu* often refers in a legal way to a state of feud.[19] It may also
explain why the wife's *monnan* "man" is *morþor hycgendne* "thinking of
murder" (20b).[20] Perhaps he, like Helgi, (*HH* II, st. 44), is also dead as
a result of feud and reflecting on his own sorrowful state.

The idea of ritual suttee, moreover, may provide a clue to the oft-
discussed meaning of lines 9–10:

> Ða ic me feran gewat   folgað secan,
> wineleas wrǽcca,   for minre weaþearfe.

> (Then I departed (= died, performed suttee) in search of service
>   (to my lord)
> A friendless exile, on account of my woeful need.)

Like *fæðu, folgað* is a technical term denoting the service due by a
retainer to his lord. It often expresses also a sense of fated destiny.[21]
After the narrator's lord has been killed, that is, she practices the
ritual service—suicide—to which the death-song may attest.

A further similarity between the *WL* and the Sigurðr legend appears in the broken oath. Sigurðr breaks his vow to Brynhildr by
marrying Gudrun—a vow restored only after death when Brynhildr
seeks to rejoin him.[22] Similarly, the narrator of the *WL* recalls:

> Ful oft wit beotedan   (21)
> þæt unc ne gedælde   nemne deað ana,
> owiht elles.

> (Often we vowed
> That us would not separate   anything except death,
> Nothing else.)

While the separation of Sigurðr and Brynhildr is specific and circumstantial, that in the *WL* is generic in two ways: as an unspecified
separation, and as a separation caused by death itself, which in the
poet's treatment blurs the circumstantiality of the past.

The genre of the death-song, then, provides a sound, if partial,
beginning in establishing a context of meaning for the poem. We seek
a reconstructed meaning of the whole that will allow us to interpret

the parts. These three Eddic women lament separation from and seek reunion with their lords, and they do so in remembrance of blood feuds. They lament, furthermore, on the verge of entering or from within the grave and world of the dead, Gudrun speaking before entering the pyre; Sigrun communing with the dead Helgi in the barrow and returning to die; and Brynhildr speaking from the underworld after her death.

There remain even so details and perspectives unique to the *WL.* Its narrator has no hope of reunion but must suffer perpetual confinement. Unlike the Eddic laments, hers is not individualized, but general, and finally, as I shall argue, "gnomic-homiletic." Her "lord" has apparently commanded her to dwell in the gloomy abode. Finally, the details of this deathly dwelling-place receive special poetic emphasis. What is stressed in the *WL,* in short, is the perpetuity of suffering in the world of the grave. It may be impossible to discover what E. D. Hirsch, Jr., has called the "intrinsic genre" of the *WL,* the compelling sense of the whole and its context that makes sense of all the details.[23] We can, however, build upon the general framework of the death-song by looking at a related Anglo-Saxon homiletic genre, for life in the grave-world receives its most thorough and graphic OE poetic treatment in the *Soul and Body* poems.

The *WL,* in other words, may represent a poetic transvaluation of the Germanic death-song in which the poet exploits homiletic possibilities of postmortem states. The idea that the separable soul can journey out of the body, for example, is witnessed in both Latin patristic and OE homiletic texts and has been applied to *The Wanderer* and *The Seafarer.*[24] The notions of the grave as an eternal house *(domus aeterna)* and of the cursed soul wandering in torment appear in Roman paganism and were inherited, if often inhospitably, by early Christianity.[25] The OE *Soul and Body* I, II, furthermore, share specific narrative and dictional similarities with the *WL,* including the motifs of dwelling, journeying, separation, punishment, and the hostility of the earthly surroundings of the grave.[26] As in the *WL,* the grave is a gloomy place of perpetual confinement; the grave-dweller's separation from its former partner hopeless; and movement around the grave or within it associated with dawn. The soul once dwelled *(eardode,* 30a) in the body as the body now inhabits an *eorðscræf* (113b). The soul is cursed to journey alone in the world of the dead *(ic ana of ðe/ut siðade* "Alone from you/I journeyed out," 52), to lament its damned state of separation from God in the face of judgment (93b–96), and to chastise the now defunct body, itself a corporeal ghost suffering the terror of worms (111–19a). Rather than treating the

horror of bodily decay and the soul's castigation of the formerly im-
moral body, however, the poet of the *WL* stresses the mental and
emotional anxiety of life in the grave through the archaic psychology
of the corporeal ghost. Like *The Wanderer* and *The Seafarer*, the elegy is
generalized, allowing the audience to experience the death-song in a
new context of homiletic implication in which "everyman" glimpses
the very worst that can happen.[27] As Tripp suggests: "just one step
out of the archaic into the spiritual literalism of an early Christian
world, death would still be something far less awesome in itself than
damnation" (353).

This approach may appear to some as yet another interpretive wild-
goose chase, in which, like Kafka's hunter Gracchus, we can never be
sure we have found the right harbor. Whether the narrator is *revenant, draugr, umbra,* or animal soul, however, seems less important poetically than that she speaks from the world of the grave and so
witnesses to the living despair of damnation.[28] This approach accounts for the probable source area of the poem—for a partially valid
"extrinsic genre"—and, if my guess about the link to the soul and
body tradition is correct, for the informing center of the poet's adap-
tations—for his intrinsic genre. The poem's conclusion, nevertheless,
seems cryptic, perhaps to allow for an epochal doubleness of interpretation. It appears to constitute a gnomic moral addressed to young
persons in general, based on the formula, *A scyle geong mon* "always a
young person must . . . ." In its generality, the conclusion would
satisfy the tenets of Northern wisdom, but would also appropriately
dramatize the price of damnation to new or would-be converts.[29] The
poet finally returns to the language of the death-song in depicting the
narrator's unhappy *freond,* who dwells in a dreary landscape very
similar to hers.[30] Given a poetic fusion of death-song and homily,
readers have erred in opting for modern psychological readings here,
such as that the wife curses her husband or lover. In the Eddic death-
songs discussed above, the lord has not departed on an earthly journey—he has *died* and entered the other world, from whence the wife
or lover implores him, one last time, to return. The poem simultaneously evokes images and values of both heroic and Christian super-
naturalism. The lord's *dreorsele* "dreary hall" (50a) is his own grave,
and his memory of *wynlicran wic* "a happier dwelling" (52a) is a discon-
solate look back at life in the body, the *sawol-hus* "soul-house" of OE
poetry.[31]

The linguistic texture of the *WL* reinforces the sense of sentient
experience in the world of the grave. The many substantives for
dwelling combine with verbs stressing endless suffering (see Martin

Green's essay, p. 123) to create a language of perpetual entombment. The frequent use of modal verbs *(mot, mæg, scyle)* signals a
special kind of compulsion and calls attention to the supramundane
limitations now inevitably in force.[32] As in *The Wanderer* and *The
Seafarer,* narrative movement oscillates between sorrowful reflection
on the (mortal) past (11. 6–28) and present (postmortem) lament (1–
5, 29–42). The conclusion integrates gnomic wisdom and homiletic
warning. My translation of lines 42–52a emphasizes these alternatives:[33]

> Always a young person   must be sober in mind,
> Firm in heart-thoughts;   likewise he should have
> A happy demeanor   along with his breast-cares
> While he experiences/suffers sin-sorrows.   Or let him
>   through himself determine
> All his earthly joys; or let him be widely outcast/dead,
> Far from the folk-land—   that (is how) my friend sits
> Under the stone-cliff,   icy with storm,
> (My) sad-minded/dead companion   covered by water:
> In his dreary hall/grave   my friend suffers
> Great cares;   too often he remembers
> A happier abode.

The poet's final appeal is multivalent: the genres of death-song and
soul-body homily unite in a voice from the grave:

> Wa bið þæm
> þe sceal of langoþe   leofes abidan.
>
> (Woeful are those
> Who must in longing   await a loved one.)

Nature, psyche, and supernature merge in the poet's religious transformation. The lament of a wife for her dead lord reverberates with
homiletic overtones of the separation of soul and body, each suffering
sentiently the terrors of a purgatorial afterlife placed poetically in the
folkloric world of the dead. It is perhaps no surprise that early Christian England should produce poetry in which the Germanic voice of
the dead speaks a warning about what finally results when life is lived
apart from God. Here, however, the damnation is not moralized as
the result of sin, but *dramatized as death.* In its broadest cultural resonances, the *WL* projects a lament of all those who suffer isolation in
the gravelike confines of this world. The desire for a permanent
dwelling and reunion in the next world is left for the reader to imagine and, by implication, for his culture to provide.

NOTES

1. For convenient summaries of nineteenth-century German scholarship on the poem, see N. Kershaw, *Anglo-Saxon and Norse Poems* (Cambridge: Cambridge University Press, 1922), pp. 28–29; and Thomas M. Davis, "Another View of *The Wife's Lament*," *PLL* 1 (1965):291–305. For coverage of more recent views, see *Three Old English Elegies*, ed. R. F. Leslie (Manchester: Manchester University Press, 1961), pp. 3–12; and Elinor Lench, "The Wife's Lament: A Poem of the Living Dead," *Comitatus* 1 (1970):3–23. There is an apparently increasing lack of consensus. W. W. Lawrence, "The Banished Wife's Lament," *MP* 5 (1908):387–405, long ago noted that "the last word about the poem has not yet been spoken" (388). Recent criticism is even more cautious. Douglas Short, "The Old English *Wife's Lament*: An Interpretation," *NM* 71 (1970):585–603, writes that "even a preliminary understanding of the poem is difficult to achieve" (585).

2. Leslie's summary comment is still representative: "Such plot as there is appears to be designed . . . to indicate the depths of misery and adversity that man can be called upon to endure: . . . in the case of a woman, desertion by her husband and rejection by his kin in a strange land" (p. 12).

3. This question also puzzled earlier editors and critics. L. L. Schücking, "Das angelsächsische Gedicht von der *Klage der Frau*," *Zeitschrift für deutsches Altertum und deutsche Litteratur* 48 (1906):436–49, writes: "Wie sollte der man, der gatte, den v. 47ff, selbst in der bedrängtesten lage im fremden lande zeigen, der frau befehlen können, im wald zu leben?" (cited in Lawrence, p. 405).

4. See n. 1.

5. Raymond P. Tripp, Jr., "The Narrator as Revenant: A Reconsideration of Three Old English Elegies," *PLL* 8 (1972):339–61.

6. Joseph Harris, "A Note on *eorðscræf / eroðsele* and Current Interpretations of *The Wife's Lament*," *ES* 58 (1977):204–8, complains: "It is incumbent upon the postmortem theorists to provide clear evidence that death has actually occurred and to deal with several positive indications that the speaker is now alive" (206). This begs the question, however, of the role of anticipated context in an archaic text and ignores the possibility that the "life" depicted represents the world of the dead—a common practice in folklore and balladry. If the convention of the death-song—a voice from the grave—was familiar to the poet's audience, then the poet would not be constrained to show that death has actually occurred. Even a cursory review of OE literature reminds us, furthermore, of a variety of nonhuman speakers, including angels, devils, the cross, and various "inanimate" objects in the riddles. The location of the narrative voice may require that we suspend our Newtonian coordinates and our humanism.

7. All references to the poem are from Leslie's edition (see n. 1).

8. Robert Stevick, "Formal Aspects of *The Wife's Lament*," *JEGP* 59 (1960):23.

9. T. P. Dunning and A. J. Bliss, *The Wanderer* (New York: Appleton-Century-Crofts, 1969), p. 48.

10. See G. V. Smithers, *The Making of "Beowulf"* (Durham: University of Durham, 1961), pp. 12–13.

11. G. Storms, *Anglo-Saxon Magic* (The Hague, 1948), p. 43.

12. Kemp Malone, "Two English Frauenlieder," *Comparative Literature* 14 (1962):106–17, suggests that *herh* is a variant of *hearg*, a word suggesting a heathen temple: the wife has been banished to a "heathenish abode" (114).

13. *Folklore in the English and Scottish Ballads* (New York: Dover, 1965), p. 101.

14. According to Sir James Frazier, ancient European groves were often burial grounds and the trees themselves were believed to be animated by the spirits of the dead. See *The New Golden Bough*, ed. T. H. Gaster (New York: New American Library, 1964), pp. 108–12. For literary analogues see Vergil's Polydorus (*Aeneid* 3:19–48); the Middle English ballad "The Marriage of Sir Gawain," in which an enchanted hag sits "betwixt an oke & a green hollen" (st. 15); and Chaucer's *Pardoner's Tale*, in which the

old man tells the youths they will find death in a grove under an oak tree (*The Complete Works of Geoffrey Chaucer,* 2nd ed. F. N. Robinson, ed. [Boston: Houghton-Mifflin, 1957], p. 153, ll. 762–65).

15. For Old Norse instances, see H. R. Ellis-Davidson, *Gods and Myths of Northern Europe* (Baltimore, Md.: Penguin, 1964), pp. 152–58.

16. "Norse Ghosts," *Folklore* 57 (June 1946):50–65; (September 1946):106–27. As OE examples, Chadwick cites the last survivor's lament and Beowulf's death speech (*Beowulf* 2247–66, 2425–37 respectively), and Bede's "Death Song."

17. References are to *Edda: Die Lieder des Codex Regius,* ed. G. Neckel, rev. H. Kuhn (Heidelberg: Winter, 1962). Translations are my own.

18. Kershaw noticed this parallel (p. 174, n. 27) but pointed out that the contexts of the Eddic passages are obscure. She speculates that the grove in the *WL* is a *griðastaðir* or sanctuary for fugitives.

19. Leslie cites F. Liebermann, *Die Gesetze der Angelsachsen* (Halle, 1906), 2:67, s.v. *fæðe,* and comments: "It cannot, therefore, refer to hostility of the husband towards his wife; personal enmity is generally expressed in Old English by *hete* or its compounds" (p. 55). *Beowulf* contains numerous examples of *fæðe,* which suggests generic enmity and at times the moral necessity of opposing an enemy (e.g., 459, 470, 595, 1207, 1333, etc.).

20. OE *morþor* often bears a more concrete sense—of death by violence—than its modern counterpart. This is suggested by compounds such as *morþorbealo* "slaughter," *morþorbed* "bed of death," or *morþorhete* "blood feud."

21. *Folgað* can suggest service as personal destiny in both social and supernatural contexts. See *Deor* 38, *Elene* 903, 929, *Christ and Satan* 328. The OI cognate *fylgð,* "a following, help, guidance" and related words, suggests a semantic field encompassing and integrating death, martial service, and the love of man and woman: *fylgð* can mean "bodyguard" (via the *comitatus*); *fylgja* "one following" refers to a fetch or female guardian spirit whose appearance forebodes death; *fylgi-kona* means "concubine." See R. Cleasby, G. Vigfusson, W. Craigie, *An Icelandic-English Dictionary,* 2d. ed. (Oxford: Clarendon Press, 1957).

22. See *Gríppispá* st. 45–46; *Völsungasaga,* chap. 22.

23. *Validity in Interpretation* (New Haven, Conn.: Yale University Press, 1967), pp. 78–89.

24. Neil Hultin, "The External Soul in *The Seafarer* and *The Wanderer,*" *Folklore* 88 (1977):39–45. Hultin (pp. 41–42) cites the *Old English Martyrology* in which St. Fursey's *gast* journeys out of his body; and St. Ambrose's *De Issac vel anima* in which St. Paul's *anima* does the same.

25. These and related customs and literary analogues are documented in detail by Franz Cumont, *Afterlife in Roman Paganism* (New York: Dover, 1950), esp. pp. 48, 55–56, 198.

26. References are to *Soul and Body* II in *The Exeter Book,* ed. G. P. Krapp and E. V. K. Dobbie (New York: Columbia University Press, 1936), pp. 174–78. The same words and phrases appear in the Vercelli version.

27. E. O. G. Turvile-Petre, *Myth and Religion of the North* (New York: Holt-Reinhart, Winston, 1964), p. 273, distinguishes three views of death in ancient Northern religion: (1) the half-life in the grave; (2) the journey—often by ship—to distant underworlds; and (3) the warrior's paradise in Valhöll. In my view, the OE elegies work variations, in homiletic contexts, on these configurations. The *WL* uses the first motif, *The Seafarer* the second, and *The Wanderer* makes a retrospective use of the third (heroic paradise in the hall is forever lost; the Christian heaven hoped for). Though narrative progression in each of these poems is discontinuous, and identification of the narrator problematical, each poem contains passages suggesting postmortem existence. See *The Wanderer* 8–14, 45–47; *The Seafarer* 58–66.

28. The Middle Ages inherited from classical antiquity several conceptions of the soul, the afterlife, and the spirit world. Though evidence is difficult to sift, it seems probable that such ideas mingled with native Germanic conceptions. For a detailed

survey of continuities in custom and belief in the change from pagan to Christian England, see William A. Chaney, "Paganism to Christianity in Anglo-Saxon England," in *Early Medieval Society*, ed. Sylvia Thrupp (New York: Appleton-Century-Crofts, 1967), pp. 67–83. Contraditions and ambiguities, however, also survive, even into the late Middle Ages. C. S. Lewis, *The Discarded Image* (Cambridge: Cambridge University Press, 1964) discusses four rival theories attempting to account for the *longaevi* or fairies, attempts "which never reached finality" (p. 134). The idea of the triple soul, as old as Plato's *Timaeus* in Western thought, was inherited by the Middle Ages. The rough equivalents, Ψυχή(*psyche*) / anima; ἐίδωλον (eidolon) / umbra; and σωμα (soma) / corpus, persist through the Middle Ages, as does the idea that the dead in or about the tomb experience a vegetating and uncertain life (Cumont, *Afterlife*, pp. 196–97). In view of such analogous concepts, a poet composing in early Christian England might have taken advantage of uncertainties or ambiguities. The parallels between the OI *draugr*, the Roman *umbra* or *simulacra*, and the medieval animal soul, for instance, could easily have provided fruitful ground for a poetic use of cognate beliefs.

29. Loren C. Gruber, "The Agnostic Anglo-Saxon Gnomes: *Maxims* I and II, *Germania*, and the Boundaries of Northern Wisdom," *Poetica* (Tokyo) 6 (1976):22–47, treats epistemological and cultural implications of the OE wisdom literature.

30. A. C. Bouman, *Patterns in Old English and Old Icelandic Literature* (Leiden: Leiden University Press, 1962) compares the use of *stanhlip* (*WL* 84a), describing the lord's dwelling, to the seven other occurrences of the word in OE poetry and concludes that the word suggests a "habitation befitting the dead" (p. 59).

31. OE *dreorig* (etym. "bloody") often describes not only the visual appearance but also the qualitative presence of death (e.g., *Beowulf* 2693, 2789; *Wanderer* 83).

32. See lines 2b, 25b, 37a, 38a, 39b, 42a, 43b, 52b.

33. I have repunctuated Leslie and indicated some important semantic alternatives.

On the Identity of the Wanderer

Ida Masters Hollowell

Among the enigmatic Old English "elegies," *The Wanderer* is especially puzzling. As Rosier notes, critics continue to enunciate problems
of considerable complexity with regard to it.[1] Bolton says, "We are
presented with so many contradictory interpretations of this poem
that the student of recent criticism might believe nothing of demon-
strable truth and validity had been or could be written."[2] Fowler
protests that the poem "has suffered as much as any Old English
poem from the analytic skills of 'higher criticism'. . . ."[3] And Cross
charges that in solving the problems presented by the poem, "research has, at times, proceeded like a game of snap in matching of
Germanic pagan sources with those from the Bible and patristic
Christian writing."[4] Our mystification is obvious; and attempts to account for it have failed. We do not know who or *what* the author was
or what the poem was written *for*.[5] And the Wanderer himself remains faceless. No one has pinned him down or made him credible. If
we could provide an identity for him, we would have made progress
toward answering some other questions. Before moving to a consideration of the Wanderer himself, however, I would like to present
certain assumptions that underlie my consideration of the poem.

    1. I assume that *anhaga* = *eardstapa* = *snottor on mode* = "Wan-
derer."

    2. I assume that all of the poem beginning with line 8 and ending
with line 110 constitutes an address by the character just referred to,
the rest being comment of the author. Lumiansky takes the view that
only lines 6–7 and line 111—the *swa cwæð* lines—are to be construed
"as necessary expository comments by the poet,"[6] and it is true that
the first five lines of the poem may reasonably be taken as spoken
either by the *eardstapa* or by the poet. However, the last lines of the
poem seem indubitably to be words of the latter. The *eardstapa* concludes his dramatic address with his climactic

Her bið feoh læne, her bið freond læne,
her bið mon læne, her bið mæg læne:
eal þis eorþan gesteal idel weorþeð.[7]

These seem to be last words. But what defines the matter is the line
immediately following, which says not only *Swa cwæð snottor on mode*,
but reports his physical position as being *sundor* and announces his
occupation: he sits *æt rune*, whatever that may be. It it difficult to take
these lines as other than editorial commentary. While the speaker of
these lines does not have to be the speaker of lines 1–5, the likelihood
is that if the composer is to be taken as uttering the last lines, he is to
be taken as uttering the first five.

3. A third assumption is that the opening and closing, so-called
Christian, lines (11. 1–5 and 114b–15) are alien to the rest of the
poem. Apropos of this assumption, I shall make some fairly extensive
comments.

Critical perspectives change over a stretch of time. A perspective is
replaced by one considered to be more scientific and more produc-
tive. And critical approaches just go out of fashion. For example, the
tendency to emend manuscripts, which once was very strong, has
abated. The tendency to see a work as a composite form has given way
to an assumption that a work is unified and that it has been transmitted substantially as the author composed it. Still more to my purpose
is the fact that following a long period—including much of the
nineteenth century and some of the present—in which scholars
sought to find "Teutonic" strains in Germanic poetry, an aversion has
developed to such a search. Bloomfield's comment, in 1963, to the
effect that "at the present, the Germanizing interpretations, dominant for many years, seem to be on the wane and Christianizing
interpretations are very common,"[8] is an understatement. It might
almost be said that scholars have turned their collective backs with
embarrassment regarding former perspectives that some of them,
and their predecessors, held.

A basic Christianizing interpretation of *The Wanderer* is that of
Huppé, who sees the poem's structure as being "built around the
themal contrast between earthly insecurity and heavenly security: a
contrast stated at the beginning, developed in the body and sum-
marized at the end of the poem."[9] Similarly, Lumiansky feels that the
poem creates a dramatic situation in which the *eardstapa* presents a
monologue "wholly Christian in tone."[10] Diekstra calls the poem "a
Christian Consolation of Philosophy."[11] Rumble, saying that few will
go as far as Robertson in interpreting the poem "in terms almost of
strict Christian allegory," still feels that it is fairly generally agreed

upon by now that the poem exists "substantially as the original poet intended it," and that it expresses "a Christian theme which is entirely in keeping with the Christian thematic matter of a great deal of other Old English literature" of its period.[12]

However, in spite of a general tendency to regard anything in Old English literature that might echo a biblical or patristic source as actually echoing that source, there is a significant hesitancy on the part of some students of Old English literature to accept a "Christian" view of *The Wanderer*. The list of those who are in some important respect hesitant is impressive and can not be ignored. The basic problem that must be faced by any analyst of the poem in exploring the degree of Christian influence is the question of the unity of the poem. The first and the last lines seem to have Christian implications. There is no doubt about 11. 114b–15, which refer to the security that rests with the Father in Heaven, and about 1. 2, which mentions *metudes miltse*. the problem is that these lines are uncongenial to the rest of the poem. Greenfield denies that there is in *The Wanderer* any "themal contrast between man's helplessness and God's mercy," pointing out, in a well-known statement, that in the poem "nothing is suggested about the Christian belief in grace and salvation as an antidote for the transitory nature of the world."[13] Gordon says, "When Dr. Huppé sees in the poem a contrast between the mercy of God and the harshness of fate, he forgets that it is *ælda scyppend* who 'thus laid waste this habitation' (1. 85),"[14] or, in Susie Tucker's words, it is the Creator who has "laid the castle waste."[15] And when the poet says, *Hu gastlic bið, þonne ealre þisse worulde wela weste stondeð* (73–74), he does not mean by *gastlic* "spiritual," as Stanley claims[16] but rather "frightening" or "depressing."[17] Thus the line does not point beyond the wasteland that is being depicted.

In fact, when we read the poem, we find the *eardstapa* rolling up a gloomy fugue, hammering out his—almost monosyllabic—*her bið feoh læne, her bið freond læne, her bið mon læne*, creating as his final construct *eal þis eorþan gesteal idel weorþeð*, and with it forecasting the coming *Dämmerung* of a world once winsome to men and inhabitable by men. The still voice of the poet comes in with its second *swa cwæð* statement, as the poet fixes what is apparently a new position for the *snottor* and thus effectively achieves a distancing maneuver. He withdraws, leaving a soft spotlight still on the former speaker, as he comments in his own pale voice, dispensing his homiletic conclusion about how *til* and how *wel* will be those who seek solace with the Father in Heaven, where all security stands.

If it were not critically fashionable today to discover unity where it has not been thought to exist, few critics would see *The Wanderer*, as it stands, to be a unified artistic achievement. The thought, point of view, the tone of the first and last segments, are at odds with those of the body of the poem. It is as if, at the end, channels have been switched on a television set, pulling a fascinated, horrified, and *involved* viewer from an apocalyptic view of the destruction of his world and flashing before his eyes a sanitized kitchen presided over by a placid voice saying, "Just put half a cup of this in your rinse water and all of your problems will vanish."

In the first place, the poem's main movement has been concluded with the dramatic last words of the *snottor: eal þis eorþan gesteal idel weorþeð*. The poet has underscored the falling of the curtain by an editorial comment and a stage direction: *Swa cwæð snottor on mode gesæt him sundor æt rune.* I would again stress the fact that the *snottor on mode* is no longer performing but is part of a silent tableau. The word *sundor* isolates him. His words, now locked away, but still vivid in our minds, have pointed no Christian moral. Rather, they have given us a dark view of the world and have pointed to an apocalyptic ending of that world. To say that an editorial "Well will it be for him who seeks solace with the Father in Heaven, where for us all security stands," simply added, without even a "therefore," even a *forþon*,[18] to tie the statement to the discourse preceding—to say that that makes for a unified production is to invite disbelief.

4. A fourth assumption is that a growth of wisdom in the Wanderer is not reflected within the confines of the poem. Pope states that the Wanderer, "having appeared to us at first as merely an *eardstapa*," succeeds in earning, "by his discourse the epithet of a wise man, a snottor on mode."[19] I do not believe that the poet intends to point to growth. The man who stops speaking at l. 110 is the same man who started some few moments and some hundred lines earlier, and it is the *snottor on mode* who is speaking throughout. Rosemary Woolf notes, "The very fact that it would only take about ten minutes to read aloud whilst the passage of time within the poem (though past is time recalled) is unchartably long, reveals that the poet is not concerned to show, with any psychological precision, how a person learns. . . ."[20] Further, although the Wanderer's lord was laid to rest *geara iu* (l. 22), there is nothing to indicate that the Wanderer himself, who has been introduced as an *eardstapa*, is not still enduring most of the hardships that he delineates so graphically beginning with line 8. He begins, "Often I have had to. . . ." Then, "There is no one *now* to whom I can tell my troubles," and besides, he says, "It is the custom to hold one's thoughts within his own breast." We also learn that the weary soul

cannot withstand fate; "nor can the troubled mind afford help." Thus there is a practical reason for staying calm and keeping one's wits about him. And this seems to be one point made. After describing what are—purportedly—his own hardships, which he generalizes eventually to cover the lot of any man, the Wanderer says, "*Therefore, I cannot think why, throughout this world, that my mind should not become dark when I think exhaustively about the lives of noblemen. . . .*" As Gordon says, he *is* saddened,[21] or this is the stand he takes. He then launches into a sermon on how wise a man must be to cope with the *status quo*. And he proceeds to sermonize off and on for the rest of the speech. The whole speech is of a piece, and it constitutes a performance that is, I believe, unified in purpose and execution, enunciated by an ordered mind that understands the tenor of the last words before it instigates the first ones.

The identity of the character who is so well integrated and talented is, of course, unsettled, as is the identity of the poet who attempts (?) so feebly to reconcile the ideas to which he devotes one hundred and five long lines with the sentiment he expresses in the opening and closing lines. The present study will point in one direction toward a possible identity for the former, although some conjectures concerning an identity of the author will be hazarded. I will explore an area that should be explored before we think of denying its significance. And I think it likely that an answer to some of the problems that *The Wanderer* has posed lies in the kind of material explored here. Briefly stated, my thesis is that the character whom we identify as the "Wanderer" is a member of a special profession, that what he is doing he is doing in line with his profession, and that an Anglo-Saxon would have identified him readily as a *woðbora* or as someone in a similar calling. He has all the earmarks of a "pro."

Elsewhere I have discussed the OE *woðbora* at length,[22] so the definition here will be brief. The word is derived partly from an IE root *uat* or *vat* meaning "to be inspired."[23] Cognate with it are nouns in several languages designating a seer or poet. Among cognate derivatives are OIr *faith*, "seer," and the name "Woden" of the Germanic god of poetry, wisdom, and magic. Also related are words having to do with frenzy or madness, such as Goth. *wods*, "possessed," OE *wod* and OHG *-wuot*, "furious" or "mad," and OS *wodian*, "to rage" or "be furious"; as well as terms having to do with poetry or song, such as Welsh *gwawd*, "poem" or "song," and OE *woþ*, "song," while OIr *faith* means "poet" as well as "seer." There is some evidence indicating that at one time the *woðbora* had been connected with a cult, in the service of which he probably achieved ecstatic inspiration through the drinking of some kind of holy *Rauschtrank* such as mead (paralleling the soma or *madhu* of the *Rigveda*).[24] In OE poetry and riddles he is represented as a poet and performer who could receive a reward for a performance. Further, he was a teacher as well as a wise man and prophet. He is repeatedly associated with wisdom. He it is who can unlock the meaning of riddles. It is a *woðbora*, according to a writer in the *Anglo-Saxon Chronicle*, who has the power to give a name to a strange visitor in the night sky: he bestows on one such phenomenon the name "comet." He is represented as a traveler in *The Order of the World* and, briefly, in the poem *Christ*. But his most revealing appearance is in *The Order of the World*.[25]

In this poem, the speaker introduces himself by title: he claims to be a *woðbora*. He also calls himself "a stranger man" *(fremdne monnan)* and asserts that he is "much traveled" *(felageongne)*. In the poem he is obviously trying to secure an audience for the lesson or sermon that he feels bound to deliver. He speaks of the natural powers in the universe surrounding man, saying that each is a clear symbol to one who can comprehend the world, and calls himself a member of "a special caste" whose members from ancient times have had "questioning minds of their own," and who have always advised men. He says that such men have, through the years, known the most about "the web of mysteries." A point that I should stress is that he is obviously a teacher. He exhorts his audience to give heed to his words: *Gehyr nu þis herespel ond þinne hyge gefæstna!* And at another point he exclaims, *Leorna þas lare!* He regales his audience with a hymn to the sun, describing the latter in such a way that he brings out its mystery and glory. He is apparently, in short, a traveling poet, seer, and teacher, who moves around and speaks his *gied* (with which he is repeatedly associated) and receives a reward.

That there were seers in Anglo-Saxon England is certain. Elsewhere I have discussed the *woðbora* and another seer figure, the Old English *þyle*. That the two were reputable in early Christian times is clear from the fact that the existence of the first is attested prominently in a number of poems in *The Exeter Book*, while the reputation of the second was honorable in clerical circles in the eleventh century. The Irish seer, the *fili*, took over much of the prestige of the druids when the latter were forced out of existence by the Christian Church, and continued to teach and write for centuries. In fact, Carney says that the Christian bishop at an Irish court stood at one shoulder of the chieftain and a court *fili* at the other, both demanding support.[26] While this precise condition is unlikely for England, there is no reason why the seer could not have continued to be attached to courts small or large. As his situation became more precarious with the spread of Latin scholarship and writing, some of his order may have taken to roaming the tracks in self-imposed exile, preaching their brand of wisdom and traditional lore to eager audiences. Or they may always have traveled.

It is one such traveler who appears in *The Order of the World*. His opening statement explicitly assumes that his status of traveler is normal and that his listeners are familiar with it. The only usage of *woðbora* in *Christ* is with reference to a character who takes a trip to the Heavenly City. This character, otherwise referred to as *witega*, the usual term for "prophet," is called *woðbora* only in connection with his otherworldly trip, and, as I have explained elsewhere,[27] the use of the title may reflect the fact that "within tradition the belief had existed in the *woðbora*'s ability to travel to a spirit realm" in a shamanistic trance induced by drink or other means.

Numerous critics have been struck by the poet's concentration on wisdom and the activity of the mind in *The Wanderer*. Clemoes refers to "the mind thinking intensely" in the poem.[28] Fowler notes the series of references to wisdom and the wise man: *wita, gleaw, wise, frod, snottor*, all of which give an air of authority to pronouncements of the speaker. Further, he points out that in 11. 65b–72 "we have a 'definition' of a wise man, in terms which imply a code of ideals neither specifically Christian or pagan."[29] Rosier perceives the poem as "a mirror of a mind in its several states and faculties. . . ." It is "an exercise in ratiocination. . . ." And, further, "The wanderer of the poem is not so much the man himself in his common life as his mind, which moves about in time past and present and finally into infinity."[30] The concentration on wisdom and the mind makes congenial the suggestion that the Wanderer had a role similar to that of a *woðbora*.

Another quality of *The Wanderer* on which there is striking agreement is the poet's tendency to generalize. Nora Kershaw notes that "the action is really timeless."[31] Ida L. Gordon finds that the poem is "concerned with the commonplaces of universal truths. . . ."[32] Leslie has identical sentiments. Such Old English poems as *The Wanderer*, he says, "illustrate typical human situations."[33] Woolf speaks of "a deliberate act of distancing" on the part of the poet to prevent "the possibility of an intimate sympathy developing between speaker and hearer. . . ." Even the dream of a lost lord and the wintry setting in which it takes place "is only by implication the Wanderer's, for it is ascribed by the Wanderer to a hypothetical *wineleas guma* and the figure is therefore an imaginary creation who stands anyway at one remove from the audience." Woolf calls the poet's handling of this scene "only one striking instance of a general peculiarity of the poem, which is that the Wanderer most often describes, not how he feels, but how someone in a comparable situation would feel," and she adds, "over half of the poem is set in this form. The intention of the poet must be to distance and generalize, and it is achieved at the deliberate expense of naturalism, for real people do not think in such a stylized way."[34] Stanley also refers to the "nonliteral conventional use of the first person" in *The Wanderer* and *The Seafarer*. He says, "The account of the events at sea, told in the third person, are the Wanderer's tale of a typical wanderer." The tale is employed by the poet, "who is using various means of expressing his teaching poetically. . . ."[35]

The "teaching" has often been referred to as "sermonizing," and the term is apt provided it is not used in a narrowly Christian sense. It is clear that the average Anglo-Saxon (like not a few of his descendants today) nodded his head appreciatively at recognizing a fact or bit of wisdom pithily phrased and made memorable by its rhythm or rhetorical ornamentation. If we examine *The Wanderer,* we find that we are looking not at something personal at all but at something impersonal—at a set piece, in fact, which presents experience of an (apparently) personal nature used as a frame on which to fasten the teaching or sermonizing passages. The poem is riddled with the exposition of teaching materials.

If we begin with line 8, we find the Wanderer introducing himself with a pathetic comment on his lot. If he is a character like the wanderer of *The Order of the World,* and the *woðbora* of the riddles, he may hope to gain sympathy for his plight and some compensation for that as well as for his performance. The words next turn immediately to gnomic or traditional matter: it is a noble custom to bind one's thoughts and troubles fast. Next we have two statements: a man with a weary spirit cannot withstand *wyrd,* nor can a troubled heart afford any help. Then we have an obvious and sermonizing conclusion: *therefore* (note that the speaker uses "therefore"—and thus achieves a link—when he wants to) one eager for good report must keep sorrow locked in his heart.

There follows what purports to be personal experience, but the message is at once made impersonal by reference to one who has experienced the hardships the speaker depicts and who knows the way things are in the world. Then we have a personal statement: "I cannot think in this world why my heart should *not* become dark when I think about the life of noblemen." Then we have sermonizing in a platitudinous chant: man must be patient, not impetuous or hasty of speech, neither weak nor reckless in combat, neither timid nor jubilant, neither covetous nor ready to boast ere he know what the issue may be. Then comes an appeal to the wise man. He must perceive how mysterious (Kerhsaw) or ghastly (the modern meaning seems justified) it will be when all the world stands wasted. And we have the future depicted for us. The whole picture is then suspended for a series of gnomic statements detailing the various ways in which a man may find death—or death may find him. The whole is pat, with the reference to being carried by birds over the sea sounding particularly formulaic.

Then, beginning with line 85, we have one of the most significant passages in the poem. The Wanderer states that the creator of men has laid waste the habitations of men, and "the old work of giants stood empty." It is immediately after this that he begins: "He who ponders thoroughly, with deep meditation, about this ruin and this dark life, wise in spirit, will call to mind the old slaughters and will voice his thoughts as follows. . . ." What follows is crucial. Here, if at any point in the poem, we have motivation for a Christian doctrine, or at least Christian sentiment; here if anywhere man's eyes should be directed to an eternal alternative. But what do we get? "He who ponders deeply about the world," we are told, will ask,

Hwær cwom mearg? hwær cwom mago? hwær cwom maþþumgyfa? hwær cwom symbla gesetu? hwær sindon seledreamas?

And then,

Eala beorht bune!   Eala byrnwiga!
Eala þeodnes þrym!

That time has gone as if it had never been. The beloved troop leave no trace save of a wonderful wall, decorated with serpent forms. Spears and weapons and Wyrd *seo mære* (the glorious) have carried off the nobles. And we have finally, as I said once before, the twilight of man's world. The speech is ended with a chant beginning, "Her bið feoh læne . . ." as the whole world runs down at last and stands idle.

Having spoken, the *snottor on mode* then seats himself *æt rune*. It is the commentator who adds a mood-destroying conclusion. That he is trying to frame the poem within the first and last line is a reasonable assumption. What stands out is the gusto with which he has presented the hundred or so middle lines.

As for the rhetorical devices used in the poem—the *ubi sunt* motif, the *sum sum* formula, and others—where they come from is not so important as how they are used. The fact that the devices are a part of the Christian homiletic tradition as well as of a Germanic tradition has been discussed many times. The point has also often been made that the devices are, in the poem, turned to the immediate purpose of the poet. The *sum sum* formula, for example, "owes much to Christian models, but the spirit which informs it has strong heroic overtones."[36] Reminding us that the *ubi sunt* passage is used in a "Christian sermon tradition in which it serves to emphasize contempt for the world," Rosemary Woolf also reminds us that in *The Wanderer* "there is no suggestion that the *maþþumgyfa* rots in the grave or that the *beorht bune* may be rusted through." And she continues: "Standing on their own, as they do in *The Wanderer, ubi sunt* questions have the reverse effect. Far from suggesting in homiletic fashion that their subjects are worthless they confer a deep nostalgic value upon them, and the very fleetingness that the questions call to mind enhances rather than diminishes their preciousness." There are "resonances of melancholy and wistfulness" that are moving but that show "more concern for natural feelings than for pure Christian teaching."[37] Dunning and Bliss are essentially right when they say that the poem never moves outside the *comitatus*.[38]

The idea that the wanderer was a seer with a professional background extending into the pagan past may be supported by evidence derivable from the puzzling lines 50b–55a. Calling them "very obscure," Salmon seeks to clarify them by considering ll. 58–64 in *The Seafarer,* which are similar but more explicit. There, the Seafarer, another lonely soul, says

> Forþon nu min hyge hweorfeð   ofer hreþerlocan,
> min modsefa   mid mereflode
> ofer hwæles eþel   hweorfeð wide,
> eorþan sceatas,   cymeð eft to me
> gifre ond grædig,   gielleð anfloga,
> hweteð on hwælweg   hreþer unwearnum
> ofer holma gelagu.

The lines seem clear. The soul is represented as leaving the body (in the shamanistic trance, it usually leaves by way of the mouth as the shaman or other psychic yawns). It roams widely over the *hwæles eþel* and *eorþan sceattas,* and comes back *gifre* and *grædig;* the *anfloga,* "lone flier," *gielleð.* Salmon represents it accurately as "screaming . . . as it flies alone, and as returning unsatisfied to the poet. . . ." Salmon continues: "This belief in the soul's ability to leave the body during life and to return again is common at some time or other in various races inhabiting regions stretching from Scandinavia to Indonesia. . . ." As he says, "The widespread nature of this belief . . . makes it less difficult to credit its presence in Old English than its absence, if not during the later Christian period at least during heathen times and the earlier days of the conversion, when heathen ideas lingered on and demanded frequent correction by the church."[39]

The evidence for belief in the disembodied soul is plentiful in Old Icelandic sources. The use of such material in forming conclusions with regard to Anglo-Saxon beliefs is warranted if similar beliefs are reflected in Old English writings. There is evidence for a body/soul dichotomy in Old English, for example that seen in compounds in *-hama: feorh-hama,* "covering of the spirit," *flæsc-hama,* "flesh-covering," and *lic-hama,* "body-covering." But the most significant *-hama* compound is *feþerhama,* a "feather-covering." A costume of feathers or one trimmed with feathers is the common covering for the shaman in most European and Asiatic cultures, including the Old Irish. *Feþerhama* occurs in Old English in *Genesis B.* There, it is a *feþerhama,* a cloak of feathers, which makes it possible for Satan to make a trip to the world. There is much other evidence for the belief in a "free-ranging soul" in Old English: for example, *floga* in compounds refers to a supernatural figure.[40]

The lines in *The Wanderer* which these comments, as well as 11. 58–64 in *The Seafarer,* may illuminate are the following (51–55a):

> þonne maga gemynd   mod geondhweorfeð:
> greteð gliwstafum,   georne geondsceawað
> secga geseldan.   Swimmað eft on weg
> Fleotendra ferð   no þær fela bringeð
> cuðra cwidegiedda.

This passage has taxed the ingenuity of would-be translators. The assumption has usually been that in l. 51, *gemynd* is the subject and *mod* the object; however, Dunning and Bliss are right, I think, in their contention that *mod* is the subject not only of *geondhweorfeð* but also of *greteð* and *geondsceawað*.[41] I would translate the passage "Then his mind [or imagination] courses over his memory of kinsmen; it greets [in the sense "works with" or "through"] gliwstafum [cf. *hearpan gretan,* "to play the harp"]. It eagerly scans the companions of men. [But] they swim afterward [or "often," retaining MS *oft*] away. The spirits of the floating ones do not bring many speech-gieds" (i.e., they are silent). The last statement shows definite use of litotes.

Gliwstafum probably signifies "with runic staves." Working with runes was part of the duties of the Germanic seer. Chanting might accompany the work, and chanting was an inseparable part of the process of inducing a tranced state for various purposes. "Greeting" or "using" gliwstaves apparently has something to do with (conjuring up?) the appearance of *secga geseldan*. Salmon suggests that the latter phrase may be used in the sense in which OI *fylgjur manna* is used. This term, also meaning "companions of men," actually involves the *fylgja*, a guardian spirit taking the form of bird or animal and thought to exist for every man. Seen sometimes by ordinary people in dreams, such figures were visible at all times to those who possessed second sight.[42]

The Wanderer is a special person of some kind. Our failure to comprehend the precise meaning of "sitting *æt rune*" has, I think, contributed to our lack of success in identifying his particular role. Because the phrase *æt rune* is to us opaque, attempts to explain the Wanderer's character have ignored it almost completely. But the poet is at pains to point out that when his speaker finishes speaking, he moves to a position apart where he is occupied *æt rune*. That the performer, his words concluded, may be actually consulting runes is an obvious notion that most critics refuse to consider. The likelihood that he is meditating in some ceremonial or at least professional capacity is a reasonable assumption to draw from the passage.

The Wanderer and his role can not be defined clearly today and may never be. The thesis of the present paper is that he is a specialist in the category of seer or preacher-teacher, a position going back to pre-Christian times, and the observations that follow are not so random as they may seem to some.

To begin with, the pagan faith and many customs and usages connected with it died hard. The Christian faith was fiercely rejected by continental kinsmen of the Anglo-Saxons and was imposed in Germany only by massacre and savage use of the sword by Charles Martel and later by Charles the Great.[43] That the Germanic people everywhere changed their deep-seated, inborn beliefs only after long passage of time and exposure to the new faith across generations is clear from fulminations of the Christian Church against the survival of pagan beliefs and practices. Meanwhile, there was some blending of the old and new. What happened to the priest Coifi after he urged Edwin of Northumbria to give up the pagan faith for the new way is not known. That he became a Christian priest is at least a possibility. Certainly that some of his kind were crossing over to the Christian priesthood in the eighth century is clear from a condemnation of the practice by the archbishop of York.[44]

Old Religious beliefs and old wisdom lore go hand in hand. As I have said before, eleventh-century respect for the terseness with which the þyle expressed wisdom is shown in a gloss holding the þyle's gnomic expression up as a model for the Christian priest. And again, the fact that the woðbora is treated sympathetically in a number of poems in the manuscript presented by Bishop Leofric to the Exeter Cathedral library is significant. The old wisdom and the gnomic expression of it were popular with Christian homilists during the Anglo-Saxon period. The rank and file of clerks and monks must have looked warmly at the old lore and the old ways of voicing it. That the thoughts of some of them turned from Christian concerns in writing secular Latin poetry as well as some verse in the vernacular is well known. The seer and professional purveyor of wisdom and the monk were brothers under the skin. That a monk could have composed a poem with nostalgic regard for a past way of life or for one that seemed to be passing requires no stretch of the imagination at all. That the central figure in his poem was someone like the woðbora is likely. And it is not fantastic to suggest the possibility that the writer had himself at one time been such a figure or had at least known such a person.

NOTES

1. James L. Rosier, "The Literal-Figurative Identity of *The Wanderer*," *PMLA* 79 (1964):366.

2. W. F. Bolton, "The Dimensions of *The Wanderer*," *Leeds Studies in English*, n.s. 3 (1969):7.

3. Roger Fowler, "A Theme in *The Wanderer*," *Medium Ævum* 36 (1967):1.

4. J. E. Cross, "On the Genre of *The Wanderer*," *Neophilologus* 45 (1961):63.

5. Cf. W. F. Klein, "Purpose and the 'Poetics' of *The Wanderer* and *The Seafarer*," in *Anglo-Saxon Poetry: Essays in Appreciation for John C. McGaillard*, ed. Lewis E. Nicholson and Dolores Warwick Frese (Notre Dame: University of Notre Dame Press, 1975), p. 209.

6. R. M. Lumiansky, "The Dramatic Structure of the Old English Wanderer," *Neophilologus* 34 (1950):105.

7. Quotations from *The Wanderer* are cited to *The Exeter Book*, ed. George Philip Krapp and Elliott Van Kirk Dobbie (New York: Columbia University Press, 1936).

8. Morton W. Bloomfield, "Patristics and Old English Literature: Notes on Some Poems," *Studies in Old English Literature in Honor of Arthur G. Brodeur*, ed. Stanley B. Greenfield (Eugene: University of Oregon, 1963), pp. 36–37.

9. B. F. Huppé, "*The Wanderer:* Theme and Structure," *JEGP* 42 (1943):526.

10. Lumiansky, "Dramatic Structure," p. 105.

11. F. N. M. Diekstra, "*The Wanderer* 65b–72: The Passions of the Mind and the Cardinal Virtues," *Neophilologus* 55 (1971):86.

12. Thomas C. Rumble, "From *Eardstapa* to *Snottor on Mode:* The Structural Principle of 'The Wanderer,'" *MLQ* 19 (1958):227–28.

13. Stanley B. Greenfield, "*The Wanderer:* A Reconsideration of Theme and Structure," *JEGP* 50 (1951):460.

14. Ida L. Gordon, "Traditional Themes in *The Wanderer* and *The Seafarer*," *RES*, n.s. 5 (1954):5.

15. Susie I. Tucker, "Return to The Wanderer," *Essays in Criticism* 8 (1958):235.

16. E. G. Stanley, "Old English Poetic Diction and the Interpretation of *The Wanderer, The Seafarer*, and *The Penitent's Prayer*," *Anglia* 73 (1955–56):462.

17. Fowler, "A Theme in *The Wanderer*," pp. 9–10.

18. Ibid., p. 13. Fowler translates: "'The world is transitory,'" and italicizes the following: "'*therefore let us place no trust in the world, but concentrate on the attainment of* God's benefits to Christians, which are permanent.'" This is the version that would have presented the argument "essential to Christian poems on mutability," an argument that is "absent" in *The Wanderer*.

19. John C. Pope, "Dramatic Voices in *The Wanderer* and *The Seafarer*," in *Franciplegius: Medieval and Linguistic Studies in Honor of Francis Peabody Magoun, Jr.*, ed. Jess B. Bessinger, Jr., and Robert P. Creed (New York: New York University Press, 1965), p. 165.

20. Rosemary Woolf, "*The Wanderer, The Seafarer*, and the Genre of *Planctus*," in *Anglo-Saxon Poetry: Essays in Appreciation for John C. McGalliard*, p. 197.

21. Gordon, "Traditional Themes in *The Wanderer* and *The Seafarer*," p. 6.

22. "*Scop* and *Woðbora* in OE Poetry," *JEGP* 77 (1978); "Was Widsiþ a *Scop?*" *Neophilologus* 64 (1980).

23. For a discussion of derivation and of cognate forms, see my "*Scop* and *Woðbora* in OE Poetry," pp. 319–20.

24. Ibid.

25. For OE references to the *woðbora*, see *The Gifts of Men*, (ll. 35–36), Riddle 31 (ll. 23–24), Riddle 80 (ll. 9–10), *Christ* (1. 301), and *The Order of the World* in *ASPR* 3; also see *Two Saxon Chronicles Parallel*, ed. John Earle and Charles Plummer (Oxford, 1892), p. 120, and p. 120, n. 6. For a discussion of the *woðbora* as he appears in Old English poetry, see my "*Scop* and *Woðbora* in OE Poetry."

26. James Carney, *The Irish Bardic Poet* (Dublin, 1967), p. 8.

27. "*Scop* and *Woðbora* in OE Poetry," p. 328.

28. Peter Clemoes, "*Mens absentia cogitans* in *The Seafarer* and *The Wanderer*," in *Medieval Literature and Civilization: Studies in Memory of G. N. Garmonsway*, ed. D. A. Pearsall and R. A. Waldron (London: Athlone, 1969), p. 62.

29. Fowler, "A Theme in *The Wanderer*," p. 8.

30. Rosier, "Literal-Figurative Identity," p. 366.

31. *Anglo-Saxon and Norse Poems* (Cambridge, 1922), p. 7.

32. Ida L. Gordon, ed., *The Seafarer*, (London: Methuen 1960), p. 27.

33. R. F. Leslie, "*The Wanderer*: Theme and Structure," in *Old English Literature: Twenty-two Analytical Essays*, eds. Martin Stevens and Jerome Mandel (Lincoln: University of Nebraska Press, 1968), p. 139.

34. Woolf, "The Genre of *Planctus*" p. 200.

35. Stanley, "Old English Poetic Diction," pp. 448 and 464.

36. R. F. Leslie, ed., *The Wanderer* (Manchester: Manchester University Press, 1966), p. 19

37. Woolf, "*The Wanderer*," p. 201.

38. T. P. Dunning and A. J. Bliss, eds., *The Wanderer* (New York: Appleton-Century, 1969), p. 94.

39. Vivian Salmon, "'The Wanderer' and 'The Seafarer,' and the Old English Conception of the Soul," *MLR* 55 (1960):1–3.

40. Ibid.

41. Dunning and Bliss, *The Wanderer*, pp. 21–22.

42. Salmon, "'The Wanderer,'" *MLR* 55:9.

43. Geoffrey Barraclough, *The Crucible of Europe: The Ninth and Tenth Centuries in European History* (Berkeley: University of California Press, 1976), pp. 18 and 41.

44. Peter Hunter Blair, *An Introduction to Anglo-Saxon England* (Cambridge: Cambridge University Press, 1962), p. 122.

The Meaning and Structure of *The Seafarer*

Roy F. Leslie

The vast majority of scholars now accept *The Seafarer* as an entity, and the explicitly Christian elements as integral parts. There is further agreement that the first part of the poem in some way exemplifies or illustrates the theme of the second. However, there are widely divergent views on how the poet achieves this unity, and therefore on how we should interpret it and on how we should define its structure. Moreover, the difficulties seem to have grown rather than to have diminished. A good solution for one crux has sometimes aggravated another. However, it is true to say that most interpretations can be classified as either literal or allegorical, albeit with different emphases. All demonstrate a clear thematic link between the halves of the poem, and many trace linguistic and other links as well.[1]

Increasingly scholars have wondered whether, perhaps, the author intended his poem to work on both levels of interpretation.[2] Perhaps the details of the seafarer's life, which are obscure and ambiguous to us, would be so obvious and unambiguous to a contemporary of the poet as to be immediately understood and taken for granted, leaving him free to appreciate the allegory. P. L. Henry believes that "a second religious and allegorical level may be and even must be assumed. It is implicit."[3] Pope, who quotes this statement, is in partial agreement with it, but warns against "accepting allegory in too relaxed a fashion and lapsing into a vaguely general and ultimately confusing reading of the poem."[4]

An interpretation that involves more than one level may well do fuller justice to the poem than one that maintains that it has only one level of meaning. However, for such an interpretation to succeed, it must be consistent; that is, each level must be consistent within itself and compatible throughout with the other, and both must be closely

related to the text. In addition, such an interpretation should establish stronger links between the first and second sections of the poem
than have been established hitherto. It is a daunting task indeed, and
one that may prove impossible to carry out. This article should not be
taken as an attempt to carry out this task, but rather as a kind of
feasibility study—a necessary preliminary for it. I should like to make
an examination of the text, and to consider the solutions suggested
for individual cruces in the context of the whole poem, and in conjunction with the solutions proffered for other cruces. In addition, I
should like to reexamine some of the generally accepted wisdom
about the less controversial parts of the text, which may have kept us
from a full understanding of the poem.

In my examination of the poem I shall refer to lines 1–33a as
section A 1, lines 33b–67 as A 2, and lines 68 to the end of the poem as
section B, purely for convenience and without implying any opinion
in the matter.

Mæg ic be me sylfum   soðgied wrecan,   f. 81^{v}
siþas secgan,   hu ic geswincdagum,
earfoðhwile   oft þrowade,
bitre breostceare   gebiden hæbbe,
gecunnad in ceole   cearsel[ð]a fela,   5
atol yþa gewealc,   þær mec oft bigeat
nearo nihtwaco   æt nacan stafnan,
þonne he be clifum cnossað.   Calde geþrungen
wæron mine fet,   forste gebunden,
caldum clommum,   þær þa ceare seofedun   10
hat ymb heortan;   hungor innan slat
merewerges mod.[5]

                                                                (1–12a)

(I can utter a true tale about myself, tell of [my] experiences, how
I often suffered days of toil, a time of hardship, have endured
bitter breast-care, experienced aboard ship many misfortunes, the
terrible rolling of the waves, where frequently the dangerous
nightwatch gripped me at the vessel's prow, when it tosses beside
the cliffs. Pierced with cold were my feet, bound with frost, with
cold fetters, where those cares sighed hot around my heart;
hunger tore within the heart of the sea-weary [one].[6])

The Seafarer opens with a formula of personal experience, lines 1–2a,
that has parallels in other Old English poems, in *The Wife's Lament* 1–
2a, in *Resignation* 96b–97, and in *Beowulf* 1723b–1724.[7]

In lines 2b–12a the seafarer particularizes his experience, the mental and spiritual anguish as well as the physical hardships of the "days
of toil" that he endured in a ship. The picture is detailed—the terrible

rolling of the waves, the "grip" of the nightwatch by the cliffs, the frostbound feet, the hunger, the seaweariness are vivid and convincing without being so realistic that we are forced to confine ourselves to a literal interpretation alone. The seafarer's *bitre breostceare* (4) is the only typical exile formula in this passage; everything else is adapted to his particular situation.[8] Moreover, he did not have to endure any of his hardships—he simply endured them, experienced them in his ship. His movement into exile took place before the beginning of his account.

> Þæt se mon ne wat
> þe him on foldan   fægrost limpeð,
> hu ic earmcearig   iscealdne sæ
> winter wunade,   wræccan lastum,   15
> winemægum bidroren,
> bihongen hrimgicelum.   Hægl scurum fleag.
>
> (12b–17)

(That the man does not know to whom on earth things happen most fortunately, how I careworn the ice-cold sea inhabited winter-long in paths of exile, deprived of friendly kinsmen, hung round with icicles. Hail flew in showers.)

In lines 12b–13b we have the first of the men whose fortunate lot in the world presents an extreme contrast to the seafarer's. What this man does not know is how the seafarer lived in exile; it is couched in typical exile imagery—*earmcearig* (14), *wræccan lastum* (15), and *winemægum bidroren* (16)—and set in a typically wintry scene, without any of the particularizing detail that we find in the description of the seafarer's hardships in lines 2b–12a. We may note that he is not bereft of a lord, merely of kinsmen, and that he did not have to stay in exile, nor is he necessarily homeless; *wunade* (15) leaves us free to surmise a literal home for him, perhaps on an island, since he lived *in brimlade* winter-long; however, we are by no means obliged to do so.

> Þær ic ne gehyrde   butan hlimman sæ,
> iscaldne wæg,   hwilum ylfete song.
> Dyde ic me to gomene   ganetes hleoþor   20
> ond huilpan sweg   fore hleahtor wera,
> mæw singende   fore medodrince.
> Stormas þær stanclifu beotan,   þær him stearn oncwæð,
> isigfeþera;   ful oft þæt earn bigeal,
> urigfeþra.   Nænig hleomæga   25
> feasceaftig ferð   f[ref]ran meahte.
> Forþon him gelyfeð lyt   se þe ah lifes wyn
> gebiden in burgum   bealosiþa hwon,

wlonc ond wingal,   hu ic werig oft
in brimlade   bidan sceolde,   30
Nap nihtscua,   norþan sniwde,
hrim hrusan bond,   hægl feol on eorþan,
corna caldast.[9]

(There I heard nothing but the sea resounding, the ice-cold wave,
sometimes the swan's song. I had for my entertainment the
gannet's cry, and the sound of the curlew for the laughter of men,
the sea-gull singing for the drinking of mead. Storms beat upon
the cliffs, where the tern answered them, icy-feathered; many a
time the eagle screamed at that, dewy-feathered. Not one of [my]
close kinsmen [my] wretched spirit could [support]. Therefore he
little believes, he who has experienced life's joy in communities,
[experienced] few harrowing things, proud and wine-flushed, how
weary I often had to stay on the ocean track. The shadow of night
grew dark, it snowed from the north, rime bound the earth, hail
fell on earth, coldest of grains.)

In lines 18–33a the pattern set in lines 2b–12a is repeated, but the
details and the imagery are different. The detailed first element (a) of
the sequence lines 18–26 concerns deprivation of worldly pleasures
rather than physical hardship; the seafarer has only the seabirds' cries
to remind him of the conviviality generally associated with the hall.
He has no protecting kinsmen to comfort his wretched soul. The
seabirds are paralleled in *The Wanderer* 45–57, but the seafarer's reaction to them is peculiarly his own.

The man in the second element (b), lines 27–29a, like his counterpart in the first sequence, seems to have everything the seafarer lacks;
he lives in a community, has few cares, and lives happily. The phrase
used to describe him, *wlonc ond wingal,* has engendered some discussion as to whether it is here just an aspect of *lifes wyn,* as it is in *The
Ruin* (34), or whether it denotes pride and immoderation. Since section B recommends humility and moderation, derogatory implications cannot be entirely ruled out. The man has precisely what the
seafarer lacks, and does not believe how the latter lives in exile.

The third element (c) of the second sequence, lines 29b–33a, is like
element (c) in the first sequence in its almost complete lack of particu-
larity and in its wintry setting; however, it is only vaguely suggestive of
exile. There is again no sense of movement. *Bidan sceolde* (30) suggests
compulsion, but is qualified by *oft* (29) and may simply mean that the
seafarer was prevented from going anywhere by storms, the description of which is vivid and evocative rather than naturalistic.

The second sequence again goes from particularized detail of the
seafarer's life in element (a), to the man who seems to have all that the

seafarer lacks in (b), to what this man does not believe—how the seafarer fared in exile—in (c).

The seafarer's exile experience seems to be somewhat atypical. He gives no reason for his exiled state; he is not the victim of a plot, or a feud; nor does he bewail the loss of a lord.[10] He is not confined; he has the sea, albeit a wintry one, yet he does not travel; and, at least in the opening lines, a *ceol* (5), yet he simply stays on the sea. We hear nothing more of the *ceol,* at least not explicitly. The land seems to loom large on his horizon; there are almost as many terms for it as there are for the sea in section A1 of the poem. We may note too that the seafarer's physical presence is not made explicit in the second sequence, whereas in the first it is: he was in a ship, his feet were cold, and hunger struck inside.

As his physical presence grows vaguer, the climate seems to become more hostile. Up to the end of line 22 it is merely extremely cold—an ice-cold sea, frost and icicles on the seafarer himself. In line 23 the first storm beats on the stone cliffs; then in lines 29b to 33a we have a crescendo of storm and cold that bind the whole earth, and the coldest of grains fall on it.

We should now take a closer look at the ignorance and disbelief of the fortunate men in element (b) of the two sequences. It is not what the seafarer suffered that they ignore, but how he is an exile; but "how" is not quite what an Anglo-Saxon familiar with his poetic heritage would expect. If he was a pious man, well-versed in Christian literature, he might have guessed what kind of an exile the seafarer was, by the end of the first sequence. If he was still unsure, the second sequence would clear up the doubt. He would come to the realization that no ordinary exile would behave in quite this way; by a process of elimination he would be led to conclude that the seafarer had a lord, was not compelled to go into exile, and was, by his evocation of the contrasting worldly man, revealing a reason for his exile—a renunciation of the temporal world for the salvation of his soul. He would also be familiar with the doctrine that the patient suffering of hardship is pleasing to the Lord. (*Resignation* lines 111b–13 states this doctrine quite specifically.) He would probably also recognize the seafarer as a metaphorical exile on earth—as a descendant of Adam.

One evocation of the seafarer's worldly opposite might well be enough to identify the purpose of the seafarer's "exile," the repetition of the motif would perhaps confirm the suspicion that the seafarer is a homilist, who has now established the theme of his homily—the transience of earthly life and the peril of being too much involved in the world.

I should like now to take account of *forþon* (27), which introduces element (b) of the second sequence. It is the first of eight occurrences of *forþon* in the poem. The difficulties of interpreting them have engendered much discussion. I have had no particular system in mind,[11] but have simply interpreted the context to the best of my ability. However, if my interpretation has accommodated one of the regular usages of *forþon,* either as an adverb or a conjunction, I have allowed myself to feel that I was on the right lines. If it can be argued that the central elements of the two sequences can be joined semantically rather than syntactically, element (b) in the first sequence with element (b) in the second, my interpretation of those sequences may possibly restore some of the connective force of *forþon* in line 27: the first man does not know, therefore the second man believes little.

There is no explicit statement as to how we are to interpret the objects of the seafarer's environment, such as we find in *Christ* 850–63, where the poet uses a simile rather than a metaphor and we therefore know what the symbols stand for. However, our poet certainly gives us no discouragement and we are perfectly free to invest incidents of the seafarer's story, such as the nightwatch, or objects of his environment, with an appropriate symbolic meaning. The poet also gives us enough information to construct a plausible literal "story" for him. The facts in the poem, augmented by some knowledge of the times, allow us to do so. He may, for instance, like Saint Columba, have had difficulty in finding a suitably remote island on which to live a life of contemplation.[12] However, I think it likely, in view of the structural emphasis the poet gives it, that he was more concerned with his central metaphor of the seafarer as exile on earth than he was with giving every incident of his creation's life and object in his environment a definite symbolic meaning, or even with giving more than the barest suggestion of a story.

For whatever reasons the seafarer suffered *bitre breostceare,* cold and hunger in the past, he looks on them now as a way of earning his place in heaven—his "ticket home." The seafarer is also making use of this experience in his present role as homilist, but he nowhere displays a "holier than thou" attitude. He has, for example, carefully planted the information that he understands the pleasures of the hall and is therefore not condemning the second worldly man's *wlonc ond wingal* state in itself, but is at pains to point out that concentration on happiness in one's earthly life alone leaves one no time to prepare for the eternal one.[13]

At this stage I should perhaps have the courage of my convictions and call the first person speaker in the poem "the homilist." However, the poet seems to have been concerned also to establish his creation as a metaphorical exile and a literal "solitary," if not actually an exile in the usual sense. I shall continue to call him "the seafarer" in the interests of clarity and unity.

After the misleadingly conventional opening, the poet gives us concentrated details of the seafarer's physical suffering and shapes them in such a way as to make us think of the seafarer as some sort of exile. Then, by a careful choice of words, the poet guides us toward the discovery of what sort of exile the seafarer is, and to a realization that he is more than an exile. We also begin to form the idea that, while he is not a literal exile, he voluntarily lives the life of one; he has no human company, he has only the seabird's cries to remind him of the sounds of the hall. This is followed by more evidence for our growing suspicion that the seafarer is also a homilist. In addition, the poet shows at least the usual skill of a poet of his time in using winter and storm imagery to set much more than the internal scene.

All in all we are well prepared for the new turn of events in A 2 and need not be surprised that they are introduced by *forþon* in line 33b.

Forþon cynssað nu

heortan geþohtas þæt ic hean streamas	f. 82^r
sealtyþa gelac sylf cunnige,	35
monað modes lust mæla gehwylce	
ferð to feran þæt ic feor heonan	
elþeodigra eard gesece.	
Forþon nis þæs modwlonc mon ofer eorþan,	
ne his gifena þæs god, ne in geoguþe to þæs hwæt,	40
ne in his dædum to þæs deor, ne him his dryhten to þæs hold	
þæt he a his sæfore sorge næbbe	
to hwon hine Dryhten gedon wille,	
ne biþ him to hearpan hyge, ne to hringþege,	
ne to wife wyn, ne to worulde hyht,	45
ne ymbe owiht elles nefne ymb yþa gewealc,	
ac a hafað longunge, se þe on lagu fundað.	

(Therefore thoughts now agitate [my] heart that I should myself try out the high seas, the salt waves' tumult, my heart's desire incites my spirit over and over again to set out so that I may seek out the home of strangers far hence. Because there is no man across the earth so proud-spirited, so generous in his gifts, so valiant in his youth, so bold in his deeds, so gracious to him his lord, that he never has anxiety concerning his voyage, as to what the Lord proposes for him, there is for him no thought of the harp, of the giving of rings, of delight in woman, of joy in the world, or about anything else save the rolling of the waves, but he always has sad yearning, he who aspires to go on to the ocean.)

The syntactical function we assign *forþon* in line 39, and the punctuation we give this passage, are crucial to its interpretation. However, without reference to these considerations, we can say that the passage naturally divides into two distinct units. The first unit, lines 33b–38, is in the first person singular, and concerns the seafarer himself. The second unit, lines 39–47, is in the third person singular,[14] and concerns a representative type of man, who is not so proud-spirited (etc.) that he never has anxiety about God's will concerning his voyage. The same man must also be the referent of *him* in line 44, and *se þe* in line 47 must refer to that category of men to which the referent belongs. Does the seafarer himself belong to this category? The answer to this question should of course accord with the meaning of the poem as a whole and should take full account of the facts of the text. However, some of these "facts" seem to be ambiguous and to contradict each other.

The interpretation of A 1 usually starts a sort of chain reaction when it fails to accord with the rest of the poem, and *forþon* (33) becomes an embarassment.[15] However, if we overcome the difficulty caused by an overly literal interpretation of A 1 by translating *cynssað* "troubles," it accords ill with *modes lust* in line 36, and if we correlate *forþon* in line 39 with *forþon* in line 33, we have the seafarer saying that thoughts now trouble his heart that he should experience the ocean himself, his heart's desire incites his spirit to seek a far-off land because there is no man on earth so proud spirited (etc.) that he never has anxiety as to God's will regarding his journey. It makes not much better sense if we treat lines 36–38 as parenthetic. We are also forced to include the seafarer and the *modwlonc mon* in the same category.

We cannot simply dismiss lines 39–47 as an adaptation of a familiar homiletic theme—an elaborate way for the seafarer to say that he has anxiety about his voyage, because he does not belong to the category of fortunate worldly men. Behind the *modwlonc mon* who does not exist, the poet has implied one who does; a man who does not have the given attributes to a high enough degree (or not at all), does have anxiety sufficient to cause him to have no thought for the harp, ring-giving, delight in woman, joy in the world, or for anything else except the rolling of the waves. This man does not seem to think about his destination, as the seafarer does, but exclusively of the rolling of the waves. It is a reasonable assumption that these pleasures would normally be enjoyed by that category of man when he was not thinking of his voyage. The seafarer does not "now" have these worldly pleasures, but he is thinking of a voyage "now." Clearly, lines 39–47 cannot include him. The other man's normal worldly pleasures identify the category of man who has anxiety about God's will concerning his journey. He is much like the other two worldly men that the seafarer has conjured up before us in lines 12b–13 and 27–29b.

It has sometimes been suggested that *longunge* (47) can be interpreted as referring to the seafarer's longing for the joys of the Lord. However, since *se þe* (47) must refer to the category of worldly men to which the seafarer does not belong, *longunge* cannot be held to refer to the seafarer. In the majority of occurrences *longung* refers to yearning or grief for something or someone already known rather than for something imagined but not yet experienced, and may here be interpreted with that meaning regardless of whether *his sæfore* (42) is interpreted as a literal journey or as the worldly man's death journey.[16]

Since nearly all meanings of *fundian* appear to have an element of desire or intention in them, it is difficult to account for its use here if *his sæfore* means "his death journey." However, if we take it as a literal journey in the temporal world, which the man wishes to make, we can still say that he would be afraid of sudden death. If he is afraid of drowning—an ignominious death for a man with his traditional Germanic attributes and tastes—it would certainly cause him to think of nothing but the rolling of the waves. Perhaps the poet meant to imply both. What seems to be much more certain is that the seafarer/homilist is holding up a third example of a worldly man whose good fortune in this world will not help him in the next.

Since the seafarer is already established as an exile in the world, there is no need to weaken the connective force of *forþon* in line 33 and we have no need to correlate it with *forþon* in line 39. The man in the passage lines 39–47 then has no thought for his usual pleasures because he has anxiety as to God's will concerning his journey. We now have two sentences, lines 33b–38 concerning the seafarer, and lines 39–47 concerning the third of the seafarer/homilist's "how not to" illustrations. Like the others, it is preceded by a passage that details the seafarer's own feelings.

I should like now to discuss the implications of the first sentence, lines 33b–38. It has one minor crux, *sylf* (35), and the phrase *elþeodigra eard gesece* (38), which has usually been considered the most crucial one for this part of the poem, if not for the whole poem.

Three possible meanings have been suggested for *sylf* (35): "myself," "of my own accord,"[17] and "alone."[18] Those who favor "myself" usually claim that the seafarer wishes to stress the "high seas" as opposed to what one is tempted to call the "low seas," as a new experience. However, the poet is already stressing the "high seas" by giving *hean* the alliteration. He is more likely to have wanted to stress another new aspect of the seafarer at this point. In addition to being an exile in this world by reason of Adam's fall, and therefore living apart from the world passively, the seafarer now wishes to be actively an exile, in the literal sense, by embarking on a *peregrinatio pro amore Dei*. In the metaphorical sense he may be said to be passively enduring his exile in the world, but he has now found out *hu we þider cumen* (118); he has found the way he must go to reach his eternal home. "Myself," the regular meaning of the word *sylf*, would seem to fit the context best.

Since Dorothy Whitelock first interpreted *elþeodigra eard gesece* as meaning a *peregrinatio pro amore Dei*[19] and G. V. Smithers[20] suggested that *elþeodigra eard* was the heavenly home of exiles in this world by Adam's fall, most interpretations of *The Seafarer* have followed one or the other, or sometimes both, to a greater or lesser degree. On the evidence of A 1 both meanings are possible here. It should be noted in passing that *elþeodigra eard* is a unique phrase in poetry, nor does it occur in the prose, as far as I have been able to discover.[21] However, Blickling Homily II, which Smithers quotes, comes very close to proving the case for the metaphorical meaning, but may postdate our poem. I think it not inconceivable that the poet, after laying the foundations carefully in A 1, coined the phrase expressly for his particular purpose here.

I have some lingering doubts as to whether the metaphorical meaning can stand alone. As with *sæfore* (42), it seems possible that with *elþeodigra eard* the poet had both levels in mind, and that he tied the two levels together by using the phrase to stand for both the literal means by which the seafarer will attain his ultimate goal and a uniquely apt metaphor for that goal—the *ham* of line 117. The literal level does not predominate, but it must be there at this stage to effect a bridge between the usual literal and the present metaphorical meaning of *elþeodigra eard*.

In A 1 we had the contrasting attitudes of the "exile" seafarer and the worldly man toward their existence in the world, whereas in lines 33b–47 we have their attitudes to movement toward the inevitable end of temporal life. The seafarer does not think of it as the end, but looks beyond it, whereas the worldly man thinks about it only when circumstances force him to consider its possible untimely arrival, and then only negatively—the *yða gewealc* (46) rather than *Dryhtnes dreamas* (65) or even their opposite.

Bearwas blostmum nimað,   byrig fægriað,
wongas wlitigað,   woruld onetteð;

ealle þa gemoniað   modes fusne,   50
sefan to siþe,   þam þe swa þenceð
on flodwegas   feor gewita[n].
Swylce geac monað   geomran reorde,
singeð sumeres weard   sorge beodeð
bitter in breosthord.   þæt se beorn ne wat,   55
e[s]teadig secg,   hwæt þa sume dreogað
þa þe wræclastas   widost lecgað.²²

(Woods take on blossoms, make beautiful the dwellings, make fair
the meadows, the world hastens: all those urge one eager of spirit,
[urge] the heart to the journey, in one who thinks to venture far
upon the seas. Likewise the cuckoo admonishes with its sad voice,
summer's herald sings, bodes sorrow bitter in the breast. That the
man does not know, the fortunate man, what those go through
who far and wide tread the paths of exile.)

Lines 48–52 may constitute the third element of the sequence of
which lines 33b–38 constitute element (a) and lines 39–47 element (b).
I do not wish to overemphasize these sequences, but there does appear to be enough of a pattern, albeit a varied one, established by
them to suggest that they constitute a conscious effort by the poet to
draw attention to the homiletic theme, and therefore to the nature of
the seafarer's exile, as well as to establish the thematic link between
the two halves of the poem.²³

The seafarer is no longer hemmed in by storms. The world around
him is growing beautiful with the coming of spring. However, this
idyllic picture is developed for only a line and a half before the by-
now-expected ominous note creeps in with *woruld onetteð* in line 49.²⁴
The world "hastens" through the seasons, from spring to summer,
but also to its end. This phrase is the first intimation of a theme that is
shortly to be treated more extensively, the transience of the world
itself.²⁵

It is noticable that the seafarer's direct references to himself are
becoming less frequent—there are six occurrences of *ic* in A 1, but
only three in A 2. His body, mind, and emotions are all overtly mentioned in A 1, but in A 2 he refers only to his mind and emotions.
Much ink has been expended on efforts to determine the nationality
of the sad-voiced cuckoo in line 53 and in *The Husband's Message*
line 23. I have myself taken part in these efforts. I still believe its
significance here, as in *The Husband's Message*, to be similar to that in
Welsh poetry, where it is a symbol of separation from loved ones,
because it accords so well with *longunge* in line 47. The cuckoo's two
roles, as herald of summer and as augur of sorrow, are not here so
contradictory as they might seem. The herald of summer is also a

reminder of the world's hastening, and therefore ultimately bodes sorrow in that role too.

In lines 55b–56a we appear, at first sight, to have another of the seafarer's worldly men. This one would be easier to interpret if his epithet, MS *eft eadig*, were not suspect. Two possible emendations have been put forward, *sefteadig* "blessed with comfort," and *esteadig* "fortune-blessed." Gordon prefers the former on the grounds that E-type lines require two alliterating staves in the first half-line.[26] However, metrical requirements must be weighed against objections such as that *seft-* does not appear elsewhere in compounds and that it is an adjective. When *-eadig* appears as the second element of a compound, the first is nearly always a noun—though this is a relatively minor objection. Neither *esteadig* nor *sefteadig* appears elsewhere, but *esteadig* has parallels in *tireadig* (*Beowulf* 2189) and *domeadig* (*Guthlac* 727 and 952). On balance *esteadig* appears to be the better of the two.

There are important differences between the two superficially similar motifs in lines 12b–15b and 55b–57. Most important are the impersonal construction of the latter—*sume* (56) as opposed to *ic* (14)—and the fact that this time the man does not know "what" exiles endure, rather than "how" they endure it.[27] In the first one the seafarer "dwelt" in exile, whereas here *sume* "lay the paths of exile far and wide." Here we have one of the common constituents of exile imagery, movement into exile, which was absent from A 1. The seafarer could well include himself in this statement, for he does not yet know what such exiles go through, since this will be a new experience for him. The only similarity between the two passages is the half-line *þæt se mon/beorn ne wat* (lines 12b and 55b). We cannot include *esteadig* or *sefteadig*, because they are the choices of editors but not necessarily of the poet. If we knew what the poet wrote in line 56a, we would be able to make a more confident judgment. However, the seafarer goes on to state, in lines 66b–67, what he himself does not believe; lines 55b–57 and 66b–67 may thus be linked to lines 12b–13 and lines 27–29a respectively in another way. The latter express the ignorance and disbelief of the worldly men, and the former those of the seafarer himself. I was led to consider this possibility by Stanley B. Greenfield's parenthetic translation of *esteadig* "filled with (Divine?) grace."[28]

Forþon nu min hyge hweorfeð   ofer hreþerlocan
min modsefa   mid mereflode
ofer hwæles eþel   hweorfeð wide   60
eorþan sceatas,   cymeð eft to me
gifre ond grædig,   gielleð anfloga,
hweteð on wælweg   hreþer unwearnum,

ofer holma gelagu,   forþon me hatran sind
Dryhtnes dreamas   þonne þis deade lif   65
læne on londe.   Ic gelyfe no
þæt him eorðwelan   ece stondeð.

(Therefore my mind now wanders beyond the confines of [my]
breast, my heart with the sea-flood across the whales' domain
traverses widely the earth's expanses, comes back to me ravening
and greedy, the lone-flyer screams, urges the heart irresistibly on
to the water-way, across the seas' expanses, because more vivid to
me are the joys of the Lord than this dear life, fleeting on land. I
do not believe that earth's riches eternally remain.)

There is a much clearer case for correlation of the two occurrences
of *forþon* in this passage (at lines 58 and 64) than for those in lines 33b
and 39.

For the last time in the poem the seafarer makes a personal statement. In A 1 he told us what the worldly man does not believe that
·enables him to live a care-free life in the world; now he tells us what
he himself does not believe, what makes it imperative for him to reject
the world.

Much has been written on the cruces in this passage. The first of
these is *hyge* in line 58. One need not agree with Gordon's interpretation of the *anfloga* (62) to recognize the good sense of her note on
hyge:

> it was not unusual in OE poetry for *hyge, modsefa* or their poetic
> equivalents to be imagined as separable entities (*hyge wæs him hinfus,*
> Beow. 755), and even as being sent over the sea (cf. *Wand.* 55–57).
> Here the poet elaborates the concept: the Seafarer's spirit passes
> beyond the confines of his breast and returns to him again, eager
> and hungering (to be gone in reality).[29]

Hyge (58) is varied by *modsefa* (59) and by *hreþer* (63). Interpretations
of this passage have sometimes strained the regular meanings of these
words in order to prove the closeness of a parallel or the certainty of a
source. For example, I find it difficult to believe that the Scandinavian
idea of the *hugr* ranging free of the body while the latter sleeps, was in
the poet's mind when he wrote this passage. The seafarer is speaking
in the present of his hopes for the future, not of a dream he has
had.[30] Vivian Salmon points out that the verb *hweorfan* is frequently
associated with the soul's departure from the body, as in *Judith* 112:
gæst ellor hwearf.[31] However, because the subject of the verb here is
gæst, not *hyge,* we should not draw too close a parallel. It should be
noted in passing that *hweorfan* is associated with movement into or in
exile as in *Genesis* 928 (Adam and Eve), 1014 (Cain), and *Guthlac* 1354

and 1379. That the seafarer's mind (or imagination) is ranging beyond its physical location, as suggested by Peter Clemoes, is entirely credible and warranted by the text.[32]

Any discussion of this text must of course take account of *anfloga* (62). It is usually taken as a metaphor for the seafarer's *hyge.*[33] However, because *anfloga* is a unique occurrence, we can never know for certain what exactly the poet meant by it, or even whether he used it in a literal or a metaphorical sense. Gordon, for example, takes it as referring back to the cuckoo in line 53. However, it is difficult to accept a reference back nine lines to *geac* in line 53. Moreover, the poet says that the cuckoo *singeð* (54), a sound that is more melodious than any that might fall within the range of *gielleð* in line 62.[34]

G. V. Smithers suggests that *anfloga* (with a short *a*) refers to the attack of disease.[35] If we were to accept his suggestion, we would have to agree to an exceptional use of *a* before a nasal, for *o* is the customary spelling for *a/o* before a nasal in this poem, and indeed in the Exeter Book as a whole. A short *a* also causes metrical difficulties. Since -*floga* consists of two short syllables, they are both required for resolution to make up a stressed syllable, and a short *a* would impair the meter, for we would need yet another short syllable after *anfloga* to complete a type A half-line. As it is, with a long *a* we have a slightly heavy but regular half-line.

John C. Pope suggests that *anfloga* be taken as a metaphor for the seafarer's *hyge,* and adds that it suggests a bird of prey, possibly a sea-eagle.[36] His suggestion seems to take the fullest account of the text. It is difficult otherwise to explain *gifre ond grædig* in a metaphorical sense, since in nearly all its occurrences the phrase (though not the words by themselves) has a pejorative sense. With Pope's interpretation, the bird of prey can have its usual "greed," but the seafarer's mind is eager for the journey and "greedy" for the joys of heaven.

Another major crux in this passage is MS *wæl weg* in line 63. Many scholars have inserted *h* before *wælweg* to give *hwælweg,* and have thereby given a more regular alliterative pattern to the line. However, I am inclined to agree with E. G. Stanley that scribal omission of *h* should be difficult to account for; moreover, *hwælweg* would, like *wælweg* be a unique occurrence. If the MS reading is retained, as a compound noun *wælweg,* there are two ways of reading it, with or without a long *æ* in the element *wæl-*. A long vowel will give us a word meaning "water," as in *wælrapas* in *Beowulf* 1610, as Stanley suggests.[37] Clearly identifiable occurrences of this element are, however, rare.

If we take the vowel as short, to give *wæl* meaning "slaughter" or "violent death," we have a much more common element, which is very active in the formation of various compound words. Smithers adopts the meaning "road to the abode of the dead" for *wælweg*.[38] However, this meaning is difficult to support, because in all its other occurrences in Old English poetry the simplex *wæl* always refers to "death by violence" and never has the general meaning "death." That it had a meaning clearly differentiated from *deað* is shown in the compound *wældeað* in *Beowulf* 695.

The seafarer's soul's impatience to find its natural eternal home does not exclude the possibility that he may also be impatient to start on a literal *peregrinatio* on earth, but for further elucidation of the nature of his impatience we must examine lines 64b–67. The word *land / lond* means "land" in the majority of its frequent occurrences; that it can mean "earth" is shown by *Phoenix* 508: *londes frætwe* "fruit of the earth." Three lines earlier in the same poem the compound *londwelan* occurs in the phrase *læne londwelan* (505) "transitory treasures of the world." In the context of the seafarer's belief that the earth's riches will not last forever, we may conclude that the poet here intended both meanings of the word *londe* (66) to be implied.

In lines 64b–66a the seafarer reveals himself fully as an exile on earth. From here to the end of the poem he develops both his themes, the danger of becoming extensively involved in the *deade lif* in this "foreign land," the earth, and the transitory nature of the earth itself. He has said all he needs to say of his own life. He will go on reminding the worldly men of the folly of their ways, but he will also hold out hope of better things.

I would like to take a brief glance back over A 1 and A 2 before going on to the overtly homiletic section of the poem. The implicitly homiletic content—the lesson of the three (four?) worldly men—has increased quantitatively throughout the first half. The worldly man in the first sequence has one-and-a-half lines devoted to him (lines 12b–13), the one in the second sequence two-and-a-half lines (lines 27–29a), and the one in the third has nine (lines 39–47). The first one is simply "most fortunate," the second one is carefree, proud, and wine-flushed—a perfectly proper state for a member of the traditional Germanic warrior class to be in, nevertheless not one that will get him closer to heaven. The third man has all the attributes of a traditional Germanic hero; by that society's standards he deserves *lastworda betst* (73) in this world. Even his entertainments are seemingly "harmless" pleasures. He is not boastful or prone to drunkenness. Yet neither his fortunate position in this world, nor his valor, can ever be enough to prevent him having *sorge* when he is contemplating a dangerous voyage. The poet has not chosen to put him in a situation where he might be killed in battle or become a hero, but in one where he is faced with the possibility of an anonymous but equally sudden death.

The contrasts not only become more elaborate as the poem proceeds, but the worldly men who figure in them become more clearly identifiable as traditionally Germanic.

It has often been observed that the seafarer's attitude to the sea undergoes a sudden change between A 1 and A 2.[39] It is, however, noticable that the terms used for the sea become progressively less pejorative. We start with *atol yþa gewealc* (6) and *iscealdne sæ* (14), but by line 30 we have the neutral *brimlade*.

The only startling differences between A 1 and A 2 are between the stormy, wintry scene that gets progressively worse through A 1, and the spring of the world in lines 48–54a in A 2, after which there are no further references to climate or season.

It is the contrary directions of sea and weather description—the one improving, the other worsening—that allegorical interpretations fail to take account of.[40] Why should a symbolic "sea of life" go from rough to icecold and then to an unqualified "ocean track," while the atmosphere above it becomes colder and stormier, until it envelops sea and land alike? There seems to be no definitive answer to the question, but I think it likely that the storms represent the seafarer's feelings about his lack of spiritual progress—he is then prevented by spiritual or literal storms from starting on his *peregrinatio*. This explanation has the merit of working on both the symbolic and the literal level—though the descriptions of storms are not factual. However, they are not so far removed from the truth as to make them totally unsuitable for literal interpretation. The worst storms of the winter around the coast of Britain often come in early spring; anyone wishing to go on a voyage would simply have to wait till they abated.[41] It should be noted that the seafarer's desire to set out is stated immediately after the description of the storms and before the signs of spring are described. It is also possible that there is a quite different allegorical significance in the storm/spring contrast, built on the idea of death and resurrection.[42]

As for the sea, one cannot help but notice that it seems to follow the same pattern as the seafarer's feelings about his situation in life. When the waves are high, so are the waves of his feelings surging about his heart. When the sea is ice cold, he is passive and static. Whether this correspondence is intentional or not is uncertain. It is perfectly possible that the sea is not specifically symbolic at all, but merely used to set a typical exile scene to introduce the anything-but-typical exile. At the beginning the literal exile is prominent, but once the exile metaphor is established, it becomes less important as the seafarer's physical being becomes less important, until at the end of A 2 he is only a mind and a voice. The homiletic voice is introduced with the exile metaphor and gradually becomes more prominent, until it is the dominant motif in Section B.

I think it entirely possible that the poet has allowed us much more freedom of interpretation in the first half of the poem than we usually allow ourselves. He has made it possible for us to carry the literal exile image right through the poem. Yet by using terms such as *elþeodigra eard* (38), *sæfore* (42), *onetteð* (49), and *londe* (66) in such a way that there is some doubt as to their exact semantic area, and by his careful modulation and control of exile imagery, he has brought to our attention the metaphorical exile behind the literal one.[43]

> Simle þreora sum   þinga gehwylce
> ær his tidege   to tweon weorþeð,   f. 82ᵛ
> adl oþþe yldo   oþþe ecghete,   70
> fægum fromweardum   feorh oðþringeð.
> Forþon þæt [bið] eorla gehwam   æftercweþendra,
> lof lifgendra   lastworda betst,
> þæt he gewyrce   ær he onweg scyle
> fremman on foldan   wið feonda niþ,   75
> deorum dædum   deofle togeanes,
> þæt hine ælda bearn   æfter hergen
> ond his lof siþþan   lifge mid englum
> awa to ealdre,   ecan lifes blæ[d],
> dream mid dugeþum.[44]   80

(Which one of three eventualities is always before his appointed day cause for doubt, [whether] illness or age or the enmity of the sword, will take life from the man fordoomed. Therefore that [is] for every man the best of memorials, the praise of those commemorating [him], of the living, which he should work for before he must depart, to act on earth against the malice of foes, [to act] with brave deeds against the devil, so that the sons of men may posthumously praise him and his fame may live afterwards for all ages among the angels, the glory of life everlasting, joy among the noble hosts.)

Gordon cites *Beowulf* 1735–39 and 1763–68 as parallels to lines 68–71.[45] There are a number of other occurrences of *adl* and *yldo*, with or without other forms of death added thereto, according to the needs of the particular context. The second of Gordon's *Beowulf* examples lists four other forms of death: by fire, flood, blade's edge, and spear's flight. None of the other occurrences in poetry states the causes of death in such an exact and exclusive way as our poem does. If the motif always appeared in this form, one could dismiss it as the formula for this particular commonplace. As it is, one wonders whether this is not another of those statements which seem unexceptional on the surface, but carry a dire warning below the surface blandness. Any Germanic hero worth his salt could shrug off the three given deaths—after all, he is in his prime, healthy, and brave; but the threat of those not stated may give him pause, especially since the seafarer has already implied that the wordly man in lines 39–47 may suffer an untimely death by drowning.

Because lines 72–80a advise on how to act in the light of the certainty of death and the uncertainty of its appointed day, *forþon* has its usual adverbial meaning "therefore." The sentence that follows is a modulation from the traditional heroic to the Christian meaning of the word *lof* (73 and 78), thereby giving the traditional concepts of *blæd* (79), *dream* (80), and *dugeþum* (80) an unambiguously Christian meaning, and thus making the point that these desiderata mean relatively little if they are confined to the temporal world. The same technique is used with *feonda* (75), but works in the opposite direction. Behind the general meaning of *feonda* "foes," stands the specifically Christian meaning of "fiends." Acting against the enmity of human foes may earn fame in this world but fiends must be prevailed against for *lof* among the heavenly host. *Deofle* (76), on the other hand, is completely unambiguous. The seafarer is in effect saying "you may earn fame in this world, with brave deeds, but if you want eternal life, you had better perform them against the devil."

As was the case earlier in the poem, there is no condemnation of traditional values; they are simply shown to be inadequate. The technique is essentially the same as that employed in lines 39–47. The seafarer states the facts and lets them speak for themselves. The type of man spoken of in the two passages is also similar.

>   Dagas sind gewitene,   80
> ealle onmedlan   eorþan rices;
> næron nu cyningas   ne caseras
> ne goldgiefan   swylce iu wæron,
> þonne hi mæst mid him   mærþa gefremedon
> ond on dryhtlicestum   dome lifdon;   85
> gedroren is þeos duguð eal,   dreamas sind gewitene.
> Wuniað þa wacran   ond þas woruld healdaþ,
> brucaþ þurh bisgo.   Blæd is gehnæged,
> eorþan indryhto   ealdað ond searað,
> swa nu monna gehwylce   geond middangeard;   90
> yldo him on fareð,   onsyn blacað,
> gomelfeax gnornað,   wat his iuwine,
> æþelinga bearn,   eorþan forgiefene.

Ne mæg him þonne se flæschoma,   þonne him þæt feorg
  losað.
ne swete forswelgan,   ne sar gefelan,   95
ne hond onhreran,   ne mid hyge þencan.

(The days are gone, all the splendors of the kingdom of the world;
there are not now kings nor emperors nor gold-givers as once
there were, when they performed among themselves the greatest
deeds of glory and lived in lordliest renown; fallen is all this noble
host, joys are departed. The weaker inhabit and possess this
world, make use of it through toil. Glory is brought low, the
nobility of the earth grows old and withers, as now does every man
throughout the world; age overtakes him, his visage grows pale,
hoary-haired he laments, knows his friend of old, child of princes,
[to be] given up to the earth. When life fails him the body cannot
swallow what is sweet, nor feel pain, nor stir a hand, nor ponder
with the mind.)

This passage consists of a series of sententious motifs. The first, in
lines 80b–85, is a version of the *ubi sunt* formula, or rather, it presents
the answers to a series of questions often asked in the formula.[46] This
is followed immediately and appropriately in lines 86–90 by the motif
of the disappearance of glory, and possession of this world by weaker
men.

In these two motifs we have a more explicit treatment of a theme
barely hinted at in the phrase *woruld onetteð* (49) "the world hastens,"
and again in the seafarer's statement in lines 66b–67 that he does not
believe that the earth's riches will stand forever. The message of lines
80b–90 is that the world is aging and nearing its end—a generally
held belief, as J. E. Cross[47] and Martin Green[48] have shown. The
belief in the weakness of later generations is also well attested (line
87).

It is the way in which the seafarer expresses these ideas that is of
particular interest here. The splendors of the earthly *duguð* (86) and
dreamas (86) have gone, and *blæd* (88) is brought low. In lines 91–96
the gloomy catalog of the ravages of time goes on. There is a sense of
time and events overtaking the individual; suddenly his lifeless body
is in its grave.

Þeahþe græf wille   golde stregan,
broþor his geborenum,   byrgan be deadum
maþmum mislicum   þæt hine mid wille,
ne mæg þære sawle   þe bib synna ful   100
gold to geoce   for Godes egsan,
þonne he hit hydeð ær   þenden he her leofað.
Micel biþ se Meotudes egsa,   for þon hi seo molde
  oncyrreð,   f. 83ʳ

se gestaþelade   stiþe grundas,
eorþan sceatas   ond uprodor.

(Although a brother desires to strew with gold the grave of his
brother born, to bury him beside the dead with various treasures
which he wishes [to go] with him, gold (when he has hidden it
beforehand while he is living here) cannot be of any assistance in
the face of god's terror, to that soul which is full of sins. Great is
the terror of the Creator, before whom the earth will turn away,
who established the firm foundations, the expanses of the earth,
and the sky above.)

Gordon follows Kenneth Sisam in emending *wille* in line 99 to
nille.[49] Sense can, however, be made of the passage without emendation. Whether we emend or not, the gist of the passage is that worldly
treasure is of no help before the terrible power of God. If we do not
emend *wille* to *nille*, we have a man strewing his brother's grave with
gold, and burying him with various treasures that he wishes to go with
the dead man, who hoarded it when he was alive—so that the gold was
available for that purpose when he died.[50]

If we emend *wille* to *nille* we get a better sense only if line 99b is
translated "that will not go with him." We must then assume that the
poem is probably of late date of composition, to justify the verb *willan*
being used to denote the future tense. Gordon suggests that there are
parallels to this passage in many Old English homilies, and that they
are closer than verses 7–9 of the West-Saxon version of Psalm 48,
which Sisam cites.[51] Whatever source or sources the poet made use of,
he incorporated the material to fit his theme. The seafarer has been
warning those who lead heedless lives and do not prepare themselves
for the world to come; now he warns those who prepare in the wrong
way that they are not helping themselves. (A good Christian would
obviously have given the money in alms to the poor.)

Lines 103–5 develop further the concept of the terrible power of
the Creator. *For þon* in line 103 makes better sense if it is taken as the
preposition *for* followed by the demonstrative pronoun in the instrumental case *þon*, than it does if the two forms are taken together as an
adverb or as a conjunction.

Dol biþ se þe him his Dryhten ne ondrædeþ;   cymeð him
    se deað unþinged.
Eadig bið se þe eaþmod leofaþ;   cymeð him seo ar of
    heofonum.
Meotod him þæt mod gestaþelað,   forþon he in His
    meahte gelyfeð.
Stieran mo[n] sceal strongum mode   ond þæt on staþelum
    healdan,

ond gewis werum   wisum clæne.   110
Scyle monna gehwylc   mid gemete healdan
wiþ leofne ond wið laþne   . . . . bealo,
þeahþe he hine fyres   fulne wille
oþþe on bæle . . . . .   forbærnedne [ne],
his geworhtne wine.   Wyrd biþ swi[þ]re,   115
Meotud meahtigra,   þonne ænges monnes gehygd.[52]

(Foolish is he who does not dread his Lord; death comes to him
unexpected. Blessed is he who lives humbl[y]; grace comes to him
from the heavens. The Creator makes steadfast his mind, because
he believes in His power. A man must control a strong mind and
keep it in place, and be true to his pledges and pure in his way of
life. Every man must behave with moderation towards friend and
towards enemy . . . . harm, although he desires [to have] him full
of fire or . . . . on a funeral pyre, a burned-out [corpse], the friend
he has made. Fate is stronger, the Creator mightier than any
mans's conception [of them].)

In line 106 we have both a summing-up of what is said before it and
a bridge to the maxims that follow it. It has often been noted that this
line bears a striking resemblance to line 35 of *Maxims I*, where the
verb is *nat* (35a), "foolish is he who does not know his Lord," whereas
our poem has *ondrædeþ*, an apt verb for the context, "Foolish is he who
does not dread his Lord." This line is the first of four expanded lines
of the type often used in Old English poetry for sententious utter-
ances.[53]

Line 107 is a modification of one of the Beatitudes as explained in
Homily XXIX of the MS Vespasian D. XIV collection: *Hwæt synd þa
gastlice þearfe bute þa eadmede, þe Godes ege habbeð?* "What are the poor
in spirit but the humble who have the fear of God?"[54]

Lines 109–15a urge moderation, in gnomic fashion, with the verbs
sceal (109) and *scyle* (111). Line 112 is the first of three lines in which
deficiencies in sense are underlined by severe metrical deficiencies.
Since there is no indication of loss in the extant manuscript, they may
result from earlier corruption. Line 112 appears as *wiþ leofne 7 wið
laþne bealo.* in the manuscript. As a standard line of Old English
poetry it is deficient in one main stress, which may be provided either
after *leofne*—possibly with alliteration—or after *laþne*. Line 113 appears as *þeahþe he hine wille fyres fulne*, which is metrically impossible
because there is no alliteration in the first half-line and there are two
in the second, namely *fyres* and *fulne*. If we move *wille* to the end of the
line, as suggested by Holthausen,[55] we can restore a measure of regularity. Krapp and Dobbie's dots after *wille* appear to indicate a belief
that something is missing from the text. Line 114 appears in the

manuscript as *oþþe onbæle forbærnedne*. Since *bæl-* and *bærn-* are the only syllables capable of carrying main stress, the line is deficient in two main stresses; possible deficiencies of sense include an infinitive after *bæle;* it must not be a verb of motion because *on* is followed by *bæle* in the dative. Another possible omission is of a masculine noun after *forbærnedne*, for which position I tentatively suggest *ne* "corpse."[56] For *geworhtne wine* in line 115a, Klaeber's translation "the friend he has made" is very attractive.

Although the precise meaning of lines 111–15a eludes us, the basic idea behind them may be discerned. Every man should behave with moderation toward both friend and enemy, although an enemy may wish him "filled with fire," almost certainly a reference to the fires of Hell, as suggested by Gordon.[57] Or the enemy may wish [to see] the man's friend of some standing on a pyre as a burned-up [corpse].

In the terse gnomic statements of lines 115b–16, we have an assessment of the twin powers of the universe, which are stronger than any man can conceive. They include not only God but fate, the traditional Germanic concept of the course of events.[58]

Uton we hycgan   hwær [w]e ham agen,
ond þonne geþencan   hu we þider cumen,
ond we þonne eac tilien   þæt we to moten,
in þa ecan   eadignesse,   120
þær is lif gelong   in lufan Dryhtnes,
hyht in heofonum.   þæs sy þam Halgan þonc,
þæt He usic geweorþade,   wuldres Ealdor,
ece Dryhten,   in ealle tid.   Amen.[59]

(Let us think where [w]e have our home, and then consider how we may go there, and we shall then labor also so that we may go there, into that eternal blessedness, where the source of life is in love of the Lord, bliss in the heavens. For that let there be thanks to the Holy One, in that He honored us, Prince of Glory, eternal Lord, for all time.   Amen.)

The closing passage of the poem, lines 117–24, is a miniature sermon in itself, opening with the familiar homiletic formula "Let us think," and continuing in the first person plural. Lines 117–19 provide a summary of the poem. In A 1 and A 2 we are told how the seafarer is following this advice. In A 1 he is an exile because he is thinking about "where we have our home" and in A 2 he is considering "how we may go there." He is also proposing to labor in his *peregrinatio* so that he may go to his heavenly home. The seafarer's postulated worldly men and the admonitions of section B provide a sort of counterpoint. A 1 and A 2 are the "how to" instructions, with a hint of what will happen if we fail to follow them, and B contains the "how not to" warnings with a hint of the rewards to be gained by following the example of the seafarer. In lines 120–22a the reward is detailed and the poem ends with thanks to God for it.

The two themes of the poem—the transience of human life on earth and the transience of the earth itself—are really two aspects of the same theme, as Cross has shown.[60] The aging of the world not only adds urgency to the quest for salvation; it adds poignancy to the struggles of the latter-day *wacran* (87) who now toil on the earth.

The two roles of the seafarer, as exile on earth and as homilist, remain the same throughout the poem and give it structural strength and unity; everything else is built around that framework. I have tried to demonstrate, by close reference to the text, that it was the poet's intention that we should recognize the seafarer's double role early in the poem. A literal exile is needed in the first place to guide us toward recognizing the metaphorical one. But, perhaps the most important function of the literal *peregrinatio* is to provide an occasion for "deeds against the devil" for the seafarer.[61]

There are two things that the Anglo-Saxon poet had in common with poets of any other age: the need to express, succinctly and forcibly, the urgent concerns of the age, and the likelihood that the recipients of his message would not all be of the same cast of mind and level of intelligence. The particular tastes that our poet had to cater to were a love of what we often dismiss as sententious commonplaces, and a taste for allusive expression. The *Seafarer* poet seems to have fulfilled his obligations admirably.[62]

The person whose mind causes him to relate what he hears (or reads) most readily to real life could picture the seafarer taking his turn on the dangerous nightwatch. He would probably assume that there were others there. However, when the words *winter wunade* (15) were reached, he would surmise that the seafarer was probably on a small island and that he was there voluntarily and virtually alone. The purpose of the reference to the fortunate man would then have occurred to him and the carefully chosen exile imagery would help to confirm the idea that the seafarer had "exiled" himself for the salvation of his own soul. In case he was too literal-minded to recognize the seafarer as an exile in the metaphorical sense in the opening twenty-six lines, the poet has given him several more opportunities to do so in the other contrasts with the worldly men. This literal-minded Anglo-Saxon would also consider it perfectly natural that the seafarer should want to embark on a journey to a foreign land. The anchorite and peregrinus images, together with a third evocation of a worldly man, would probably confirm his suspicion that the seafarer was also a homilist. It would come as no surprise to him that the seafarer's longing for the heavenly home expressed in lines 58–64a leads him to reject all the pleasures of this familiar land, because they are so transient that they are already dead—or soon will be when all such things come to an end. It is of course perfectly natural that such a "seafarer" would deliver a farewell homily before setting out.

Sitting next to this literal-minded man, his opposite may be imagined, the man who could and did turn almost any experience or phenomenon into a metaphor. The first passage of curiously incomplete exile imagery would probably reveal to him the nature of the seafarer's exile. He would need only one mention of the *ceol* (5) and the *nihtwaco* (7) to construct a vivid image of this Christian on the spiritual nightwatch in his frail ship of faith, about to be dashed on the rocks of temptation.[63] He would already have been predisposed by the numerous metaphors of this kind in his regular reading toward understanding the poem in this way. he would hardly need the idea of a literal *peregrinatio* and would automatically interpret *deade lif/lœne on londe* (65b–66a) as referring to the whole transitory world. He would hardly notice that the seafarer was no longer referring to the sea, since it was a metaphorical sea to begin with, and the seafarer is no longer speaking of the faithful.

My two imaginary Anglo-Saxons are extremes, whereas the poet was almost certainly aiming at the majority in between who, by using the literal level to locate and inform the metaphorical level, would come to a full appreciation of this poem that he constructed with such care.

NOTES

1. For details of early scholarship see I. L. Gordon, ed., *The Seafarer* (London: Methuen, 1960), hereafter referred to as Gordon, and E. G. Stanley *The Search for Anglo-Saxon Paganism* (Cambridge: Brewer, 1975), a reprinting of articles first published in *Notes and Queries* (1964–65), pp. 53–64.

2. For example T. A. Shippey, *Old English Verse* (London: Hutchinson, 1972), especially pp. 69–71.

3. P. L. Henry, *The Early English and Celtic Lyric* (London: George Allen and Unwin, 1966), p. 134.

4. John C. Pope, "Second Thoughts on the Interpretation of *The Seafarer*," *Anglo-Saxon England* 3 (1974):80.

5. The text is based upon the unpublished half of my Ph.D. dissertation of 1955, with modifications made over the years. It is listed in the catalog of the University of Manchester as follows: "LESLIE (Roy Francis) 'An Edition of the Old English Elegiac

poems 'The Wanderer' and 'The Seafarer,' with a 'Study of Old English elegiac poetry.' by R. F. Leslie 1955 (Typewritten copy of thesis 3 vols.)"

For my discussion of *cearselða*, see *Old English Poetry: Essays on Style* ed. Daniel G. Calder (Berkeley: University of California Press, 1979), pp. 111–25.

6. Translations of all texts (except where otherwise stated) are my own.

7. All textual references to Old English poems, except *The Seafarer*, are to the editions in *The Anglo-Saxon Poetic Records*, ed. G. P. Krapp and E. V. K. Dobbie (New York: Columbia University Press, 1931–53).

8. Definitions of exile imagery are according to Stanley B. Greenfield, "The Formulaic Expression of the Theme of 'Exile' in Anglo-Saxon Poetry," *Speculum* 30 (1955):200–206.

9. Line 26 *f[ref]ran:* MS *feran.*

10. Many commentators take *nænig hleomæga* to refer to the seafarer's lordless state, e.g., Michael D. Cherniss in *Ingeld and Christ* (The Hague: Mouton, 1972), *"Juliana and The Seafarer,"* p. 212, Jerome Mandel in "The Seafarer," *NM* 77 (1976):541. I do not consider this assumption to be warranted by the text. The seafarer is saying that not any one of a number of protecting kinsmen could comfort him, not that one of them had been his lord. Henry, *The Early English and Celtic Lyric*, p. 133, justified MS *feran* (26) by translating "Not one of the kinsmen, not a single wretched soul could travel (sail)," which conveys the meaning of lines 25b–26 admirably. However, I do not feel quite able to "stretch" the text to such a distinctly modern idiom as "not a single wretched soul," though I recognize this as a subjective judgment.

11. Such as W. F. Bolton's in *Modern Philology* 57 (1959–60), 260–62, "Connectives in *The Seafarer* and *The Dream of the Rood*." O. S. Anderson, *The Seafarer: An Interpretation* (Lund: Gleerups, 1937), pp. 8–9, states that all the occurrences of *forþon* in *The Seafarer* can be translated "therefore." He has recently partially retracted the statement (as O. Arngart) in *"The Seafarer:* a Postscript," in *ES* 60 (1979):250.

12. John T. McNeill, *The Celtic Churches: A History, A.D. 200 to 1200* (Chicago: University of Chicago Press, 1974), pp. 89–90.

13. O. Arngart, in *"The Seafarer:* A Postscript," p. 250, emphasizes that the seafarer "wishes to persuade rather than condemn."

14. E. G. Stanley, "Old English Poetic Diction and the Interpretation of *The Wanderer, The Seafarer* and *The Penitent's Prayer,"* *Anglia* 73 (1955):413–66 states that it is "relevant" to *The Seafarer* that there is confusion between the first and third person singular in *The Penitent's Prayer*. However, I do not think that there is any confusion of person either here in lines 33b–47, or elsewhere in the poem.

15. Gordon, *The Seafarer*, p. 3, footnote 1, cites just such a case.

16. Cf. *Daniel* 29 *langung* and *Beowulf* 1879 *langað.*

17. Stanley B. Greenfield in *"Min, Sylf,* and Dramatic Voices in *The Wanderer* and *The Seafarer," JEGP* 68 (1969): 212–13.

18. John C. Pope in "Second Thoughts on the Interpretation of *The Seafarer*."

19. Dorothy Whitelock, "The Interpretation of *The Seafarer,"* in *The Early Cultures of North-West Europe: H. M. Chadwick Memorial Studies*, ed. Sir Cyril Fox and Bruce Dickins (London: Cambridge University Press, 1950), pp. 262–72.

20. G. V. Smithers, "The Meaning of *The Seafarer* and *The Wanderer," Medium Aevum* 26 (1957):137–53, abbreviated as Smithers, 1957. Also G. V. Smithers, "The Meaning of *The Seafarer* and *The Wanderer* (continued)," *MÆ* 28 (1959):1–22, abbreviated as Smithers, 1959, and G. V. Smithers, "The Meaning of *The Seafarer* and *The Wanderer:* Appendix," *MÆ* 28 (1959):99–105, abbreviated as Smithers, 1959 Appendix.

21. Henry, *The Early English and Celtic Lyric*, pp. 36–37 and 195–96, and Whitelock, "The Interpretation of *The Seafarer,"* pp. 267–72, on the other hand, give many examples of *in elþeodignesse lifian* denoting literal *peregrinatio.*

22. Line 52 *gewita*[n]: MS *gewitað   e*[*s*]*teadig:* MS *efteadig*

23. A. D. Horgan in "The Structure of *The Seafarer," RES*, n. s. 30 (1979):41–49, recognizes the structural function of the worldly men, but interprets the contrast as one

of poverty and riches. I do not believe this to be the main theme of the poem but our interpretations are in some respects complementary.

24. J. E. Cross in "On the Allegory in *The Seafarer*—Illustrative Notes," *MÆ* 28 (1959):104–5, first pointed out that there was no need to give *onetteð* anything other than its usual meaning "hastens" here.

25. Norman Blake in *N & Q* 207 (1962):163–64 has shown that lines 49–50 may be interpreted as a symbol of the resurrection of man at the Day of Judgment. He links these lines with lines 31–33a, the winter storm at the end of A 1, and goes on to say: "The description of winter and spring would then symbolize respectively the death of man together with the period of waiting in the grave and the resurrection of man at the Day of Judgement."

26. Gordon, *The Seafarer*, pp. 40–41.

27. T. N. Toller in *An Anglo-Saxon Dictionary: Supplement* (London: Oxford University Press, 1921), gives "to do, perform, commit, perpetrate," for *dreogan*, any one of which would also fit the context here.

28. Stanley B. Greenfield, "The Old English Elegies," in *Continuations and Beginnings: Studies in Old Engish Literature* ed. E. G. Stanley (London: Nelson, 1966), p. 156.

29. Gordon, *The Seafarer*, p. 41.

30. Smithers, 1959, pp. 16–20.

31. Vivian Salmon, " 'The Wanderer' and 'The Seafarer', and the Old English Conception of the Soul," *MLR* 55 (1960):1–2.

32. Peter Clemoes, "*Mens absentia cogitans* in *The Seafarer* and *The Wanderer*," in *Medieval Literature and Civilization: Studies in Memory of G. N. Garmonsway*, ed. D. A. Pearsall and R. A. Waldron (London: Athlone, 1969), pp. 62–77.

33. For example F. N. M. Diekstra, "*The Seafarer* 58–66a: The Flight of the Exiled Soul to its Fatherland," *Neophilologus* 55 (1971):433–46, and Vivian Salmon.

34. Gordon, *The Seafarer*, pp. 41–42. Neil D. Isaacs, "Image, Metaphor, Irony, Allusion and Moral: the Shifting Perspective of 'The Seafarer,' " *NM* 67 (1966):278, suggests that *anfloga* is the seafarer's spirit and is like the cuckoo.

35. Smithers, 1959, pp. 20–22.

36. John C. Pope, "Dramatic Voices in *The Wanderer* and *The Seafarer*," in *Franciplegius: Medieval and Linguistic Studies in Honor of Francis P. Magoun, Jr.*, ed. Jess B. Bessinger, Jr., and Robert P. Creed (New York: New York University Press, 1965), pp. 192–93, n. 39.

37. E. G. Stanley, Review of Ida L. Gordon's edition of *The Seafarer* in *MAE* 31 (1962):56.

38. Smithers, 1957, p. 138. It should be noted that Professor Smithers does not insist on this reading. See also O. Arngart/ O. S. Anderson, "*The Seafarer:* A Postscript," p. 250, where he justifies emending *wælweg* to *hwælweg* despite the fact that his interpretation is similar to Smithers'.

39. E.g. Gordon, *The Seafarer*, p. 3, and Stanley B. Greenfield, *A Critical History of Old English Literature* (New York: New York University Press, 1965), p. 220.

40. E.g. Daniel G. Calder, "Setting and Mode in *The Seafarer* and *The Wanderer*," *NM* 72 (1971):266.

41. I fully agree with E. G. Stanley, "Old English Poetic Diction and the Interpretation of *The Wanderer, The Seafarer* and *The Penitent's Prayer*," pp. 436–37, that Old English descriptions of winter are often figurative, but feel that here figurative and literal meanings coincide.

42. Norman Blake, in *NQ* 207. I think it perfectly possible that the poet intended this allusion to heighten the drama of his poem; it is not, however, essential to recognize it in order to understand the poem.

43. T. A. Shippey, *Old English Verse*, p. 68, believes *The Seafarer* to be a good example of the kind of poem that "maintains in tension disparate but loosely-related elements of thought and emotion, forcing the reader or listener to supply his own interpretation, if he feels the need."

44. Line 69 *tidege to tweon*, for MS *tide geto tweon*, on analogy with *mældæge* in *Genesis* 234, which also refers to the future. Line 72 *bið* not in MS. Line 79 *blæd:* MS *blæð*; for examples of *ð* written instead of *d* in the Exeter Book, see Carleton Brown, "*Poculum Mortis* in Old English," *Speculum* 15 (1940):389–90, n. 3 (#(2) on p. 390).

45. Gordon, *The Seafarer*, pp. 42–43.

46. J. E. Cross, "*Ubi Sunt* Passages in Old English—Sources and Relationships," *Vetenskaps-Societetens Årsbok í Lund* (Lund: Gleerup, 1956), pp. 25–44. For discussion of this passage in relation to the *ubi sunt* theme in *The Wanderer*, see Roy F. Leslie, *The Wanderer* (Manchester: Manchester University Press, 1966), pp. 18–20.

47. J. E. Cross, "Aspects of Microcosm and Macrocosm in Old English Literature," *Comparative Literature* 14 (1962):1–22, and especially 16–18.

48. Martin Green, "Man, Time, and Apocalypse in *The Wanderer, The Seafarer,* and *Beowulf,*" *JEGP* 74 (1975):502–18.

49. Kenneth Sisam, "Seafarer, Lines 97–102," *RES* 21 (1945):316–17. Gordon, *The Seafarer*, pp. 45–46.

50. E. G. Stanley, "Old English Poetic Diction . . .", p. 456, has a very similar interpretation of lines 97–102 to my own.

51. Gordon, *The Seafarer*, p. 23, also p. 45n.

52. Line 110 *mo[n]*: MS *mod.* Line 114 *[ne]* not in MS. Line 115 *swi[þ]re:* MS *swire.*

53. Cf. *The Wanderer* 111–15, *Solomon and Saturn* 453–60.

54. See Homily XXIX of *Early English Homilies from the Twelfth Century MS. Vesp. D. XIV*, ed. Rubie D-N. Warner (London: Early English Text Society, 1917), o.s. 152, p. 74.

55. F. Holthausen, "Zur altenglischen Literatur VII," *Anglia Beiblatt* 19 (1908):248.

56. The simplex in Gothic is *naus* and in Old Icelandic *nár*. It is, however, a second element in two compounds in Old English: *orcneas* (*Beowulf* 112) and *drihtneum* (*Exodus* 163); it is an initial element in *nefuglas* (*Genesis* 2159), *neosiþum* (*Vainglory* 55), *neobed* (*Phoenix* 553) and *niobed* (*Genesis* 3430).

57. Gordon, *The Seafarer*, p. 47

58. Cf. especially *Resignation* 44 for God as ruler of *wyrda* and *Maxims* II 5 for a close parallel to *The Seafarer* passage, *wyrd byð swiþost.*

59. Line 117 *[w]e:* MS *se.*

60. Cross, "Aspects of Microcosm and Macrocosm in Old English Literature," especially pp. 1–2.

61. Greenfield, "The Old English Elegies," pp. 156–57, argues against a purely metaphorical *elþeodigra eard gesece* on the same grounds.

62. See W. F. Klein, "Purpose and the 'Poetics' of *The Wanderer* and *The Seafarer*," in *Anglo-Saxon Poetry: Essays in Appreciation for John C. McGalliard*, ed. Lewis E. Nicholson and Dolores Warwick Frese (Notre Dame: University of Notre Dame Press 1975), pp. 208–23. I agree with Klein that the poet was no "languid monk" making a "scissors and paste" collage, but not that he owed anything to Oðin or to his two ravens.

63. J. E. Cross, "On the Allegory of *The Seafarer*—Illustrative Notes," p. 106. See also Marijane Osborn, "Venturing upon Deep Waters in *The Seafarer*," *NM* 79 (1978):1–6.

Time, Memory, and Elegy
in *The Wife's Lament*

Martin Green

Time broods heavily over most Old English literature, but especially over its poetry. The speech of King Edwin's retainer in Bede's account of the conversion of Northumbria expresses what is perhaps an authentic traditional Germanic feeling for man's place in time. Man's life in time, the retainer says in this famous figure, is like a warm hall in the winter through which a bird flies; "but after a very short space of fair weather that lasts for a moment, it soon passes again from winter to winter. . . . So the life of man here appears for a short season, but what follows or what has gone before, that surely we know not."[1] Even if this speech is a fiction—an expression of Bede's Latin literary training rather than an authentic piece of the Germanic *Weltanschauung*—it still speaks eloquently of a feeling for time that is expressed elsewhere in the literature.

For us who see all of Old English literature whole and simultaneously it sets up sympathetic resonances elsewhere. For example, when Beowulf prepares to descend into the murky waters of Grendel's mere, his response to Hrothgar's cautions derives from a sense that for the warrior intent on his *dom,* each episode of conflict and testing is reduced to a moment of crisis; time is brief and fleeting and of the essence:

> "Ure æghwylc sceal   ende gebidan
> worolde lifes;   wyrce se þe mote
> domes ær deaþe;   þæt bið drihtguman
> unlifigendum   æfter selest."[2]

(Each of us must experience the end of life in the world; let him who can perform valorous deeds before death; that is the best thing afterwards for a dead man.)

Like the speech of Edwin's retainer, this passage emphasizes the shortness of man's life in the face of a hostile world, and the full narrative of Beowulf's exploits puts that moment of the hero's life (or the three moments, as Tolkien suggested)[3] in the wider temporal perspective of the movement of time in legendary and scriptural history. The perspectives of *Beowulf* are objective and comprehensive; man's life in time is seen against the background of the cycles of the rise and fall of empires and dynasties, and, perhaps, against the linear movement of Christian history framed by Creation and Doomsday.[4]

The Old English poems traditionally called the elegies present a concise expression of a major portion of the Old English sense of time. They are preeminently concerned with the relation of past and present, and as lyrics, they are more concerned with subjective response than with cosmic perspectives (although cosmic perspectives are not far removed from the concerns of some of them). The elegies' special sense of time has been a major reason for their being so labeled. As Alvin A. Lee remarks, "the essential element [in the elegies] is always a melancholy sense of the passing away of something desirable, whether that something be a life, a civilization, a human relationship. . . ."[5] But the term *elegy,* as we have often been reminded recently, is equivocal and imprecise, and thus, any generalization about elements common to the group of poems is difficult to sustain. This is especially true of any generalization about the sense of time in the poems. The sense of time in the elegies is a complex of attitudes, as a reexamination of *The Wife's Lament* makes clear.

If generalizations are difficult to sustain about the elegies in general, they are particularly difficult to sustain about *The Wife's Lament.* The extensive scholarship and criticism of the poem have emphasized how little consensus there is about this short poem of 53 lines. Perhaps the only certainty is that the poem is difficult to interpret, and much "ingenious desperation," in Bruce Mitchell's phrase,[6] has been invested on it to elucidate its obscurities. The obscurities are as basic as the essential elements of the narrative situation of the poem. A speaker, presumably a woman,[7] is separated from her lord, *hlaford,* and bewails her plight. The *hlaford* has gone abroad, "heonan of leodum/ ofer yþa gelac" (6b–7a), but the reasons for his journey are never stated. The relationship of the speaker to the lord is not clear either; is she his wife or his lover? The lord's kin (*þæs monnes magas,* 11) have been plotting to separate the lord and the speaker; but why? Is she in exile abroad or at home?[8] Beyond the lack of solid information about the "plot," there are the technical obscurities of the syntax and semantics of the poem. Is the "geong mon" referred to in line 42 the same person as the *hlaford* or the *gemæcne mon* of line 18? Lines

42–54, which contain the reference to the *geong mon,* are difficult to construe. The verb mood here is subjunctive, but what does that imply: a curse or a gnomic reflection?[9] Lines 17a–20 are obscure in sense not only because of the reference to the *gemæcne mon* but also because his actions (*morþor hycgende,* 20b) are not precisely defined, and the temporal relationship of these lines to the lines preceding is not clear despite what appears to be a precise arraying of adverbial markers (*ærest, Ða, ongunnon*).

The obscurity of the situation, the vagueness of the identity of the speaker, and the opaqueness of the language would seem to be formidable blocks to any interpretation. The poem is a mysterious one that yields to understanding only reluctantly if at all. Yet, paradoxically, these very obscurities throw the sense of time in the poem into relief. By obscuring elements of narrative or plot, the poem places emphasis squarely on the present circumstances of the speaker.

These circumstances are not defined until relatively late in the poem (ll. 27–41). The speaker is in exile far from home and friends; she (I call the speaker "she" for convenience, although the gender of the speaker is not crucial to my argument) sits in isolation under an oak tree (*under actreo,* 28a) that grows at the mouth of a cave (*eorðscræfe*).[10] The sketchy details of the surrounding landscape emphasize the speaker's isolation. The cave is in a wasteland surrounded by dim valleys and high hills that in the speaker's metaphoric associations constitute a fortress (*burgtuna,* 31a), a joyless and bitter place overgrown with briars. The grim landscape externalizes the speaker's mood and feelings; it could be said that her mind, like the surrounding valleys, is *dimme* and *brerum beweaxne.* The oak tree and the earth-hall are such concrete entities in a poem that is otherwise devoid of concrete detail, they force themselves on the reader as potential carriers of meaning. Like the hills, valleys, and briars, they can be seen as embodiments of the speaker's isolation. Their place in the landscape, their very rootedness and fixity, are objective correlatives of the speaker's imprisonment in mental and physical space. They mark out the narrow limits of her movement in comparison to the expansion of the world beyond, where she cannot go. She is condemned to wander within the cave under the tree.

The rootedness and fixity of the earth-cave and tree may also suggest the temporal dimensions of the speaker's situation. They are expressions of the unchanging, static quality of the speaker's present that is defined elsewhere in this passage by the reference to the summer-long day (*sumorlangne dæg,* 37b) through which she must sit and weep for her sorrows (*wræcsiþas,* 38b). The image of the summer-long day combined with the image of the cave and tree creates a sense of temporal suspension. Her time is all present—a present without end. Her days are all summer-long days, one day like the next. While the Wanderer and the Seafarer's misery is defined by the physical pain and suffering of exile—cold, ice, and endless sea—hers is defined by its temporality.

The presentness and interminableness of the speaker's temporal stasis is further underscored by the striking juxtaposition of phrases in line 29. Contemplating her dwelling, she says:

> Eald is þes eorðsele,   eal ic eom oflongad.
> (Old is this earth-hall,   I am full of longing.)

The parataxis of the line links the age of the cave with the deep intensity of the speaker's present longing and misery. The juxtaposition makes it appear as if the fact of the cave's age—its link with an indeterminate past—is enough to intensify present misery and to make it that much more unbearable. This is, indeed, what the poem has suggested up to this point, although here it is expressed in a line of great economy and intensity. The speaker exists in an interminable present; that present is all that exists, and her pain and suffering are as unrelenting as the summer-long day. But that unrelenting present is given its intensity by a past, fragments of which are "present" in the memory of the speaker.[11]

In the earlier portion of the poem (ll. 1–26), the relationship between past and present is developed as the overriding preoccupation of the speaker. The first five lines establish the pattern for the rest of the poem as the verb tenses shift back and forth between present and past and as the syntax encloses the past tense verbs in and envelope of the present tense:

> Ic þis giedd wrece   bi me ful geomorre,
> minra sylfre sið.   Ic þæt secgan mæg,
> hwæt ic yrmþa gebad,   siþþan ic up weox,
> niwes oþþe ealdes,   no ma þonne nu.
> A ic wite wonn   minra wræcsiþa.
>
> (1–5)

The stress is thus on the "presentness" of the speaker's situation. Her present misery is greater than any she has experienced since she grew up (siþþan ic up weox). That she feels a compulsion always to recount her wræcsiþa underscores the sense that the present is felt by the speaker as being interminable.

The shift in line 6 to the past events that have led up to the present moment of the speaking of the poem suggests the beginning of a detailed account of the circumstances. Adverbial markers in lines 6 and 9 further reinforce the suggestion of circumstantiality and provide seemingly precise indications of the train of events. First *(Ærest)*, her *hlaford* left his people and went over the sea; the speaker was concerned about his whereabouts. Then (*Ða*), she herself went on a journey *(feran gewat,* 9a), whose purpose is ambiguously expressed by the opaque phrase *folgað secan.*[12] The next circumstance narrated, however, is introduced without any adverbial indicator:

> Ongunnon þæt þæs monnes   magas hycgan
> þurh dyrne geþoht,   þæt hy todælden unc,
> þæt wit gewidost   in woruldrice
> lifdon laðlicost,   ond mec longade.

(That man's kin began to think in secret thought that they might separate us, that we two widely separated in the world might live miserably, and I yearned.)

The placing of these lines and the absence of temporal connectives suggests continuity—that the plotting of the kinsmen took place after the speaker's departure. Similarly, the command of the lord that she *herheard niman* (15)—another crux—seems to be subsequent to events previously narrated, although the sequence is not altogether logical.[13]

The difficulty with these lines is that as we read them, we experience them successively in time. As Harry and Agatha Thornton and A. A. Lind point out, this successiveness is true of all language: "All acts of speech consist of successive items experienced in time."[14] This temporal linearity of language reinforces the strong sense of sequence in lines 6–20 of *The Wife's Lament.* But the relationship of the events remains equivocal because the syntactic markers of temporality are missing at key places. What the relationship might be is suggested by the Thorntons and Lind's discussion of style in the Homeric poems. Quoting the German linguist Ammann, they define the mode of the Homeric poems as appositional; that is, there is a "piecemeal building up of a sentence out of a 'sentence kernal which is self-sufficient in content, and loosely added supplements and expansions' " (p. 75). On this basis they go on to characterize what they call "an appositional mode of thought," which, they argue, implies a conception of time different from a linear and sequential one, one in which the various dimensions of time are less clearly separated. As they put it: "What distinguishes appositional utterance is that it is an experience of a minimum of a future that is certainly to be expected and in part predetermined. As for the past, it is not strictly separated from the present as a past that has been and is no more, but it is always close behind the present, intensifying and illuminating it. One might go so far as to say that it is still part and parcel of the present as immediately experienced by the narrator and listener" (p. 86).

Although the style of *The Wife's Lament* in particular and Old English poetry in general differs from Homeric style—the former being relatively terse and compressed in comparison to the elaborate piling up of elements of the latter—it is still primarily appositional. The parataxis of lines 6–21 cuts the narrative into distinct segments, yet links them together in such a way that there is a strong suggestion of the rush of memory that is not necessarily sequential. As T. A. Shippey notes: "[*The Wife's Lament* presents] with great force the image of a mind circling over past events, unable to find a position of rest."[15] The lack of sequence is confirmed to an extent by the juxtapositions contained in lines 21–25. After having returned from the memory of the past to remark on the intensity of her present misery, she again recurs to the past to recall the oaths she and her lord swore never to be parted except by death:

> Forþon is min hyge geomor,
> ða ic me ful gemæcne   monnan funde
> . . . .
> Bliþe gebæro   ful oft wit beotedan
> þæt unc ne gedælde   nemne deað ana
> owiht elles;   eft is þæt onhworfen,
> is nu * * *   swa hit no wære
> freondscipe uncer.
>
> (17b–25a)

(Therefore is my mind the sadder, that I found the fully equal mate. . . . Happily we often vowed that nothing else would separate us but death itself; now is that changed, our friendship is as if it had never been.)

In a logical sequential narrative, one would expect the fact that the lord and the speaker swore oaths of undying loyalty to be placed anterior to the details of the lord's departure. But the poem presents this detail afterward; thus what seems important is not the sequence but the emotive weight of the events as they are juxtaposed in the memory of the speaker. Further, lines 21–25 conclude the first half of the poem in a way that sums up how the temporal relationships are apprehended in the poem. So much has change come about in the speaker's fortunes, so wretched is her present, that her past has all but disappeared. Her past is not, as Leslie has said, something with which she steadies herself in moments of greatest distress;[16] the love she and her lord shared in the past has gone and become as if it never had been—*swa hit no wære*.

Intensifying further the misery of the present is the lack of a future in the consciousness of the speaker. She seems irrevocably trapped in her present. There is no further *onwhorfen* expected or contemplated, only more summer-long days when she will sit by her tree and *wepan mine wræcsiþas*. Her mind, she says in lines 39–41, is forever restless:

> forþon ic æfre ne mæg
> þære modceare   minre gerestan. . . .

And the word *æfre* in its absoluteness indicates the extent to which she is trapped and the extent to which her memory defines her present without any glimpse of release.

The final lines of the poem (42–53) can be seen to emphasize this lack of future consciousness no matter which way we construe them. If we accept the more likely interpretation that they are a gnomic reflection on the wretched state of exile and the bitterness of solitude—a reflection that begins with a generalized *geong mon* and then shifts to a hypothetical picture of the exiled lord whom the speaker imagines is sharing her loneliness and isolation—then the focus is clearly on the present. The speaker is resigned to her lot and sees no fundamental change occurring. Like her lord, she is trapped *on dreorsele,* a phrase that, as Karl Wentersdorf has suggested, may have a temporal rather than a spatial reference.[17]

The picture of absolute passivity and hopelessness, of a person suspended in time, emerges strongly from *The Wife's Lament* and contrasts markedly to the other elegies. In many of them some future different from the present is implied, whether that future is defined as the vague hope for some *edwendan,* "change," as in *Deor,* or the more specific hope for an eternity beyond this life, as in *The Wanderer* and *The Seafarer.*[18] This difference has been noted before by all commentators who have felt *The Wife's Lament* to be a different kind of poem from the others. One might say that *The Wife's Lament* comes closest to being a pure form of elegy,[19] one that deals with "the passing away of something desirable"; but this characterization misses what I have been trying to suggest about the poem's sense of time; its concern is not primarily with what was, but with what is.

The Wife's Lament presents a sense of time that is almost all pure subjectivity. There are no references to history, to cosmic process, to any dimension of time beyond the human mind contemplating its own existence. This sense of time is strongly modern, for twentieth-century attempts to grapple with the mysteries of time have emphasized its very subjectivity. As a noted twentieth-century philosopher has put it: "Strictly speaking, no time can be common to two selves. . . . There are as many time-series as there are selves who perceive things in time."[20] Or, as Auden has put it more poetically: "we have no time until/ we know what time we feel."[21] But the subjective psychology of time is not a twentieth-century discovery. Augustine, in Book 11 of the *Confessions,* eloquently examined the dimensions of the human problem of time, and central to his analysis was his discovery that the objective basis for knowing time provides little that is certain or measurable. Looked at logically, the past no longer exists, the future has yet to come, and the present is the point of least duration because "it is measured while it is passing; when it has passed by it is not measured, for then there will be nothing to measure."[22] It passes in a flash, he says elsewhere. Yet paradoxically, Augustine argues, it is in the present where all times exist: in the present of the mind (11.20). There is a "present of things past, a present of things present, and a present of things future. . . . The present time of things past is memory; the present time of things present is sight; the present time of things future is expectation." Augustine caps his extended exploration of these paradoxes with an apostrophe to his mind that gathers up past, present, and future: "It is in you, my mind, that I measure time. . . . As things pass by they leave an impression in you; this impression remains after the things have gone into the past; and it is this impression which I measure in the present, not the things which, in their passage, caused the impression" (11.27).

Thus far, Augustine's formulations provide a paradigm for what I have been suggesting about the "presentness" of *The Wife's Lament.* But one essential difference should be noticed. As E. D. Blodgett has noted, for Augustine the problem of what Blodgett calls the "restlessness of the heart in time" is the springboard of Christian ethics.[23] Augustine moves from his examination of the human temporal paradoxes to a celebration of God's eternality. This, Blodgett argues, is in contrast to ancient pagan attempts to escape from the riddles of time through "withdrawal into stasis" by an "extension" of the soul's present. The Christian soul, on the other hand, withdraws from the fragmenting change of the temporal present by tending toward the complete presence of eternity. It is perhaps the failure of the speaker in *The Wife's Lament* to transcend her present that underscores the poignancy of her sad song and defines the poem's difference from the other elegies.[24]

NOTES

1. Bede, *Ecclesiastical History*, bk. 2, chap. 13. I have modified the translation of J. E. King in the Loeb Classical Library volume: *Baedae opera historica* (Cambridge, Mass.: Harvard University Press, 1930), 1:285.

2. *Beowulf*, ll. 1386–89, quoted from *Beowulf and the Fight at Finnsburg*, 3d ed., ed. Fr. Klaeber (Boston: D. C. Heath, 1950).

3. J. R. R. Tolkien, "Beowulf: The Monsters and the Critics" in *Proceedings of the British Academy* 22 (1936):245–95.

4. See my article "Man, Time, and Apocalypse in *The Wanderer, The Seafarer,* and *Beowulf,*" *JEGP* 74 (1975):502–18.

5. Alvin A. Lee, *The Guest Hall of Eden: Four Essays on the Design of Old English Poetry* (New Haven, Conn.: Yale University Press, 1972), p. 128. See also Stanley B. Greenfield, *A Critical History of Old English Literature* (New York: New York University Press, 1965), p. 214.

6. Bruce Mitchell, "The Narrator of *The Wife's Lament:* Some Syntactical Problems Reconsidered," *NM* 73 (1972):222–34. The lack of consensus has been a long-standing problem; see W. W. Lawrence, *"The Banished Wife's Lament,"* *MP* 5 (1907–8):387–405.

7. On the identification of the speaker as *not* a woman as traditionally thought, see Rudolph C. Bambas, "Another View of the Old English *Wife's Lament,*" *JEGP* 62 (1963) as reprinted in *Old English Poetry: 22 Analytical Essays,* ed. Martin Stevens and Jerome Mandel (Lincoln: University of Nebraska Press, 1968), pp. 230–36, and Martin Stevens, "The Narrator of *The Wife's Lament,*" *NM* 69 (1968):72–90. For contrary views, see Mitchell, *NM* 73; Angela Lucas, "The Narrator of *The Wife's Lament* Reconsidered," *NM* 70 (1969):282–97; and Lee Ann Johnson, "The Narrative Structure of *The Wife's Lament,*" *ES* 52 (1971):497–501.

8. Some solutions to the textual obscurities have been offered by, among others, Douglas Short, "The Old English *Wife's Lament,*" *NM* 71 (1970):585–603, who sees the situation involving the narrator's illicit relationship with a second man; Johnson (see n. 7 above), who sees the poem as the "plight of a wife whose husband is a criminal"; R. P. Fitzgerald, *"The Wife's Lament* and the Search for the Lost Husband," *JEGP* 62 (1963):769–77, who links the poem to the folklore theme of the search for a super-natural male who disappears when some taboo has been violated; Raymond Tripp, Jr., "The Narrator as Revenant: A Reconsideration of Three Old English Elegies," *PLL* 8 (1972):339–61 (see also William Johnson's essay in this present volume). Two unusual solutions involving allegorical interpretations of the poem are offered by Michael J. Swanton, *"The Wife's Lament* and *The Husband's Message,*" *Anglia* 82 (1964):269–90, and W. F. Bolton, *"The Wife's Lament* and *The Husband's Message:* A Reconsideration Recon-sidered," *Archiv für das Studium der neueren Sprachen und Literatur* 205 (1969):337–51. Main line interpretations can be found in Roy F. Leslie, *Three Old English Elegies: The Wife's Lament, The Husband's Message, The Ruin* (Manchester: Manchester University Press, 1961); Alain Renoir, "A Reading Context for *The Wife's Lament,*" in *Anglo-Saxon Poetry: Essays in Appreciation,* ed. Lewis E. Nicholson and Dolores Warwick Frese (Notre Dame: University of Notre Dame Press, 1975), pp. 224–41, and "A Reading of *The Wife's Lament,*" *ES* 58 (1977):4–19; and Matti Rissanen, "The Theme of Exile in *The Wife's Lament,*" *NM* 70 (1969):90–104. The most recent study of the problems in the poem is Karl P. Wentersdorf, "The Situation of the Narrator in the Old English *Wife's Lament,*" *Speculum* 56 (1981):492–516.

9. The construing of the last lines as a curse was proposed by Stanley B. Greenfield, *"The Wife's Lament* Reconsidered," *PMLA* 68(1953):907–12. Greenfield later recon-sidered his initial judgment in his essay on the elegies in *Continuations and Beginnings,* ed. E. G. Stanley (London: Nelson, 1966), p. 166. See also Wentersdorf, *Speculum* 56 and his earlier article, "The Situation of the Narrator's Lord in *The Wife's Lament,*" *NM* 71 (1970):585–603, for consideration of the problems in these lines.

10. The *eorðscræf* has been interpreted as a grave by Tripp and William Johnson, and

by Elinor Lench, "*The Wife's Lament:* A Poem of the Living Dead," *Comitatus* 1 (1970): 3–23. For contrary views see Joseph Harris, "A Note on *eorðscræf / eorðsele* and Current Interpretations of *The Wife's Lament*," *ES* 58 (1977): 204–8, and Wentersdorf, *Speculum* 56.

11. Cf. Renoir, *ES* 58:15 and T. A. Shippey, *Old English Verse* (London: Hutchison, 1972), p. 74.

12. Wentersdorf, *Speculum* 56, provides a detailed discussion of this phrase which he interprets as "refuge, protection." For other views, see Short and Lee Ann Johnson.

13. Short points up the contradiction in the time sequence (*NM* 71:587). Lee Johnson sees the adverbials and verbals as conspicuous and intentional, a sign of careful construction (*ES* 52:499).

14. Harry and Agatha Thornton and A. A. Lind, *Time and Style: A Psycho-Linguistic Essay in Classical Literature* (London: Methuen, 1962), p. 75.

15. Shippey, *Old English Verse*, p. 72. Wentersdorf, *Speculum* 56:493, resolves the illogical sequence of events by suggesting that ll. 1–10 provide a summary of the narrator's plight (her husband has gone; she has sought refuge) and ll. 10 ff., beginning with *ongunnon*, present a recapitulation of the story in more detail and in sequence: the kinsmen plot against the speaker and her lord; the lord orders her to seek refuge since he is plotting revenge *(morþor hycgende):* they vow devotion unto death. This interpretation is appealing and accounts for many of the cruces of these lines; my own view is that such logical ordering is unnecessary.

16. Leslie, *Three Old English Elegies*, pp. 3–4.

17. Wentersdorf, *NM* 71.

18. See Roy F. Leslie, *The Wanderer* (Manchester: Manchester University Press, 1966), p. 15, and Shippey, *OE Verse*, p. 58, on the sense of the future in these poems; see also my article cited in n. 4 above.

19. The characterization was made by B. J. Timmer, "The Elegiac Mood in Old English Poetry," *ES* 24 (1942): 33–47 and echoed by Greenfield, *Continuations and Beginnings*.

20. T. M. E. McTaggert, *The Nature of Existence*, quoted in A. A. Mendilow, *Time and the Novel* (1952; reprint ed. New York: Humanities Press, 1972), p. 63.

21. Quoted in Mendilow, *Time and the Novel*, p. 118. See also Hans Meyerhoff, *Time in Literature* (Berkeley and Los Angeles: University of California Press, 1960), p. 26.

22. *The Confessions of St. Augustine*, trans. Rex Warner (New York: New American Library, 1963), p. 273.

23. E. D. Blodgett, "The Unquiet Heart: Time and the Poetry of Antiquity and the Middle Ages," *Filolški Pregled* 1–4 (1971): 55–83.

24. See, for example, James Doubleday's characterization of the development of *The Wanderer:* "The poem, in brief, moves through three major stages. In the first, the speaker recalls his past hardship. But in venting his grief . . . the healing process begins. . . . In the second stage, he comes to understand fully that his lot is part of the general mutability of the world. . . . In the third stage he perceives the remedy for that mutability in the grace of the unchanging lord. . . ." "The Three Faculties of the Soul in *The Wanderer*," *Neophilologus* 53 (1969): 189–93.

On *Resignation*

Marie Nelson

The incomplete poem this paper is about has been called *Resignation*[1] and classified as an elegy; but the title fits only its last two lines, and, at least at first glance, it seems that less than half of what remains of the poem can be regarded as an elegy. But let the title stand. No one is likely to be misled by a title given an Old English poem in the last century or two. And let the classification stand also. A working definition like "a relatively short reflective or dramatic poem embodying a contrasting pattern of loss and consolation, ostensibly based upon a specific personal experience or observation, and expressing an attitude toward that experience"[2] will not exclude *Resignation;* nor should *Resignation*'s concern for the hereafter cause it to be seen as essentially different from other elegies like *The Wanderer, The Seafarer,* and perhaps *The Husband's Message.*[3] Also, despite Bliss and Frantzen's convincing demonstration that half of a leaf of the Exeter Book is missing after line 69,[4] I think we can allow the poem to retain the integrity it has in Krapp and Dobbie. The missing half leaf need not have been, as Bliss and Frantzen believe, the end of one poem and the beginning of another.

I do not think that we who labor in the vineyard of Old English criticism are obligated to establish the unity and coherence of every poem in the Anglo-Saxon Poetic Records; but then neither do we have to assume that *Resignation* is a prayer with an elegy tacked on, as it was once assumed that *The Seafarer* was an elegy to which a sermon was added. The order of *Resignation*'s two parts is the opposite of the *Seafarer* order, and the speaker of *Resignation* does not reach the assurance with which *The Seafarer* and *The Wanderer* end. But this failure does not negate his singleness of purpose. Indeed, his failure to express an absolute faith that his soul will find its way to God may well be what makes *Resignation* an elegy, for it is that failure that communicates a sense of personal experience.

The *Resignation* we have is not a whole poem. Even so, I think a determined effort to see it whole will show that it is an elegy. Its two parts are different, but this is not an untypical structure for an Old English poem.[5] And if we read the first part as a *commendatio animae,* as Malmberg suggests, and take the sea journey of the second for the voyage of the soul after death, the whole poem can be seen to have a single purpose. Its purpose is to prepare the mind and soul for death.

That preparation is most difficult, as close examination of the language of the poem reveals. Both the prayer of part one and the consideration of exile in part two show a conflict between faith and fear. Although the speaker directly entrusts his soul to God in the prayer, his requests are qualified by confessions that show that he knows he has no right to receive the safe conduct he asks for. And although he claims his determination in part two, his desire is again undercut by qualifications. First he distances his desire to leave the world by expressing it, in part, through third person narration; and even when he returns to the directness of the first person and verbally divests himself of all that could bind him to the world, he finds he is still unable to depart.

We first see the speaker of the poem as a penitent who addresses God. He asks His help; commits himself to Him; and then requests a sign, protection, and forgiveness. The request for forgiveness leads to the speaker's reason for asking: he has committed sins in the past. A description of his present condition (he is stained with sin and afraid for his soul) leads to another reference to the past: he has angered God. Nevertheless, the speaker expresses his gratitude for the trials he has already undergone and finds courage, and even joy, in anticipating the difficult journey to come. He then links his own experience to that of an exile he describes. He himself is impelled to go wretched from his homeland,[6] and though he is now "bound fast in [his] heart" (which I take to mean determined and resolute), his having angered God in the past is paralleled by God's anger with the exile. As the poem concludes, the speaker wishes to embark on a sea journey, but is unable to do so.

The whole account is presented in the first person except for ll. 89b–96b, when the life of the *anhoga* is described. Though we may see in the speaker's brief switch to the third person a certain temporary distancing from the immediate experience in which he is engaged,[7] his narrative focus on the present is quite consistent; and the present of the elegies (with the exception of *The Husband's Message*) is a time of woe. Whoever experiences the hardships of *Resignation*, whether it is the *ic* who speaks or the traditional figure with whom he identifies himself, experiences it *now*. The verbs are present indicatives. The sinner repents. The exile laments, men give him alms, his heart is always sorrowful, his mind distressed. The speaker does not know what he can purchase a boat with, has no money or friends, cannot carry out his desire to leave a world in which he suffers. And yet he remembers that remedy rests with God. The *persona* continues to live in the world, taking some consolation, I think, in the belief that a voyage to the heavenly *patria* will someday be possible. This, then, is the experience the speaker of *Resignation* presents.

Elegies, however, do more than tell about experiences involving loss and consolation. They also present attitudes. One way to get at those attitudes is to ask what the speaker does as he presents his experience, or, to say it another way, what speech acts he performs.[8] I will digress a little here to consider the general subject of speech acts in the elegies before giving specific attention to the speech acts of *Resignation*. This, I think, will help establish a perspective for considering *Resignation* as an elegy.

We find a variety of speech acts being performed in the elegies. *Describing* is the essential act of *The Ruin* and is the act that the *Wanderer* speaker performs when he tells of walls that stand blown by winds and hung with hoar-frost (75–77). *Asserting* takes a positive form when the speaker in *Wulf and Eadwacer* claims it is Wulf's absence that has made her heartsick (13–15) and a negative one when the speaker of *The Seafarer* says he does not believe that the wealth of the world stands eternal (66b–67). The *Riming Poem* speaker *predicts* when he says that "when the body lies dead the worm eats the members, carries the expectation, and consumes the feast" (75–76). The *Wulf and Eadwacer* speaker *threatens* when she says that Wulf will bear the "whelp" to the wood (16b–17), and the *Wife's Lament* speaker *philosophizes* when she says "Woe is to him who must endure longing for love" (52b–53), if she does not *curse*.[9] The *Wanderer* speaker *laments* with "Alas the bright cup! Alas the byrnied warrior! Alas the glory of the prince!" (94–95b). The *Seafarer* and *Riming Poem* speakers *exhort* their listeners when they say "Let us consider where we have a home" (116) and "Let us now, like the holy ones, shear away our sins . . . in order to see the true God and rejoice forever in peace" (83b–87). The speakers of the elegies also perform acts of *commanding*, as when the message, or message-bearer, of *The Husband's Message* orders the receiver to embark on a sea journey (24–29), and of *thanking*, as in the Seafarer's "For this be thanks to the Holy One" (123b). But *narrating* is the speech act most frequently performed in the elegies.

And *narrating* is an act to which attention is often called. The Wanderer's monologue is introduced with a *swa cwæð*. His opening line, "Often I must alone each dawn bewail my sorrow," suggests that *lamenting* will follow; but, after comments on the absence of audience and the custom of silence, *narrating*, or the presentation of events in sequence, begins. *The Wife's Lament* also begins with references to acts of speaking. The *persona*'s first statement, "I utter this song about myself full sadly," suggests a lament, but then "I can say that . . ." prefaces a simple narration of, not a continuous complaint about her experience. *The Seafarer* begins with a speaker's assertion of his ability to tell his own story; and *The Husband's Message* begins with "Now I wish to tell you . . . ." The "I wish to tell my experience" formula comes in line 35 in *Deor;* and in *Resignation* the speaker says "I speak these words eager from the heart" in 83b–84a, and, twelve lines later, "I tell this sorrowful story most strongly [or mainly] about myself," again drawing attention to the act of narration.

As E. G. Stanley and others have noted, the *Resignation* poet uses two different modes of presentation.[10] The first is quite explicit, and the second is metaphoric in a traditional way. Only two explicit speech acts are to be found in *Resignation,* and they, as might be expected, are in the first part of the poem. However, examination of the various speech acts of the poem, both explicit and implicit, may lead to a stronger sense of the speaker's purpose and the significance of his failure to achieve it.

When the *persona* says *Ic þe, mære god, mine sawle bebeode* (5b–6a) and *Gesette minne hyht on þec* (37b), he is, in saying those words, committing his soul to God and placing his trust in Him. He does not say "I praise" in the long prayer section of the poem, but nevertheless, with every variation with which he addresses his Creator, he implicitly pays tribute to the power, the holiness, the wonderfulness, the everlastingness, the wisdom, the justice, and the mercy of God. Neither does he say "I request," "I assert," "I thank," "I confess," or "I repent," but he also performs these acts. Even less explicitly, near the end of the poem he may be saying, or attempting to say, "I dare," or "I willingly accept whatever challenge God sends me." It will be the purpose here to show how the explicit and implicit speech acts that the *Resignation* speaker performs give structure to a poem that becomes a testament of courage.

Resignation is different from the other elegies in that its primary speech act is the request. In fact, the poem derives much of its coherence from the repeated requests for God's help with the task the speaker has set for himself. Requests dominate the first part of the poem, and, seen in the perspective established by the prayer that precedes it, the elegiac second section seems to function as an indirect request. Indeed, as direct attention to the poem itself will show, repeated requests provide the basic structure of *Resignation*.

Resignation begins with two parallel clauses, *Age mec ælmihta god,* and *helpe min se halga dryhten* (May the almighty God have me, may the holy Lord help me). A direct expression of commitment follows the double request of the opening lines,

> Ic þe, mære god,
> mine sawle bebeode   ond mines sylfes lic,
> ond min word ond min weorc,   witig dryhten,
> ond eal min leoþo,   leohtes hyrde,
> ond the manigfealdan   mine geþohtas.

(5b–9)

> (I to you, Glorious God,
> commit my soul   and my own body,
> and my word and my work,   Wise Lord,
> and all my members,   Guardian of Light,
> and my manifold thoughts.)

Having totally committed himself to God, the speaker continues to request His help. The grammatically imperative verbs *Getacna* (10a), *læt* (15b), and *Forgif* (19a) succeed the subjunctives of the opening lines and function as key words in requests[11] that the speaker be shown how he can do God's will, that God not allow thieves to harm him, and that he be forgiven for sins. This series ends with a humble assertion, *Ic þa bote gemon, cyning wuldor, cume to, gif ic mot* (20b–21) (I am mindful of the remedy, King of Glory, would come to it, if I am permitted).

Further requests follow in an envelope passage that extends from ll 22–37a.[12] Two uses of *forgiefan* (which now means "grant," not "forgive" as it did in 19a) mark the passage. The first, *forgif,* functions as the verb of a request that God prepare the speaker, giving him the time, understanding, patience, and mindfulness for each test that will be sent him. The relationship between God and the supplicant is given syntactic realization here (as it was in the speech with which the speaker committed himself to God) by the juxtaposition of *þu* and *me*. *þu* and *me* come together in 22a and 24a as the speaker refers to the things "You grant me" and the tests "You send me." Repetition of the second and first person pronouns continues the development of the grammatical, and personal, relationship as the speaker requests that God, Who knows his sins, cleanse him and prepare him to seek the life after this one. This section closes with *Hwæt, þu me her fela * * * forgeaf* (36b–37a) (Lo, you have granted me many [favors] here); and it is at this point that the speaker performs the explicit speech act of placing his trust in God, saying,

> Gesette minne hyht on þec,
> forhte foreþoncas,   þæt hio fæstlice
> stonde gestaðelad.

(37b–39a)

> (I place my trust in You,
> my fearful forethoughts, so that they may stand
> firmly established.)

Another series of requests provides the basic structure of ll. 39b–64. They are: lift up my heart; cleanse me; permit me to depart; save my soul; permit angels to bring me to Thy presence; do not allow the devil ever to lead Thy offspring on a loathly journey. The last two requests of this series, which involve permitting, are introduced by *forlæt* (49b) and *ne læt* (52b); and the repetition draws attention to the speaker's anxiety. He digresses briefly, calling very directly on the *commendatio* tradition, to consider the possibility that the devils, if they triumph, may think themselves higher than Christ; but he returns almost at once to his main concern, praying, "Defend me and restrain them [the devils] when the storm comes against my soul; keep it [my soul] whole and sustain it."

Comments on the speaker's spiritual state, which include simple statements of need, acts of confession, and an expression of eagerness, support the 39b–64 series of requests. In 41–43a two uses of *nu* focus on the present urgency,

> Nu ic fundige to þe,   fæder moncynnes,
> of þisse worulde,   nu ic wat þæt ic sceal,
> ful unfyr faca.

> (*Now* I would hasten to You, Father of Mankind,
> from this world, *now* I know that I must [depart],
> in a very short time.)

At this point the speaker seems to find consolation in a belief that he will leave the world soon and in his faith in the mercy of God, but his use of *þeah* clauses shows a certain lack of assurance. In 47b he asserts that he takes comfort in God, but in an immediately following *þeah* clause he admits that he has learned little mercy in the time he has lived. In 49b–51a he requests that God allow the angels to take him to His presence, but a following *þeah* clause undercuts his request: he has committed many sins in his days. But the two conditional clauses show two things: the speaker understands that God's grace is given, not earned; and he is making progress toward self-understanding.

The *þeah* clauses just discussed also function as indirect acts of confession. The speaker confesses more directly when he says,

Min is nu þa
sefa synnum fah,   and ic ymb sawle eom
feam siþum forht,   þeah þu me fela sealde
arna of þisse eorþan.

(64b–66a)

(My heart is now
stained with sins,   and I am sometimes [a litotes]
afraid for my soul,   though You have given me many
blessings on this earth.)

The penitent seems to gain a deeper sense of his unworthiness as he
confesses it. Here, besides acknowledging his generally sinful condition, he confesses the specific sin of fear.[13] Whereas before the fearful
þeah clauses qualified movements toward faith, now a *þeah* clause diminishes the effect of an admission of fear. The penitent's progress is
tortuous indeed, but in the "though you have given me many blessings" clause a *þu me* juxtaposition once more affirms his relationship
with his God.

The first part of *Resignation* ends with a rendering of thanks that
uses the appropriate subjunctive and another *þu me* construction.
Even as the speaker thanks God for the rewards and favors He has
given him, however, with another qualification (*No ðæs earninga
wæron*) he denies that he has deserved those gifts. He not only conditions his requests: he also qualifies his acceptance.

The conjunction with which l. 70 begins suggests to me that the
poem's missing half leaf may have contained further presentation of
the difficulties and imperfections of the speaker; but all we know is
that, despite what may have gone before, the mood is now one of
determined readiness.

hwæþre ic me ealles þæs   ellen wylle
habban ond hlyhhan   ond me hyhtan to,
frætwian mec on ferðweg   ond fundian
sylf to þam siþe   þe ic asettan sceal,
gæst gearwian,   ond me þæt eal for gode þolian
bliþe mode,   nu ic gebunden eom
fæste in minum ferþe.

(70–76a)

(Yet I wish in all this to have courage
and to rejoice and trust in myself,
to clothe myself for the journey forth and hasten
on the journey that I must set for myself,
prepare my soul, so that I may endure all for God
with a happy mind, now that I am firmly
resolved in my heart.)

The speaker has chosen the *forðweg*[14] and asserts his readiness to depart with courage and even joy. It may be that some interpreters would see this as an act of resignation, but I can not see it as resignation, at least not in any common sense of the word. This is too active and self-motivated a choice to be a simple acceptance of whatever comes.

In the immediately following lines the penitent again asserts his unworthiness, but, considered in relationship to what he requires of himself, this assertion may constitute a paradoxical (and certainly unintended) demonstration of his worthiness. These are his words:

> Huru me frea witeð
> sume þara synna   þe ic sylf ne conn
> ongietan gleawlice.   Gode ic hæbbe
> abolgen, brego moncynnes.
>
>   (76b–79a)
>
> (In truth, God punishes
> certain sins in me   that I myself am not able
> to perceive wisely.   I have angered God,
> the Lord of Mankind.)

Conscious that he is not able to know all his sins (and that he may well be further punished for them), the speaker still dares to make his choice. Three *for þon* clauses present the cause-effect reasoning that supports his decision. First, he has angered God. *For this reason,* he says, he is punished before the world. The following detail relates the degree of his sin to the degree of the retribution: his transgressions were great and thus his punishment has been severe. Second, he is not wise in judgment, wise before the world. *For this reason* (in order to become wiser, it can be assumed) he speaks these words of determination eagerly from the heart, so that he may endure more anguish than other people.[15] He asks to be permitted to suffer in the belief, it is again fair to assume, that it will purify his mind and soul. In l. 86, a *god ealles þonc* for hardships to endure is inserted, a parallel to the thanks for favors granted of 67b–68. The third *for þon* is not prefaced by a confession of guilt or incapability, but can be related to the whole section that precedes it.[16] *For this reason*—all of the above, I take it— the speaker is impelled to go forth, wretched, from his homeland; and his soul-searching preparation carries him into a third person description of the life of the exile:

> Ne mæg þæs anhoga,
> leodwynna leas,   leng drohtian,

wineleas wræcca,   (is him wrað meotud),
gnornað on his geoguþe,
ond him ælce mæle   men fullestað,
ycað his yrmþu,   ond he þæt eal þolað,
sarcwide secga,   ond him bið a sefa geomor,
mod morgenseoc.

(89b–96a)

(The lonedweller cannot,
deprived of the joy of fellowship,   long endure,
the friendless exile,   [God is angry with him!],
he laments in his youth,
and men always support him with alms,
increase his distress, and he endures all that,
the wounding speech of men, and his heart is always sad,
his mind morning-sad.)

In this brief section of the poem the speaker distances the emotions that accompany his effort to come to terms with the thought of his own death in two ways: he calls upon the formulas of an established tradition, and he switches to third person narration. From 83b on it is as easy to see why the second part of *Resignation* should be considered elegiac as it is to see why the first part has been called a prayer. In the first part we see all these variations for God: *ælmihta god, halga dryhten, wundorcyning, ece dryhten, mære god, witig god, leohtes hyrde, tungla hyrde, meotud, soðfæst cyninge, wuldorcyninge, dryhtne, lifgende god, cyning wuldor, min frea, halges heofoncyninge, arfæst god ecan dreames, gæst god cyning, fæder moncynnes, wyrda waldend, leofra dryhten, nergende cyning, mihtig dryhten, ece god, frea, God brego moncynnes, dryhten min,* and *meahtig mundbora.* Here, in addition to the *fus on ferþe* of 84a, which strongly suggests the Seafarer's eagerness, we have *ic afysed eom* and *of minum eþle* (both of which relate to the essential condition of exile); *yrmþu* and *modðearfoða* (for hardships the exile experiences); *þolade, drohtian,* and *gnornað* (verbs for suffering); *anhoga* and *wineleas wræcca* (nouns that refer to the lonedweller); and *earm, sefa geomor,* and *mod morgenseoc* (words that relate to his emotional state).[17]

But it is the *exile* who cannot live long, and the *exile* who must endure well-meant charity and hurtful words; and through his use of third person narration the speaker even displaces the anger of God, causing it to fall upon the exile rather than on himself. The experience described has all the marks of the elegiac *sarspel,* but this is not yet the personal experience of elegy. The speaker, however, has identified himself with the exile; and with another elegiac formula, "I tell my own story," he returns to first person narration.

Ic bi me tylgust
secge þis sarspel   ond ymb siþ spræce,
longunge fus,   ond on lagu þence,
nat min * * *
hwy ic gebycge   bat on sæwe,
fleot on faroðe;   nah ic fela goldes
ne huru þæs freondes,   þe me gefylste
to þam siðfate,   nu ic me sylf ne mæg
fore minum wonæhtum   willan adreogan.
Wudu mot him weaxan,   wyrde bidan,
tanum lædan;   ic for tæle ne mæg
ænigne moncynnes   mode gelufian
eorl on eþle.   Eala dryhten min,
meahtig mundbora!   þæt ic eom mode [.]eoc,
bittre abolgen,   is seo bot æt þe
gelong æfter [.]fe.   Ic on leohte ne mæg
butan earfoþum   ænge þinga
feasceaft hæle   foldan [. . . .] unian;
þonne ic me to fremþum   freode hæfde,
cyðþu gecwe [. . . . .]   me wæs a symle
lufena to leane,   swa ic alifde nu.
Giet biþ þæt selast,   þonne mon him sylf ne mæg
wyrd onwendan,   þæt he þonne wel þolige.

(96b–118)[18]

(I tell this sad story most strongly
[mainly] about myself, and, striving forward with longing,
speak of a journey and think of the ocean.
My * * * does not know
how I can buy a boat for the sea,
a ship for the ocean; I do not have much money
or indeed many friends [a double litotes] who would help me
on my voyage. I cannot carry out my purpose now
myself because of my poverty.
The wood may flourish for them,[19] await fate,
bring forth branches; I, because of blame,
cannot love in [my] heart any lord of mankind
on the earth. On, my Lord,
mighty Protector! I am sick at heart,
bitterly aggrieved. [For] that the remedy is with You
after life. I, a wretched man, cannot by any means
live without hardship in the light on this earth.
As I have lived now, when I had peace with strangers,
a pleasant home, sorrow was always the return of loved ones.
Yet it is best, when a man cannot himself
turn fate aside, that he then endure it well.)

Bliss and Frantzen not only challenge the integrity of *Resignation*,
they also deny that the poem they call "Resignation B" (K–D 70–118)
is an elegy. They see the assertion of the speaker's desire presented

here as a simple wish to escape present hardships. I find lines 114–16 as enigmatic as the opening lines of *Wulf and Eadwacer*. There we do not know what hostility may greet the *him* who may come with force, or whose hostility it may be. Here we have a similar sense that hostility is involved without understanding why it should be so. Do those whom the speaker has loved reject him because he made peace with people they do not know? Has he incurred their enmity because he made friends with strangers they consider to be enemies? And who could the strangers be? It is impossible to say.

The people to whom the *him* of 105a refers (this is assuming it is a plural pronoun) are no more identifiable than the strangers and loved ones of 114a and 116a, but here at least a parallel is possible. In 105–8a the speaker may suggest the same kind of contrast between the desires of those who wish to live in the world and the desires of the man who seeks spiritual wisdom that we find in *The Seafarer*.[20] The wood may flourish for those who dwell on the land, but not for the penitent. The joys of companionship are for others, not for the man who would embark on a lonely journey.

Bliss and Frantzen consider the *persona*'s inability to actually set forth on his journey an embarrassment to critics who place *Resignation* within the penitential tradition. In penitential poems speakers carry through their intentions to leave the world, or at least we are convinced that they will do so. Nevertheless, the *Resignation* speaker's failure does not make his intention less penitential. His failure to depart is an act of confession, and the sin confessed is fear.

Earlier in the poem, the *Resignation* speaker spoke of fear even as he entrusted his soul to God. The words he used were, "I place my trust in You, my *fearful* forethoughts, so that they may stand firmly established." He confessed his fear indirectly a number of times with qualifying *þeah* clauses, and he also confessed it directly. As he approached the elegiac section he minimized his fear with a litotes (he was afraid for his soul "a few times," 66a); and in the elegiac sequence of 89b–96a he displaced God's anger, causing it to fall on the exile (91b), not on himself, as in 78b–79a. Now, as the speaker returns to first person narration, fear once again defeats his intentions.

In the passage cited above, the speaker wants to buy a boat and set out to sea, but he has neither much wealth nor many friends, a double litotes, since an exile suffers poverty and has *no* friends. This, I think, is not the simple complaint that Bliss and Frantzen take it to be. In the context established here, which makes full use of the themes of deprivation and loneliness, the speaker, even as he claims his inability to depart, verbally divests himself of all the things that might deter him

from his purpose: possessions, helpful friends, pleasure in the frui-
tion of the earth—all of life's transitory joys. This attempted act of
faith, like the more direct acts of confession, repentance, and prayer
that preceded it, seems to be one of a series designed to prepare the
speaker for death. And yet—he cannot leave. The question we cannot
help asking is why.

The practical answer of course is that it simply is not time yet.
There is a time to die and that time has not come. Now it is time to
prepare to die. But, as we can see, the penitent has been eagerly striving to reach a state of readiness and he has not succeeded. Why has he
failed? The answer is, once again: he has the sin of fear. In attempting
to overcome that sin the poet has drawn on the tradition of penitential
prayer and on the conventions of elegy. Now an elegiac formula, "I
speak for myself," has led to one of the most telling confessions of
fear we have yet seen. It is as if we have been permitted to enter the
speaker's actual experience. We learn that he must go someplace. He
is obligated to go. He even wants to go. But he cannot leave. He
cannot buy a boat. He cannot pay the fare. And there is no one he can
ask for help.

I have been speaking all this time as if the first person narration of
the elegies is a simple first person account of personal experience. It is
not. The ethopoeic "I" of the elegies is an inclusive first person; and
the speaker of *Resignation* both confesses and avoids confessing the sin
of fear. If we can remember the dream in which we must *be* somewhere, but the car will not start, the bus will not come, we cannot pay
for the cab, and the friends we could call are all out of town, I think
we will recognize the very human fear of *Resignation* as our own.

The *Resignation* poet seems to have chosen the traditional prayer
for the departing soul, with its acts of petition and confession, as a way
of performing his responsibility to remember that he must die. This
was an act of wisdom, for as the gnomic poet said,

> Dol biþ se þe his dryhten nat,   to þæs oft cymeð dead unþinged.
> Snotre men sawlum beorgað,   healdað hyra soð mid ryhte.[21]
>
> (Foolish is he who does not know his Lord,   to such death often
>   comes unexpected.
> Wise men protect their souls,   guard their truth with
>   righteousness.)

Guided by the same sense of responsibility, the poet of *Resignation*
called upon the traditional metaphor of the sea journey as another
way to keep the knowledge that he must die always before him. This
too was a wise choice, for it enabled him to acknowledge the fears that

threatened to overwhelm him, and to use them for the good of his soul. As the "Storm" riddle poet says:

> Dol him ne ondrædeð   ða deaðsperu;
> swylteð hwæþre   gif him soð meotud
> on geryhtu   þurh regn ufan
> of gestune læteð   stræle fleogan,
> farende flan.
>
> (83–87a)[22]

> (Foolish is he who does not dread the deathspear;
> nevertheless he dies if the true God
> through the rain from above causes
> an arrow, a travelling arrow, to fly
> straight from the whirlwind.)

The *Resignation* speaker makes no bargain with death. It is *life* and its vicissitudes that he resigns himself to in the last two lines of the poem. But the failure of the penitent to overcome his fears does not detract from the genuineness of his desire to dare the attacks of devils and the onslaught of the storm. Indeed, his courage in the face of the dangers that may beset his soul seems all the more genuine *because* it is qualified by fear.

No one would argue that *Resignation* has the poetic power of *The Wanderer* or *The Seafarer*, the poignance of *Deor* or the *Frauenlieder*, the verbal skill of *The Riming Poem* or *The Ruin*, or the bright promise of *The Husband's Message*. Nevertheless, if we choose to see it whole, *Resignation* is an elegy that presents the moving experience of a man engaged in the contemplation of his own death. If we accept the spiritual progress of ll. 1–69 as part of the poem, and I think I have provided adequate reason for doing so, the journey of part two may also be seen as an expression of a desire to face death, a greater trial than any the speaker has yet endured. To make such a request goes beyond an act of simple resignation, or passive acceptance. It is one thing to accept whatever happens; it is quite another to choose to venture forth to where one must accept whatever comes. To ask what the *Resignation* speaker asks is to perform an act of courage, and the fact that he is not yet ready to accept the trial he has requested does not really negate the courage of the act itself. I think we can say that the human document that survives as the record of that kind of courage deserves to have endured the ravages of time.

NOTES

1. George Philip Krapp and Elliot Van Kirk Dobbie, eds., *The Exeter Book, ASPR* 3 (New York: Columbia University Press, 1936), publish the poem under this title. Lars Malmberg retains the title *Resignation*, but publishes the poem as "Resignation A" and "Resignation B" in *Resignation* (Durham: Durham and St. Andrews Medieval Texts, 1979). Citations will be taken from *ASPR*. Translations will be my own unless otherwise indicated. Paraphrases included within paragraphs will be freer representations of meaning, often more "sense for sense" than "word for word."

2. Stanley B. Greenfield, "The Old English Elegies," *Continuations and Beginnings,* ed. E. G. Stanley (London: Nelson, 1966), p. 143.

3. Margaret E. Goldsmith, "The Enigma of 'The Husband's Message,'" *Anglo-Saxon Poetry: Essays in Appreciation for John C. McGalliard,* ed. Lewis E. Nicholson and Dolores Warwick Frese, (Notre Dame: University of Notre Dame Press, 1975), pp. 242–63, does not see the speaker of *HM* as a cross, as did Robert Kaske, "A Poem of the Cross in the Exeter Book," *Traditio* 23 (1967): 41–71, but does provide additional reasons for taking the message of the poem as the Lord's call to his beloved.

4. Alan Bliss and Allen J. Frantzen, "The Integrity of Resignation," *RES,* n.s. 27 (1976): 385–402.

5. This, of course, does not mean that even poems with very obvious divisions cannot be interpreted as unified wholes. See, for example, the discussion of the unity of *The Seafarer* by Jerome Mandel, *NM* 77 (1976): 538–51.

6. W. S. Mackie, *The Exeter Book,* Part II, EETS 194 (London: Oxford University Press, 1934), p. 169, translates 88b–91a, "So I have been driven in wretchedness from my home; thus solitary and deprived of social joys, a friendless exile can no longer live," taking *forþon* as a connective between the situations of the speaker and the exile figure.

7. James L. Boren, "The Design of the Old English *Deor,*" *AS Poetry,* pp. 264–76, shows that the "Deor" speaker gains sufficient perspective to be able to relate his misfortune to that of others by "fictionalizing" his own experience. The temporary distance that the "Resignation" speaker gains by "traditionalizing" his experience seems comparable.

8. I am using "speech act" in the sense developed by J. L. Austin, *How To Do Things With Words* (Cambridge, Mass.: Harvard University Press, 1962), and J. R. Searle, *Speech Acts* (New York: Cambridge University Press, 1969).

9. I find sufficient reason for taking the speech act as *philosophizing* in P. L. Henry's discussion of *WL* within the context of gnomic style and content of Old English, Old Icelandic, and Early Irish and Early Welsh poetry in *The Early English and Celtic Lyric* (London: Allen and Unwin, 1966), pp. 91–132.

10. "Old English Poetic Diction and the Interpretation of *The Wanderer, The Seafarer,* and *The Penitent's Prayer,*" *Anglia* 73 (1956): 413–66. Thomas A. Bestul, "The Old English *Resignation* and the Benedictine Reform," *NM* 78 (1977): 18–23, places the first part of the poem within the tradition of confessional prayer and sees the second as a metaphor for the life of the penitent. Titles given the poem by early editors show a strong tendency to regard it as a prayer. They include B. Thorpe's "A Supplication," R. P. Wülker's "Gebet," E. Sieper's and L. L. Schücking's "Klage eines Vertriebenen," and W. S. Mackie's "The Exile's Prayer," in *Codex Exoniensis* (London, 1842), *Bibliothek der angelsächsischen Poesie,* B. II (Leipzig, 1894), *Die altenglische Elegie* (Strassburg, 1915), *Kleines angelsächsisches Dichterbuch* (Cothen, 1919), and *The Exeter Book,* EETS 194, respectively.

11. Austin, *How To Do Things With Words,* p. 73, discusses various uses of the imperative mood. The use of the grammatical imperative was not confined to commands, but did include commands, along with other acts like exhortations, permissions, consents, dares, etc.

12. A. C. Bartlett, *The Larger Rhetorical Patterns in Anglo-Saxon Poetry* (New York: Columbia University Press, 1935), pp. 9–20, develops the idea of the "envelope."

13. John Donne's "A Hymn to God the Father" provides a striking parallel in its placement of the confession of fear.

14. Malmberg concurs with the usual emendation of *ferð weg* to *forðweg* and, rejecting the possibility that the speaker's attitude was sufficiently contrite for him to consider a spiritual journey, takes *forðweg* as a euphemism for death. Though my interpretation of attitude differs, I also take *forðweg,* as well as *sið* (97b) and *siðfate* (103a), as the familiar locution.

15. The fear-determination sequence is comparable to that of *The Dream of the Rood* (*The Vercelli Book, ASPR* 2, ed. G. P. Krapp [New York: Columbia University Press, 1932], pp. 64–65) when the dreamer, having just told of the great fear that was the response to Christ's question of how many would be willing to "taste of death," says that he wants to be permitted to seek the cross alone "more often than all men."

16. My translation differs from Mackie's (given above in n. 6) both in regard to *forþon* and *afysed.* It takes the *forþon* of 88b as a cause-effect conjunction and implies more self-direction than Mackie's "driven forth."

17. Stanley B. Greenfield, "The Formulaic Expression of the Theme of Exile in Anglo-Saxon Poetry," *Speculum* 30 (1955):200–206, presents status, deprivation, state of mind, and movement in or into exile as aspects of the exile state.

18. There are several holes in the MS here. Easy emendations are *seoc* (109b), *life* (111a), and *gewunian* (113b); and *gecweme* (Mackie's solution, supported by Krapp and Dobbie) works well enough in 115a as "pleasant" modifying *cyðþu,* "home." K-D and other editors supply *selast* in 117a.

19. Perhaps the *him* of 105a refers to land-dwellers.

20. Jerome Mandel, " 'The Seafarer,' " *NM* 77 (1976):538–51, develops the contrasts between the concerns of the Seafarer and those of the land-dwellers in some detail. I think the same kind of contrast may be barely suggested here.

21. "Maxims I," 35–36, *Exeter Book,* p. 157.

22. "Riddle 3," 53–57, *Exeter Book,* p. 182.

The Old English *Ruin:* Contrastive Structure and Affective Impact

Alain Renoir

Although I do not believe that the anonymous Old English elegy known as *The Ruin* has yet turned up on the *New York Times'* list of best-sellers or is likely to do so in the near future, I hope not to exhibit incontrovertible symptoms of incurable optimism if I suggest that the fascination that it has held and still holds for professional literary people has earned it a respectable place on the unwritten list of enduring poems of the English language. Ever since 1826, when John Josias Conybeare's edition was published posthumously along with his Latin translation and a Modern English version,[1] the poem has been edited and reedited more than twenty times, translated over and over again by some of the most distinguished translators, and made the object of innumerable studies by scores of formidable scholars. It is significant in this respect that, in an age that stands out for its methodical rejection of the past and its passionate concern for the immediate or near immediate, a glance at the *MLA International Bibliography* indicates that the scholarly interest accorded *The Ruin* may well be on a par with that accorded to many current and recent authors.[2]

Despite all the scholarly energy that it has generated, however, *The Ruin* tends to remain excluded from elementary courses in Old English,[3] presumably because it presents an array of textual and other problems that might well prove discouraging to beginning students. Conversely, those literary theorists who look upon Old English as excess baggage in the English curriculum may well be tempted to suspect that the stimulus for this energy ought to be sought in the problems in question rather than in the inherent literary quality of the poem. It is, in fact, difficult to deny the quasi-irresistible scholarly challenge of a short text packed with as many tantalizing problems as this one, as a few samples will illustrate. The only medieval transcript, in the Exeter Book, is preserved on parchment so badly burned out in places that fourteen of the poem's forty-five manuscript lines have been affected—nearly all of them seriously enough to render their contents almost completely conjectural and the concluding one so drastically as to leave nothing discernible except the bottom half of four characters[4]—so that it is impossible to assess empirically such a basic fact as the exact number of two-hemistich verses. Kemp Malone has accordingly reminded us that the text has been "printed in 48 or 49 lines" because "we cannot be sure of the number,"[5] which Stanley B. Greenfield lists as "some forty-nine."[6] Moreover, the frame of reference is so protean that great quantities of ink have been used to demonstrate why the ruin described is unquestionably the city of Bath or why it is Chester or why it is Hadrian's Wall or why it is the Babylon of the Apocalypse or how it may conceivably be no particular place at all.[7] Finally, the precise date of composition remains so uncertain that even such a thorough student of the text as Roy F. Leslie can only conclude that the evidence "would appear to support the usual attribution . . . to the eighth century."[8] There can be no doubt that the poem in its present manuscript shape constitutes a heart-warming sight for the antiquarian, the literary detective, the paleographer, or the imaginative translator, and every student of Old English shares some stated or unstated interest with one or more of these. Yet I find myself in agreement with the view that literary quality alone more than warrants the attention that has been lavished on the poem, and I should like to argue that one need not be a professional student of Old English to respond to the text regardless of the problems that beset it.

Since the previous remarks have been largely concerned with the state of the manuscript and the observations that follow presume to deal with the text as it has come down to us and as it affects the audience, consistency would require that references be to the facsimile edition of The Exeter Book. For the sake of simplicity, however, all my references to and quotations from Old English poetry are from *The Anglo-Saxon Poetic Records*,[9] where *The Ruin* is printed in forty-nine lines, and I have indicated such differences between the printed text and the manuscript as may prove relevant to my argument. The line numbers in this essay may accordingly be used to refer to any standard edition of relatively recent vintage.

The Ruin stands out from the other Old English elegies insofar as it is a series of tableaux rather than a narrative or philosophical monologue, and Alvin A. Lee has accordingly noted that it comes "very close to what we in the twentieth century know as an 'imagist' poem."[10] *The Wanderer, The Seafarer, Wulf and Eadwacer, The Wife's Lament, The Husband's Message, Deor,* and *The Riming Poem* describe or at least mention some kind of human action that explicitly affects or has affected or will affect the speaker or a major character in the poem, and *Resignation* has its speaker ask for God's help and describe his own situation. Over half of these formulate or suggest a philosophical lesson; all of them make clear the speaker's state of mind, and most of them give us enough evidence to ascertain or at least to argue his or her sex and status in the world. In contrast, *The Ruin* contains no philosophical statement[11] and offers no cue whatsoever regarding the status, sex, situation, or state of mind of its speaker. In effect, it has a speaking voice but no speaker, and no actual human action takes place within its time frame or is mentioned as having taken place or being about to take place. Such activity—in contrast to action—as we are asked to evoke is purely imaginary, is of a general nature, would have taken place generations before, and claims no connection with the speaking voice or any specific person in the poem. In other words, whereas the physical frame of reference is merely ambiguous and accordingly enables dedicated scholars to hold out for Bath or Chester or some other location, the emotional frame of reference is a total vacuum, which the modern reader must fill from his or her own reading of the text. As a result of this vacuum, the specific quality of the extant text—that is to say, such aspects thereof as produce its effect upon the audience—must perforce become a focal point for the reader intent upon enjoying the poem as well as for the critic attempting to analyze it.

Greenfield aptly refines a critical consensus when he writes that "the *Ruin*'s specific quality . . . inheres in its use of alternation: between the present ruins and past beauty, between the dead builders and kings and the once-breathing and once-strutting warriors in their halls, with the climax narrowing in focus from the 'far-flung kingdom' to the pride of the city, its baths."[12] The juxtaposition of contrasting times, concepts, and scenes is indeed the key to the structure of the poem, as may be observed in the following abstract, where line references are used to separate contrasting scenes or visions of life and decay[13]—positive and negative scenes, as they will occasionally be called hereafter—which stimulate respectively feelings of joy and sorrow: *This stonework is splendid (1a), demolished by fate (1b). The sites of the city have crumbled, undermined by age; the earth holds the builders, and hundred generations have died (2a-9a). This wall has survived one kingdom after another (9b–11a); the high gate has crumbled (11b). . . . The bold in mind built the foundations. The dwellings were glorious, and there were bath-*

houses, all kinds of impressive buildings, and mead-halls filled with rejoicing human beings (19b–23b) until fate changed all that: days of pestilence came, the city crumbled, and those who might repair it lay dead. Therefore all these things are in ruin, and the place fell to the ground (24a–32a), where in days of old many a happy man in splendid war trappings gazed on treasures and on the glorious city of the spacious kingdom; there were the stone courts where the hot baths ran hot over the stone. . . . That is a royal thing . . . (32b–49b).

Whether contrast be used by Catullus to emphasize Lesbia's dismay at the death of her pet sparrow,[14] or by the *Beowulf*-poet to emphasize the significance of Beowulf's prowess in Heorot,[15] or by Chaucer to emphasize the awe-inspiring grimness of the tower in which Palamon and Arcite are imprisoned,[16] or by Shakespeare to emphasize the courageous honesty of Cordelia's relationship to her father,[17] it is a time-hallowed rhetorical device often used to make something good or pleasurable stand out against an evil or unpleasant alternative, or *vice versa*. It is commonly associated with the Old English elegies, where it repeatedly emphasizes the unpleasantness of the present against the imagined or remembered pleasantness of the past.[18] The abstract above shows that the general principle applies to *The Ruin*, where it takes on a structured and complex form. The structured quality results from the fact that the initial statement signals what Daniel G. Calder has called a "pattern"[19] that extends throughout the poem, where the juxtaposed contrasting units progress from short to long, starting out with one half-line opposed to another half-line (1a vs. 1b) and ending with eight-and-one-half opposed to seventeen-and-one-half lines (24a–32a vs. 32b–49b). The complexity results from the fact that the otherwise fairly regular progression is inter-rupted by a partially ambiguous group of two-and-one-half lines, of which one half-line (11b) has a clearly negative connotation while two lines (9b–11a) may take on a positive or negative connotation depend-ing upon the audience's point of view,[20] and especially from the fact that past and present occasionally alternate within the same scene (e.g., 24a–32a), so that the relationship between the concept of time and the processes of life and decay yields a somewhat flexible rather than rigid equation.

The very nature of this complexity and flexibility brings up another important difference between *The Ruin* and the more popular Old English elegies. Here the contrasts between juxtaposed scenes or im-ages are particularly sharp and effective, but the occasional disjunc-tion between time and mood tends to tone down the sense of sudden transition that we associate with the other elegies. To be sure, we are told that life in the once-thriving city was good "up to the point" (24a:

"oþþæt") when fate intervened negatively, but the total disintegration
into the present lifeless ruin took place as a slow process after the
death of those who might have repaired the crumbling walls (28b–
31a), and we are soon returned to visions of well-being in the same
location (32b ff.). The difference to which I am calling attention may
be illustrated with a glance at *Deor,* where the speaker contrasts his
former happiness to this present wretchedness. Using the very same
conjunction for the same purpose as *The Ruin,* he tells us that everything was going according to his liking "until now" (39b: "oþþæt . . .
nu"), at which point his luck ran out with his lord's decision to give his
job and possessions to someone else. The addition of the adverb *now*
(nu), however, conveys a sense of immediacy that has no equivalent in
The Ruin, and there is nothing in the remainder of the poem to
suggest any subsequent change or progress: the speaker has passed
from happiness to wretchedness within a half-line, and his situation
has neither worsened nor improved since. The same kind of negative
comparison can be made with *The Wanderer,* where the beginning of
the speaker's woes coincides precisely with the burial of his lord (22b–
23a), as a consequence of which he has somehow been forced to take
up the same life of exile "over the commingling of waves" (24b: "ofer
waþema gebind") which he still endures now, and nothing in the text
suggests the least amelioration or deterioration in his lot since that
time. Even *The Husband's Message,* which is generally taken to an-
nounce the probable end of a period of forced separation between the
man who sent the message and the woman to whom it is addressed,[21]
fits the pattern of *Deor* and *The Wanderer,* because the emphasis is
largely on the woman, whose presumably unpleasant situation seems
to have developed with the man's departure (19b–20a) and to have
remained unchanged to the present, since such improvements as may
or may not affect that situation are clearly in the future and will take
place only "if" (47b: "gif") the man can solve certain unspecified
problems, and since such strokes of luck as the message claims for him
have taken place outside the actual action of the poem. In addition to
The Ruin, only one obvious exception to this pattern immediately
comes to mind, and that is *The Wife's Lament,* where the speaker's woes
increase in clearly detectable stages: "First" (6a "Ærest") her lord departs; "then" (9a: "Ða") she must also leave home like a "friendless
exile" (10a: "wineleas wræcca"); immediately thereafter (11a ff.), her
lord's relatives begin plotting to make her hateful to him, and they
presumably succeed, since he orders her to take up a life of dreary
seclusion (15a ff.) "in this earth cave" (34b: "geond þas eorðscrafu").[22]
This is not to say that the contrast between happiness and sorrow in

The Wife's Lament and the contrast between the joyful human activities of the past and the decaying stillness of the present in *The Ruin*[23] are anything but powerful, but rather to point out that the means whereby the impact of the latter affects us differ considerably from those commonly associated with the Old English elegies.

The means in question differ from those of the other elegies in yet another noticeable respect, for *The Ruin* steers clear from the rather common practice of establishing a clear-cut correlation between a given situation or mood and geographic proximity or separation. As I have already noted, the speaker of *The Wife's Lament* tells us that her emotionally depressing problems began when her husband first went away (6a–8b), thus correlating her woes not only with a point in time but with a geographic separation as well, and the remainder of the poem elaborates upon the lamentable effects of that separation. Precisely the same principle applies to *Wulf and Eadwacer,* whose speaker blames much of her woes on the separation necessarily brought about by the fact that "Wulf is on an island [and she] on another" (4a–b: "Wulf is on iege, ic on oþerre"),[24] and the problems that have faced and may still face the woman of *The Husband's Message* are openly connected with the separation that came between her and the author of the message when the latter "was driven away from the victory-people by a feud" (19b–20a: "Hine fæhþo adraf / of sigeþeode"). The speaker of *The Wanderer* likewise bemoans not only the death of his lord but also his own concomitant separation from home, which began when he departed over the waves (23a–24b), and the speaker of *The Seafarer* grows restless when he muses upon the hardships he has endured at sea and allows his mind to wander "far away toward a land of foreigners" (37b–38b: "feor heonan / elþeodigra eard"). In *The Ruin,* on the contrary, there is absolutely no actual or even imagined change of location, and such contrasting changes of scenery as affect the mood of the poem are strictly the result of imagined changes in chronology.

To recapitulate the foregoing observations, my contention is that *The Ruin* produces its effect upon the modern reader through the structured juxtaposition of scenes of life and of decay that are respectively but not in every respect correlated with past and present and that, unlike the other Old English elegies, it has no speaker, no actual action, no stated or clearly implied philosophical lesson, and no empirical or imaginary geographic separation. The remainder of this essay will be devoted to the examination of a few details that may be considered illustrative of this contention, and students of Old English will recognize the extent of my debt to an especially important study

in which Greenfield has pointed out that "much of the poem's poignancy" derives from the kind of alternative movement mentioned
here but that "the diction and synctatic and rhetorical patterns contribute even more to its poetic effectiveness."[25]

I have mentioned above that the principle of contrasting concepts
and times stands illustrated in the opening line: "Wrætlic is þes wealstan, wyrde gebrǣcon" (1 [Splendid is this stonework, demolished by
fate]). The second hemistich, however, poses a problem, since we may
side with either the majority of translators in construing the verb as
the past participle, which the thrust of the sentence leads us to expect,
or with Burton Raffel in construing it as the preterit plural, which the
form -brǣcon normally indicates, but nevertheless translating it as a
perfect singular for the sake of Modern English idiom: "Fate has
smashed. . . ."[26] My siding with the majority in this case is almost
purely arbitrary[27] and should not be taken to reflect negatively upon
one of the finest achievements of one of our finest translators. Even
though the choice of either interpretation must perforce affect our
perception of the grammatical aspect, it need not alter the essential
fact that the demolition we are asked to observe took place in the past
but is being observed in the present, so that the superficially simple
opening statement actually presents us with a bewildering array of
clashing or nearly clashing concepts: a splendid work of masonry is
also a dilapidated ruin, the dilapidation that we observe now actually
took place in the past over an unspecified period of time, and the
now-dilapidated splendor that has been called to our attention must
presumably have been a reality before the onslaught of decay. In
other words, the positive and negative reactions elicited from the
reader are intricately but logically interwoven with the concepts of
past and present.

The contrast and the implied relationship between splendor and
decay are particularly effective for the reader somewhat familiar with
Old English poetry because the way in which they are expressed is
unexpected and therefore noticeable. To be sure, it is a commonplace
of Old English elegiac poetry that, with the contrast between past and
present, splendor must in time give way to decay like everything else
in human affairs,[28] but the adjective *wrætlic* has a decided tendency to
appear as a headword in a first hemistich followed by a second hemistich whose contents either are neutral or reinforce the concept of
splendor.[29] One finds this pattern clearly illustrated in such familiar
pieces as *Beowulf*, where the phrase "splendid wave-sword" in the first
hemistich is followed by "the illustrious man" in the second (1489):
"wrætlic wæsweord, widcuðne man"), or *The Phoenix*, where the breast

plumage of the wondrous bird is described with the statement that "splendid is the breast below" in the first hemistich, followed by "wondrously fair, / bright and beautiful" in the second hemistich and the next line (307a–8a: "Wrætlic is seo womb neoþan, wundrum fæger,/scir and scyne").

Even when ruins or presumed ruins are mentioned, the focus is on either the decay or the splendor rather than on the contrast between them. In *The Wanderer*, for instance, the speaker imagines how dreary the world will be when everything in sight will have fallen to ruin, "just as now, here and there throughout this world, walls stand swept by the wind, covered with hoarfrost . . ." (75a–77a: "swa nu missenlice geond þisne middangeard / winde bewaune weallas stondaþ . . ."); and we find the other alternative in a passage from *Maxims II* that has been likened to *The Ruin*[30] and where we are told of presumably Roman ruins[31] that "cities are visible from afar, the skillful work of giants, those which are on this earth, splendid stonework" (1b–3a: "Ceastra beoð feorran gesyne, / orðanc enta geweorc, þa on þysse eorðan syndon, / wrætlic wealstana geweorc"). If we share the increasingly common view that a reader's response to a given text depends in part on expectations fostered by previous experience,[32] we must agree that much of the impact of the initial line of *The Ruin* is due not only to the contrast between splendor and decay but also to the fact that the second of these contrasting elements causes momentary puzzlement in the reader by totally reversing the normal expectations in a manner not unlike that which John Donne has made famous with his initial line, "At the round earth's imagined corners. . . ."

The element of momentary puzzlement might be even stronger if we knew only the manuscript text. Since we should then have no access to a modern editorial title to warn us that the subject matter is a ruin, we might conceivably suppose the splendid stonework of the first hemistich to be a functional building still in use—something like the "splendid and gold-adorned hall" of *Beowulf* (307b–8a: "sæl . . . / geatolic ond goldfah")—which we should be understandably shocked to find crumbling to pieces in the second hemistich. The shock effect would probably be compounded if we were also to heed Fred C. Robinson's perceptive and thoroughly documented advice that "when we read an Old English literary text we should take care to find out what precedes it in its manuscript state and what follows it."[33] What precedes *The Ruin* in the manuscript is *The Husband's Message*, and the separation between the two is far less obvious than the separation between the former and the poem that follows it or even than the separations between sections of the latter.[34] Accordingly, anyone reading through the manuscript would almost automatically be pro-grammed to associate briefly the stonework of the first hemistich of *The Ruin* with the residence where the man who sent the message in *The Husband's Message* (37b) lives in such opulence that he "experi-ences no lack of joys or of horses or of treasures or of mead-pleasures or of any princely treasures over the earth" (44b–46: "nis him wilna gad, / ne meara ne maðma ne meododreama, / ænges ofer eorþan eorlgestreona"); and there are no grounds for assuming this resi-dence to be in anything but perfect condition, and certainly not in a shambles. What I have been trying to suggest here is that the impact of the first line of *The Ruin* is even stronger if we read the poem in the light of the context within which the Old English compilers of the manuscript intended it to be read than if we read it in the quasi-vacuum unavoidably created by modern editorial practices.

Temporary puzzlement necessarily calls attention to the contrast that I have been discussing, but the power of the line derives from the statement that the destruction has been caused "by fate" (1b: "wyrde"), for the presence of the word *wyrd* within an Old English context rules out the possibility of mere accident and assures us that the scene we are asked to imagine represents the only possible out-come of an inexorable process that affects all human undertakings. Professional students of English literature have learned from *The Wanderer* that "fate is absolutely inexorable" (5b: "Wyrd bið ful aræd"), or from *Beowulf* that "fate always goes as it must" (455b: Gæð a wyrd swa hio scel"), and the medievalists among them have run across similar statements over and over again and may wish to agree with B. J. Timmer's suggestion that this view of fate possibly provides "the explanation for the elegiac spirit in Anglo-Saxon literature."[35] They will also recall that the notion of immutable fate so bothered early English Christians that they apparently had to grant it a quasi-formal hierarchical status immediately below God, who accordingly became the "controller of fate" *(wyrda wealdend)*. The expression stands out because it usually appears in the first hemistich of a verse,[36] and the concept it expresses remained alive long enough to turn up in Chaucer's *Troilus and Criseyde,* where we read of "the fatal desty-ne/That Joves hath in disposicioun" (5. 1–2) and find a precise ac-count of the relationship between ourselves, fate and God:

> But O Fortune, executrice of wyrdes,
> O influences of thise hevenes hye!
> Soth is, that under God ye ben oure hierdes.

> (3. 617–19)

Returning to the first line of *The Ruin*, we may further note that this same inexorable fate which is the agent of destruction carries the alliteration in the second hemistich, so that its destructive inexorableness becomes linked in our mind both with the stonework manifestly erected by human labor and with the very concept of splendor that has provided the introduction to the poem ("Wrætlic . . . wealstan, / wyrde"). This same fate, as noted earlier in a different context, reappears halfway through the poem, where the alliteration makes it impossible to ignore the fact that it is held solely responsible for the destruction of the happy life that used to go on in the city "until fate the mighty changed that" (24: "Oþþæt þæt onwende wyrd seo swiþe").

My previous argument that the key elements of the line under scrutiny stand out partly because of a rhetorical structure different from what we should normally expect does not mean that the thoughts thus called to mind are anything but typical of assumptions found elsewhere in Old English poetry. We have already heard the speaker of *The Wanderer* evoke an image of decaying stoneworks, and we may recall that he goes on to tell us how "the creator of men"—the same God who controls fate— "laid waste this dwelling-place so that the cities, the ancient work of giants stood silent and empty" (85–87: "Yþde swa þisne eardgeard ælda scyppend / oþþæt burgwara breahtma lease / eald enta geweorc idlu stodon") and how it was "fate the illustrious" (100b: "wyrd seo mære") that brought death to the warriors of these cities. We likewise need not have gone very far into *Beowulf* to be familiar with the assumption that even Heorot, the most splendid and "greatest of hall-buildings" (78a: "healærna mæst") ever erected by human beings is so unquestionably doomed to eventual destruction that from the very instant of its completion "it waited for the hostile-flames, for the hateful fire" (82b–83a: "heaðowylma bad, / laðan liges"). The first line of *The Ruin* makes no statement about the fate of human endeavors; yet, approached in the light of the natural context that I have tried to suggest, it almost inevitably reminds us that all human splendor, like human beings themselves, is doomed to destruction and oblivion, or, as Edward B. Irving has put it, that "man . . . erects and binds together walls and civilizations. The universe unbinds and levels them."[37] The thought is admittedly provided by the reader, but I believe that it sets the tone for the remainder of the poem.

The presence of a paradigmatic opening that sets the tone for the remainder of the work and provides an outline of the action or inaction therein places *The Ruin* within a rhetorical tradition that includes such widely acclaimed medieval masterpieces as the *Nibelungenlied,* the *Gunnlaugssaga Ormstungu,* and *Troilus and Criseyde.*[38] Considered independently from the materials they introduce or the traditions to which they belong, these openings would almost certainly seem as uninteresting to the reader as Chaucer's eight-line summary of the misadventures of Lucifer, in *The Monk's Tale* (ll. 1999–2006), seems to current undergraduates who may never have heard of the Fall of the Angels and its traditional consequences. In brief, just as the initial synopsis prepares us for the body of the text, so the body of the text helps us appreciate the initial synopsis in retrospect; and this interaction is especially effective in a short poem that we can consider as a whole instead of a sequence of connected episodes, as we usually do with longer works.

In *The Ruin,* each contrasting scene builds upon the initial paradigm, so that the concepts found there are transformed into vivid realities, which in turn add to the impact of these concepts. For instance, the notion in the second hemistich that the "splendid stonework" of the first hemistich has been "demolished by fate" is so elaborated in the next eight-and-one-half lines (2–9a) that we visualize the details of a process only suggested by the concept. We see that at some point in the past the various "sites of the city came tumbling down" (2a: "burgstede burston"); we see that now "the roofs have caved in and the towers are in ruin" (3: "Hrofas sind gehrorene, hreorge torras"); and we are made to appreciate the human significance of these actual and imagined facts when we are told that now "the grip of earth holds the master builders" (6b–7a: "Eorðgrap hafað / waldend wyrhtan") who once erected these buildings. In a subsequent contrasting section (12–23),[39] which elaborates on the first hemistich of the poem, we are likewise made to appreciate the former splendor of the ruined city and to imagine the human joy that once found expression therein. We see that "the halls of the city were magnificent [and] the bathhouses numerous" (21: "Beorht wæron burgræced, burnsele monige"), and we are made to respond to the heart-warming sight and sounds of "many a mead-hall filled with the joys of men" (23: "meodoheall monig [mon]dreama full"). The exhilarating atmosphere of wealth and carefree conviviality is reminiscent of *Beowulf* and the great hall Heorot filled with "joy" (88b: "dream") as well as with "the sound of the harp, the sweet song of the scop" (89b–90a: "hearpan sweg, / swutol sang scopes"). Furthermore, just as it is at the very conclusion of these festivities that the monster Grendel makes his entrance into *Beowulf*—and we are in fact told that they lasted "until" (100b: "oþþæt") he decided to put a violent end to

context: in the first place, the appearance and activities attributed to these warriors in the immediately subsequent lines suggest nothing but the happiest possible life; in the second place, the mere mention of human beings affords a welcome relief from the immediately preceding scene of total desolation, and the introductory function of the adverb "where" (19b: "þær") emphasizes the contrast by stressing the imagined fact that it was on the site of this very same wasteland that human beings formerly lived in luxury and happiness. When the poem is considered as a whole, it is of course this and the preceding contrasts that call forth in the reader the reflective mood associated with elegies.

The passage examined above also calls attention to two other kinds of contrasts that affect the impact of *The Ruin*. One results from the fact that the verbal units expressing destruction are almost consistently single words, as in "the place *collapsed* into *ruin*, *levelled* to the hills" (31b–32a: "Hryre wong *gecrong* / *gebrocen* to beorgum"), while those expressing pleasant things are often compounds or phrases, such as "precious-gems" (35b: "searogimmas") or "of the spacious kingdom" (37b: "bradan rices"). The other results from the fact that the semantic units expressing destruction are almost consistently active words, while those expressing pleasant things are predominantly passive. To return to the examples examined above, the noun *hryre*, which begins the sentence and which I have rendered with the passive Modern English word *ruin* for the sake of convenience, carries a strongly active connotation that the modern reader realizes as soon as he or she recalls the obvious connection of this noun with the verb *hreosan*, which means *to fall* or *to collapse* or *to cave in* and whose plural past participle (*-hrorene*) we have already encountered in the third line of the poem.[42] The active significance of the subsequent verb *to collapse (cringan)* has been suggested above in regard to its two previous appearances in the poem (25a–28b), and that of the verb *to level* or *to break (brecan)* is obvious enough to need no elaboration here. Conversely, the compound *precious-gems (searogimmas)*, the adjective *spacious (brad)*, and the noun *kingdom (rice)* carry no intrinsic implication of action, even though they may well acquire such an implication within a given context. I believe that the latter observations apply to nearly all the words and groups of words italicized in the passage under observation, with the obvious exception of the verb *to shine (scinan)*, the probable exception of the compound noun *war-trappings (wighyrsta)*, and the possible exception of the compound adjective *flushed-with-wine (wingal)*, which suggests at least a modicum of active elation.

The extent to which the contrasts discussed here may be considered typical of the poem as a whole may be inferred through the juxtaposition of two passages. The first passage comes from a negative scene, and the active words suggestive of some kind of destruction are set off in italics:

> burgstede *burston,*　*brosnað* enta geweorc.
> Hrofas sind *gehrorene,*　*hreorge* torras,
> hrungeat *berofen,*　hrim on lime,
> *scearde* scurbeorge　*scorene, gedrorene,*
> ældo *undereotone.*
>
> (2–6a)

(the sites of the city came tumbling down; the work of giants crumbles. The roofs have caved in; the towers are in ruin, despoiled of their gates; hoarfrost is on the cement, the roofs are mutilated, cut away, collapsed, undermined by age.)

Even if we wish to ignore that the adjective *hreorig*—which I have rendered by "in ruin"—bears to the verb *hreosan (to collapse)* the same kind of relationship that has been outlined above in respect to the noun *hryre,* we can see at a glance that nearly fifty percent of all the words in the passage are both active and suggestive of some kind of destruction. The second passage comes from a positive scene, and the words or groups of words suggestive of pleasant things have been set in italics while those which are likewise passive have also been underlined:

> *Beorht* wæron *burgræced,*　*burnsele monige,*
> *heah horngestreon,*　*heresweg micel,*
> *meodoheall monig* [*mon*]dreama full.
>
> (21–23)

(The sites of the city were glorious, the bathhouses many, the multitude of gables lofty, the martial sound loud, many a mead-hall filled with human joy.)

We can see that, within context, only one word (21a: "wæron") out of the total thirteen keeps a neutral connotation, while the remainder— or over ninety percent—suggests some kind of pleasant experience; and, in contrast to the negative passage, only two groups of two words (22b: "heresweg micel"; 23b: "[mon]dreama full")—or below thirty-one percent of the total number of words—are clearly active, while the remaining nouns and adjectives are passive. The difference between active and passive here may be ascertained by noting that the adjective *glorious (beorht)* implies no ongoing action, since it often applies to inanimate objects or to human beings passively enjoying a reputation that they earned in the past or inherited from their ancestors, but that the phrase "filled with human joy" *([mon]dreama full)* calls to mind the various activities in which human beings indulge when in a joyous mood.

Not only do the verbal suggestions differ between positive and negative passages, but the very mechanics of suggestiveness differ as much as the suggestions themselves. As already argued, concepts of destruction in the poem tend to find expression in single words, while pleasant concepts tend to find expression in phrases and compound words, and the negative passage examined above bears out that contention insofar as all of its nine words suggestive of destruction are single words whose negative connotations would endure equally strongly even if we were to remove their various prefixes (e.g., *underetan: to undermine / etan: to consume, to corrode*). We should also note that, with the single exception of the adjective *hreorig (in ruin)*, these words are verbs, whether used as indicatives or as past participles. In contrast, all but one (21a: "beorht") of the semantic units with pleasant connotations in the positive passage are either phrases or compound words without a single verb among them, and the only verb in the entire passage is *to be (wesan)*, which implies no action of its own.

Whether formally studied by the professional literary scholar or more casually apprehended by a general audience, the facts observed above must of necessity influence our response to the poem, as a glance at two of their many implications will illustrate. The first implication has to do with phrases and single words, since common sense tells us that the latter carry with them the makings of their respective connotations while the former must often rely upon interaction between individual words. When the poet Ron Loewinsohn opens a "pastoral" with the single word *Death*[43] standing alone in the first line, for example, we perceive a reasonably firm connotation that affects our approach to the rest of the poem; but when he mentions the smell "of fresh-churned butter" eight lines later, we derive the connotation from the whole phrase, and each individual word would acquire a very different connotation if the reference were to fresh-churned cement or rancid butter. In *The Ruin*, the phrase "many a mead-hall" (21a: "meodoheall monig") carries extremely pleasant connotations of opulence ("many") and of communal festivities ("mead-hall"), which would both vanish if we were to replace either word. Phrases like "a dilapidated mead-hall" or "many a rat-hole," for instance, would carry connotations of neither opulence nor communal festivity. The resultant principle is that, whereas the connotation of the individual word may prove fairly secure, that of the phrase is likely to be much more precarious. In accordance with this principle, the many gables of the imagined city would not appear nearly so impressive if they were not as "lofty" (22a: "heah") as they are numerous, and the uplifting martial strains that fill the place might well strike us as pathetic if their sound were represented as weak or squeaky instead of "loud" (22b: "micel").

The second implication has to do with single words and compound words. Here again, common sense tells us that the former are likely to deliver their meaning more quickly and not seldom more forcefully than the latter, which normally require us to associate at least two different concepts before we may make sense of the compound. For most of us, the single word *pretty* conveys its meaning rather more quickly than the equivalent compound *eye-pleasing,* and the single word *God* is easier to grasp and in most cases more forceful than the equivalent compound *Tetragrammaton*. In keeping with this principle, such compounds as *horngestreon (multitude of gables)* or *mondream (human joy)* in the positive passage under discussion have a less immediate and less forceful effect than such verbs as *brosnian (to tumble down)* or *gedreosan (to collapse)* in the negative passage. One is tempted to say that, just as the latter suddenly hit us with the full shock of the destructive force they convey, so the former more deliberately lead us to reflect upon the pleasant situation they suggest. This contrast is even stronger in the manuscript, since Old English scribes did not think themselves bound by the practices of modern editorial scholarship, with the twofold result that all six units printed as compounds are actually recorded as pairs of separate words (e.g., f. 124a, l.17: "here sweg") potentially subject to the same kind of connotative mutability that I have discussed in respect to phrases.

The features of *The Ruin* that I have pointed out in the course of the present essay are admittedly self-evident, but I believe that considering all of them together instead of separately may provide the modern reader with at least some means of responding to the poem in a methodical and rewarding manner. If my analysis be not completely mistaken, the negative passages are both more active and more immediate in their effect than the positive passages. Since the former convey images of destruction while the latter present us with pictures of opulence and happiness, the contrast emphasizes an obvious reality, for—as the text itself tells us unequivocally with the statement that the city was happy and opulent until fate "changed" (24a) all that happiness and opulence into ruin—destruction is necessarily a form of change, and change is by definition a form of action that affects whatever state of affairs was previously in effect. The unstated assumption that we are thus made to illustrate in our mind's eye is that—like mankind itself—even the proudest human achievements are no match for the process of destruction. Because the destruction took place in the past (e.g., 2a) but continues in the present (e.g., 2b), we are reminded that the process is pragmatically eternal, while the fact that the splendid city that once was is now no more illustrates the disturbing truth that everything human is circumscribed by time. Finally, the contrast between the connotative firmness of the expressions suggestive of destruction and the connotative mutability of those suggestive of opulence and happiness emphasizes the fateful fragility of human accomplishments at their peak. It is significant in this respect that what appears to be the concluding statement of the poem[44] assures us that we can still perceive "something regal" (48b: "cynelice þing") in the ruins of the once-splendid city that is no more. The poem thus comes to an appropriate end with an allusion to the same contrast between splendor and decay that was so clearly expressed in the opening line with the passive adjective *splendid (wrætlic)* opening the first hemistich and the active verb *to demolish (gebrecan)* closing the second.

As stated near the beginning of this essay, I believe that the modern reader of *The Ruin* must somehow compensate for the fact that the poem has a speaking voice but no speaker, that it includes no actual action within its own time frame—unless we wish to count as action the slow disintegration that goes on with the passage of time—and that it formulates no philosophical lesson. The task is an easy and natural one because the several contrasting scenes and techniques illustrate and emphasize what most of us already take for granted about the evanescence of human affairs. After all, those of us who grew up a few decades ago in practically any relatively large city of the industrialized world need only return to find the familiar sites reduced to wastelands by the demolition crew or metamorphosed into gray-concrete skyscrapers by the dismal magic of architectural engineers, and I suspect that even the most fervent believers in urban renewal experience a feeling of loss not dissimilar to that which comes upon us at the sight of ancient ruins. By thus striking a familiar chord, the poem prompts us to draw the lesson that it does not formulate and to become, as it were, the speaking voice's partners in witnessing the real stillness of the present as well as the imagined activities of the past. Because the process requires that we contribute—wittingly or otherwise—from the store of our personal experience, the decaying city whose former splendor we have been made to imagine becomes at least in part our very own. This process is, I suspect, the sort of thing that has prompted Greenfield to note that the Old English elegies tend to "reflect a sense of personal loss. . . . And if we read these poems with this expectation in mind we find a particular kind of meaning in them that has satisfied many critics, and struck a resonant chord in the general reader's mind, down to the present day."[45]

Since I have tried to make it clear that my remarks were primarily intended to illustrate some of the ways in which *The Ruin* might affect a modern reader equipped with only such knowledge of Old English poetry as may be expected from a lettered person in the English-speaking world, I should acknowledge here the hypothetical but very legitimate objection that I have taken no account of what the author of the poem may have intended. I fear that I can only plead guilty, but I see no reason to exaggerate my sense of guilt. For aught I know, the poem may have been originally intended as a come-on to prospective visitors to the city of Bath or as a guidebook for tourists interested in Hadrian's Wall, or it may represent an Old English attempt to appropriate a Medieval Welsh topic[46] or to compose in the spirit of Venantius Fortunatus's *De Excidio Thoringiae*[47] or Boethius's *Consolatio Philosophiae*.[48] I have, regrettably, no means of ascertaining which of these and other theories may be correct, and because their respective proponents exhibit a decided tendency to reject each others' views as demonstrably worthless, I can see no great harm in trying an initial approach that suits all the current theories equally well while enabling the reader to apprehend some of the essential power of the text. I should also like to suggest the possibility that the approach that I have illustrated may conceivably help us respond to the poem in a manner not totally different from that of Old English audiences.

In the course of my argument I have called attention to certain ways in which even a minimal familiarity with the practices of Old English poetry can influence our response, and any professional scholar of Old English will think of many additional examples. Since Old English is no longer spoken and most of us have learned it too late in life to feel as naturally at ease with it as we should like, and since the number of poems known to us only by inference or through diminutive fragments tells us that we have access to only part of what may once have been a substantial canon,[49] we need not stretch the credibility gap very far to assume that those native speakers of Old English who would listen to poetry or read through *The Exeter Book* must have been rather better attuned than we are to the implications of the poetic patterns that I have discussed.

To single out one piece of supporting evidence for my contention, we may assume that an audience constantly exposed to what Arnold V. Talentino has termed the "preoccupation with the implacable destructiveness of fate"[50] in Old English poetry would be better attuned than we are to the function of fate in the poem. One may likewise wish to consider the possibility that, regardless of the manner in which it was actually composed, *The Ruin* belongs to that oral-formulaic tradition which Jeff Opland has shown to have conceivably endured through most of the Old English period.[51] I have no intention of arguing here whether the poem does in fact belong to that tradition, but the hypothesis is worth noting because John Miles Foley speaks in part for Greenfield, Adrien Bonjour, Donald K. Fry, and other scholars when he cogently argues that a given formulaic element can affect the audience's reaction to a text by locating the contents "with relation to archetypal paradigms,"[52] and one may not reject offhand the possibility that some of the many similarities and contrasts between *The Ruin* and other Old English poems[53] are in fact positive and negative expressions of archetypal paradigms presumably familiar to the audience for whom the poem was originally intended and that they accordingly contribute to the kind of impact that I have discussed.

One may also, and equally legitimately, object that approaching literature from the audience's point of view must perforce lead us on the path to confusion since no two readers or listeners are likely to bring precisely the same frame of reference to their literary experience. The resultant unlikelihood of ever providing a definitive interpretation to which everyone must subscribe in every detail is, of course, the most obvious shortcoming of what Stanley E. Fish has taught us to call "affective" criticism. But we need by no means share his stated conviction that "the objectivity of the text is an illusion"[54] to admit that there is something to be said in favor of recognizing the fact that the same sequence of words often affects different and yet equally competent readers in totally different ways,[55] and that the annals of literary criticism provide abundant illustrations of this phenomenon.[56] Although Old English audiences probably enjoyed a more homogeneous social and literary background than we do—and they probably did not feel so mercilessly hounded as modern scholars by the necessity to produce new and ever-so-clever interpretations—I suspect that they were not essentially different from modern readers of books or watchers of motion pictures. If I be correct in my suspicion, then the approach that I have illustrated is likely to prove as harmless and potentially rewarding as I have claimed, but it will be so only as long as we remember that it is only one of many equally harmless and equally rewarding approaches over which it has no right to claim the least superiority.

NOTES

1. John Josias Conybeare, *Illustrations of Anglo-Saxon Poetry*, ed. William D. Conybeare (London, 1826), pp. 251–55.

2. For instance, the 1978 *MLA International Bibliography*, vol. 1, prints two entries on *The Ruin* (3188 and 3189) but only one on Oscar Williams (11991) and Joan Didion (5851) respectively, and the 1979 volume likewise bears out my contention with once again two entries on *The Ruin* (3489 and 3490), two entries on Joan Didion (10875 and 10876), and none on Oscar Williams.

3. I have not examined every textbook ever used in beginning Old English, but neither I nor any colleague whom I have consulted can think of a textbook widely used in the English-speaking world that includes *The Ruin*, and Fernand Mossé's *Manuel de l'Anglais du Moyen Age* (Paris: Editions Montaigne, 1950) is the only available elementary text that immediately comes to mind as including the poem. Roy F. Leslie, ed., *Three Old English Elegies* (Manchester: Manchester University Press, 1961), has accordingly noted that *The Ruin* belongs to a group of poems that "have tended to remain the preserve of scholars . . ." (p. vii).

4. For verification, consult the facsimile edition by Raymond W. Chambers et al., *The Exeter Book of Old English Poetry* (London, 1933), ff. 123b (last line)–24b, ll. 8–15 (i.e., 7–14 on f. 124a) and 40–45 (i.e., 8–13 on f. 124b) have been affected; they correspond to ll. 12a–18a and 42b–49b in standard printed editions of the twentieth century.

5. Kemp Malone, "The Old English Period," in Albert C. Baugh, ed., *A Literary History of England* (New York: Appelton-Century, 1948), p. 88.

6. Stanley B. Greenfield, *A Critical History of Old English Literature* (New York: New York University Press, 1968), p. 214.

7. The argument in favor of Bath seems to have been first formulated in print by Heinrich Leo in his *Carmen Anglosaxonicum in Codice Exoniensi Servator Quod Vulgo Inscribitur Ruinae* (Halle: Formis Hendeliis, 1865), p. 5. It has had numerous adherents since that time and is generally accepted today, though with some caution, e.g., by C. L. Wrenn, who writes in his *A Study of Old English Literature* (London, 1967), that archaeological investigation "seems strongly to support the identification" (p. 154) but nevertheless insists that "it must remain only an attractive hypothesis" (p. 154); a less hesitant identification with Bath has been formulated by Karl P. Wentersdorf in his "Observations on *The Ruin*" *MAE* 46 (1977): 171–80. The most important arguments have been clearly outlined by Leslie in his *Three Old English Elegies*, pp. 22–27; and Cecilia A. Hotchner has conveniently listed in her *Wessex and Old English Poetry, with Special Consideration of The Ruin* (Lancaster, Pa.: Lancaster Press, 1939) theories advanced up to 1939 (pp. 11–12), with special attention to those concerned with the possible relationship of *The Ruin* to Venantius Fortunatus's *De Excidio Thoringiae* (pp. 103–34). The candidacy of Chester has been supported by Gareth W. Dunleavy in his "A 'De Excidio' Tradition in the Old English *Ruin*?" *PQ* 33 (1959), where he argues that the poet "could have drawn on either first- or second-hand knowledge of the events and sights at Chester" (p. 118). The candidacy of Hadrian's Wall has been proposed by Stephen J. Herben in "Correspondence," *MLN* 53 (1939): 37–39 and earnestly defended in his "*The Ruin* Again," *MLN* 59 (1944): 72–74, and the Babylonian theory has been advanced by Hugh T. Keenan in his "*The Ruin* as Babylon," *Tennessee Studies in Literature* 11 (1966): 109–17. Greenfield, in his *Critical History*, both sums up the prevalent view and mentions an eminently reasonable alternative with the statement that the

ruined site is "usually taken to be Bath, though it is quite possible the scene is an amalgam of various locales" (p. 214).

8. Leslie, *Three Old English Elegies*, p. 35.

9. *The Anglo-Saxon Poetic Records: a Collective Edition*, 6 vols., ed. George P. Krapp and Elliott Van Kirk Dobbie (New York, 1931–53). Quotations from *The Ruin*, the other Old English elegies, and *The Phoenix* are from vol. 3 (*The Exeter Book*, ed. Krapp and Dobbie [1936]): quotations from *Beowulf* are from vol. 4 (*Beowulf and Judith*, ed. Dobbie [1953]); quotations from *Maxims II* are from vol. 6 (*The Anglo-Saxon Minor Poems*, ed. Dobbie [1942]).

10. Alvin A. Lee, *The Guest-Hall of Eden: Four Essays on Old English Poetry* (New Haven, Conn.: Yale University Press, 1972), pp. 150–51.

11. The contrary view is perhaps best illustrated in James F. Doubleday's incisive and carefully supported argument, in his "*The Ruin:* Structure and Theme," *JEGP* 71 (1972):369–81, that the poem provides an explicit Christian lesson for the future. Doubleday appropriately makes much of the statement "oþ hund cnea / werþeoda gewitan" (9b–10a ["until hundred generations will depart"]), but a majority of scholars consider "gewitan" a preterit, as Leslie points out (*Three Old English Elegies*, p. 69), and I am accepting the more conventional view while recognizing that Doubleday's argument may not be safely ignored.

12. Greenfield, *Critical History*, p. 215.

13. The guiding principle behind the selection of contrasting units is obviously arbitrary, since one could equally logically use past and present as a basis, in which case the result of the analysis would be approximately the same but the process would be complicated by a substantial increase in the number of contrasting units. For the sake of communication, I have likewise selected my points of separation between contrasting units according to Krapp and Dobbie's punctuation, even when I have reservations about it, so that new units begin with or after a period, a semicolon, or a conjunctive word like *oþþæt* or *þær*. Although there were occasions where working according to a different system of punctuation would affect the analysis of a given segment, the effect on the interpretation of the poem as a whole would be small enough to be disregarded here.

14. C. Valerius Catullus, *Carmen 3*, ll. 3–5, in *Catullus*, ed. C. J. Fordyce (Oxford: Clarendon Press, 1961): "Passer mortuus est meae puellae, / passer, deliciae meae puellae, / quem plus illa oculis suis amabat" (My girl friend's sparrow is dead, the sparrow that was my girl friend's joy, that she loved more than her own eyes").

15. *Beowulf*, 913b–15b: "He [Beowulf] þær eallum wearð, / mæg Higelaces, manna cynne, / freondum gefægra; hine [Heremod] fyren onwod" ("In this respect Beowulf, Hygelac's kinsman, became very dear to his friends, to the race of men; crime took possession of Heremod").

16. Geoffrey Chaucer, *The Knight's Tale*, ll. 1051–60, in *The Works of Geoffrey Chaucer*, ed. Fred N. Robinson (Cambridge, Mass.: Houghton-Mifflin, 1957), where contrast with Emily's carefree behavior serves to emphasize the grimness of the prison tower where Palamon and Arcite are incarcerated: "She walketh up and doun, and as hire liste / She gadereth floures, party white and rede, / To make a subtil gerland for hire hede; / And as an aungel hevenysshly she soong. / The grete tour, that was so thik and stroong, / Which of the castel was the chief dongeoun. . . ." All subsequent quotations from Chaucer are from the same edition.

17. William Shakespeare, *The Tragedy of King Lear*, ed. Alfred Harbage (Baltimore: Penguin, 1962): whereas Goneril answers her father's query about the extent of her love for him with, "Sir, I love you more than word can wield the matter; / Dearer than eyesight, space, and liberty . . ." (I, i, 54–55), while Regan declares that same speech "too short" (I, i, 72) of the appropriate sentiments and proclaims herself "an enemy to all other joys" (I, i, 73) but the love of her father, Cordelia can only state the fact that she has nothing to add: "Nothing, my lord" (I, i, 87).

18. See, e.g., Greenfield, *Critical History*, p. 214.

19. Daniel G. Calder, "Perspective and Movement in *The Ruin*," *NM* 72 (1971): 442; Calder's divisions differ from mine, but the principle remains the same.

20. The connotation of these lines is likely to seem positive if we focus on the fact that the wall therein has survived all these years, but it is likely to seem negative if we focus on the fact that the kingdoms left behind by the wall are no more.

21. See, for example, Malone, "Old English Period," p. 91; or David M. Zesmer, *Guide to English Literature from Beowulf through Chaucer and Medieval Drama* (New York: Barnes & Noble, 1961), p. 51. Greenfield, *Critical History*, correctly mentions "the brave new terrestrial world envisaged by the speaker of *The Husband's Message*" (p. 214), and Leslie, *Three Old English Elegies* equally correctly thinks that the man writes to the woman that he "has repaired his fortunes and can offer her a position and degree of property commensurate with that which the two of them had enjoyed in days gone by" (p. 13).

22. As already stated in my "A Reading of *The Wife's Lament*," *ES* 58 (1977), my use of the feminine pronoun to refer to the speaker of the *Lament* is purely "pragmatic and by no means intended as a rejection of its opposite" (p. 4), which has been notably argued by Rudolph C. Bambas in his "Another View of the Old English 'Wife's Lament,'" *JEGP* 62 (1963), especially pp. 307–8, and Martin Stevens in his "The Narrator of 'The Wife's Lament,'" *NM* 69 (1968): 72–90.

23. The similarities suggested between the two poems should be especially obvious to those scholars who view the speaker of *The Wife's Lament* as actually dead, as argued independently by Elinor Lench in her "*The Wife's Lament*: a Poem of the Living Dead," *Comitatus* 1 (1970): 3–23, and by Raymond P. Tripp, Jr., in his "The Narrator as Revenant: A Reconsideration of Three Old English Elegies," *PLL* 8 (1972): 339–61.

24. Here as in the case of *The Wife's Lament*, my assumption that the speaker is a woman should be considered a purely pragmatic acceptance of majority opinion, as I explained many years ago in my "*Wulf and Eadwacer*: a Noninterpretation," in Jess B. Bessinger and Robert P. Creed, eds., *Franciplegius: Medieval and Linguistic Studies in Honor of Francis Peabody Magoun, Jr.* (New York: New York University Press, 1965), especially pp. 146–48 and 150.

25. Stanley B. Greenfield, "The Old English Elegies," in Eric G. Stanley, ed., *Continuations and Beginnings: Studies in Old English Literature* (London: Nelson, 1966), p. 145.

26. Burton Raffel, trans., *Poems from the Old English* (Lincoln: University of Nebraska Press, 1964), p. 71. Because the plural of *fate* usually implies a personification which, as illustrated by Leslie (*Three Old English Elegies*, p. 67), a majority of scholars seems to consider out of place here, the hemistich is usually construed in the singular rather than by " . . . shattered by the fates," as Nora Kershaw translates it in her *Anglo-Saxon and Norse Poems* (Cambridge: Cambridge University Press, 1922), p. 55; and the verb is usually construed as a past participle, as illustrated in Robert K. Gordon's *Anglo-Saxon Poetry* (London: Dent, 1949), p. 92 ("broken by fate") or in Charles W. Kennedy's *An Anthology of Old English Poetry* (New York: Oxford University Press, 1960), p. 8 ("wasted by Fate"). A notable exception is Edward B. Irving, Jr., who, in his "Image and Meaning in the Elegies," in Robert P. Creed, ed., *Old English Poetry: Fifteen Essays* (Providence: Brown University Press, 1967), translates the opening line as "Wonderful is this wall stone, the fates have broken it" (p. 154).

27. The text is otherwise consistent in its spelling of strong past participles (e.g., 3a: "gehrorene" or 4a: "berofen" or 5b: "scorene, gedrorene"), so that we should normally expect the past participle of *brecan* to appear as *brocen* or *gebrocen* and accordingly construe *bræcon* or *gebræcon* as a preterit. On the other hand, one may not wish to overlook the possibility of a scribal slip caused by unwitting analogy with the preterit "gespræconn," which happens both to be the very last word in the immediately preceding *Husband's Message* and to be so located in the manuscript that the letters *-conn* occur immediately above the first four letters of the verb under discussion and that the two verbs are connected by a slash symbol.

28. Greenfield, *Critical History*, notes that the Old English elegies "have in common

two overlapping concerns: (1) a contrast between past and present conditions, and (2) some awareness of the transitory nature of earthly splendor, joy, and security" (p. 214).

29. Jess B. Bessinger, Jr., and Philip H. Smith, Jr., *A Concordance to the Anglo-Saxon Poetic Records* (Ithaca, N.Y.: Cornell University Press, 1978), pp. 1469–70, list nine instances of the adjective *wrætlic* used as a headword in the first hemistich, and only the one in *The Ruin* departs from the principle mentioned here.

30. See, e.g., Leslie, *Three Old English Elegies,* p. 67.

31. Joseph Bosworth and T. Northcote Toller, *An Anglo-Saxon Dictionary* (London, 1898–1921), p. 149, suggest that names ending in *-ceaster* must belong to sites originally constructed by the Romans; and Francis P. Magoun, Jr., and James A. Walker, *An Old English Anthology: Translations of Old English Prose and Verse* (Dubuque: W. C. Brown Company, 1950), translate the opening of the relevant passage as "(Roman ruined) cities are visible . . ." (p. 91).

32. See, e.g., Stanley E. Fish's discussion of the effect of Milton's *Paradise Lost,* 1., 292–94, upon readers whose expectations have developed through familiarity with Virgil's *Aeneid,* in Fish's *Surprised by Sin* (New York: St. Martin's Press, 1967), pp. 24–25. The principles at work have been studied by Norman H. Holland in his *The Dynamics of Literary Response* (New York: Oxford University Press, 1968), pp. 1–30 and 90–91, as well as in other studies of his.

33. Fred C. Robinson, "Old English Literature in Its Most Immediate Context," in John D. Niles, ed., *Old English Literature in Context: Ten Essays* (Cambridge and Totowa, N. J.: D. S. Brewer and Littlefield, 1980), p. 11.

34. In the manuscript of *The Exeter Book,* the scribe has skipped a line between the last line of *The Ruin* (f. 124b) and the first word of the next poem *(Riddle 61),* and *The Husband's Message* (ff. 123a–23b) is divided into three sections separated from each other according to the same principle; in contrast, there is no separation whatsoever between the first word of *The Ruin* and the last line of *The Husband's Message,* and we might wish to keep in mind that the current classification of the text into different poems with individual titles is the work of modern editors.

35. B. J. Timmer, "Wyrd in Anglo-Saxon Prose and Poetry," in Jess B. Bessinger, Jr., and Stanley J. Kahrl, eds., *Essential Articles for the Study of Old English Poetry* (Hamden: Archon, 1968; reprinted from *Neophilologus* 26 [1940]: 24–33), p. 157, who traces the history of *wyrd* on the preceding pages (124–57). Bessinger and Smith, *Concordance,* pp. 1488–89, record fifty-two instances of *wyrd,* twenty-two of *wyrda,* and fourteen of *wyrde,* most of which occur in statements with direct or indirect implications similar to those of the statements which I have quoted.

36. See *Exodus* 433a, *Andreas* 1056a, *Elene* 80a, *Resignation* 44a, all in *Poetic Records.*

37. Irving, "Image and Meaning," p. 156.

38. *Das Nibelungenlied,* ed. Karl Bartsch, rev. Helmut de Boor, 12th ed. (Leipzig: F. A. Brockhaus, 1949), 2 : 1–4; *Gunnlaugssaga Ormstungu,* ed. Peter G. Foote and Randolph Quirk (London: Thomas Nelson & Sons, 1957), p. 317; *Troilus and Criseyde,* I, 1–5 and 53–56. I have discussed the synopsis aspect of the opening of the *Gunnlaugssaga* in my "The Inept Lover and the Reluctant Mistress: Remarks on Sexual Inefficiency in Mediaeval Literature," in Edward Vasta and Zacharias P. Thundy, eds., *Chaucerian Problems and Perspectives* (Notre Dame: University of Notre Dame Press, 1979), especially pp. 192–93; and a discussion of the respective forms and functions of these paradigmatic openings will be found in my "Bayard and Troilus: Chaucerian Non-Paradox in the Reader," *Orbis Litterarum* 36 (1981): 116–40.

39. The section mentioned here (12a–23b) could be considered immediately subsequent to the section previously examined (2a–9a) if we construed the intervening lines (9b–11b) as illustrative of destruction and accordingly to be seen as part of the following section, but it has already been noted (n. 20) that the connotation of 9b–11b seems ambiguous.

40. Gary I. Rubin, "A Rhetorical Analysis of *Deor, The Ruin,* and *The Wanderer,*" in *Dissertation Abstracts International* (A—The Humanities and Social Sciences), vol. 35

(1975), no. 10, p. 6680–A, is primarily concerned with the juxtaposition of past and present verbs.

41. The principle invoked here is the same whereby Erwin Panofsky has explained certain differences between the medieval and Renaissance attitudes toward Classical Antiquity, in his "Renaissance and Renascences," *Kenyon Review* 6 (1944):201–36.

42. The difference between the active *hryre* and the passive *ruin* illustrates the problems facing literary translators of the poem. Raffel, *Poems from the Old English*, has brilliantly circumvented the problem by using the expression "the ruined site" (p. 27), in which the past participle implies that action has in fact taken place.

43. Ron Loewinshon, "Pastoral," l. 1, in Donald M. Allen, ed., *The New American Poetry* (New York: Grove Press, 1960), p. 376.

44. Since only four words—"þæt is cynelic þing" (f. 124b, l. 44)—are unequivocally identifiable in the last four manuscript lines, one may not safely assume anything more than a strong probability about the form and contents of the concluding statement.

45. Stanley B. Greenfield, *The Interpretation of Old English Poems* (London and Boston: Routledge and Kegan Paul, 1972), p. 12.

46. Thematic similarities between *The Ruin* and certain Welsh materials have been recognized since Conybeare's edition; see, e.g., Leslie, *Three Old English Elegies*, p. 30.

47. For the relationship between *The Ruin* and the *De Excidio Thoringiae*, see, e.g., Malone, "Old English Period," p. 88, as well as Hotchner's *Wessex and Old English Poetry*, pp. 103–34.

48. In my "The Least Elegiac of the Elegies: a Contextual Glance at *The Husband's Message*," *Studia Neophilologica* 53 (1981):69–76, I have pointed out certain thematic similarities between the Old English elegies and the *Consolatio Philosophiae*, especially the seventh poem of the second book.

49. See R. W. Chambers, "The Lost Literature of Medieval England," in Bessinger and Kahrl, *Essential Articles*, pp. 3–26 (reprinted from *The Library* 5, no. 4 [1925]), and Richard M. Wilson *The Lost Literature of Medieval England* 2d ed. (London: Methuen, 1970), esp. pp. 1–23; I have pointed out some implications of the problem in my "*Beowulf:* a Contextual Introduction to Its Contents and Techniques," in Felix J. Oinas, ed., *Heroic Epic and Saga* (Bloomington: Indiana University Press, 1978), p. 99.

50. Arnold V. Talentino, "Moral Irony in *The Ruin*," *PLL* 14 (1978):3; on pp. 5–10, Talentino discusses the connotation of many important words that I have left unmentioned.

51. Jeff Opland, *Anglo-Saxon Oral Poetry* (New Haven and London: Yale University Press, 1980), considers the possibility that the "scop disappeared from certain courts and may well have disappeared altogether by the ninth century" (p. 265) as well as the alternative possibility that "practicing scops still survived in Anglo-Saxon courts in 1066" (p. 266). Tripp, "Narrator as Revenant," argues in favor of the view that the Old English elegies may "be connected with the oral ballad tradition" (p. 339).

52. John Miles Foley, "Formula and Theme in Old English Poetry," in Benjamin A. Stolz and Richard S. Shannon, eds., *Oral Literature and the Formula* (Ann Arbor, Mich.: Center for the Coordination of Ancient and Modern Studies, 1976), p. 218; see also his "*Beowulf* and the Psychohistory of Anglo-Saxon Culture," *American Imago* 34 (1977), where he argues that oral-formulaic elements present us "time and again with a verbal montage of the group's poetic models and thereby with the data which these models encode" (p. 134). Stanley B. Greenfield, "The Formulaic Expression of the Theme of Exile in Anglo-Saxon Poetry," *Speculum* 30 (1955), has argued that "association with other contexts using a similar formula will inevitably color a particular instance of a formula so that a whole host of overtones springs into action . . ." (p. 205); Adrien Bonjour, "*Beowulf* and the Beasts of Battle," *PMLA* 72 (1957), believes that the use of formulaic themes can make us see things "in advance" (p. 556) and affect our response accordingly; and Donald K. Fry, "The Heroine on the Beach in *Judith*," *NM* 68 (1967), believes that formulaic themes "prove to be a mnemonic device as much for the audience as for the poet; they provide the audience with a supply of associations . . ."

(p. 181). I have tried to illustrate the principle in my "Germanic Quintessence: the Theme of Isolation in the *Hildebrandslied*," in Margot H. King and Wesley M. Stevens, eds. *Saints Scholars and Heroes: Studies in Medieval Culture in Honour of Charles W. Jones* (Collegeville, Minn.: Hill Monastic Library, Saint John's Abbey and University, 1979), 2:143–78, and I discuss its critical implications in my "Oral-Formulaic Context: Implications for the Comparative Criticism of Mediaeval Texts," in John Miles Foley, ed., *Oral Traditional Literature* (Columbus, Ohio: Slavica Publishers, 1981).

53. For a handy list of such similarities, see Leslie, *Three Old English Elegies*, pp. 67–76.

54. Stanley E. Fish, "Literature in the Reader: Affective Stylistics," *New Literary History* 2 (1970):140.

55. See, e.g., Norman N. Holland, *Poems in Persons* (New York: Norton, 1973), who shows how a given reader "recreates a literary work" (p. 100) in various ways.

56. To verify the point in reference to Old English elegies, one need only recall that *Wulf and Eadwacer* has been interpreted as practically everything from a riddle to a touching story about dogs (see my "*Wulf and Eadwacer:* a Noninterpretation," pp. 146–47, for references and additional interpretations), and that *The Wife's Lament* has been interpreted as dealing with a heathen god, a dead woman, a plea for the reunion of Christ and the Church, and various other things (see my "Christian Inversion in *The Wife's Lament*," *SN* 49 [1977]:20, for reference and additional interpretations).

The Text and Context
of *Wulf and Eadwacer*

Marijane Osborn

Because of its brevity and an apparently casual allusiveness, *Wulf and Eadwacer,* the most evocative and personal of all the Anglo-Saxon lyrics in the *Exeter Book,* has been subjected to what is probably the widest range of interpretations of any poem in the Anglo-Saxon corpus. It has been identified, for example, as an episode in the Sigurd story, a canine love song, and a charm against wens. But as Alain Renoir has shown, it may be appreciated as a poem when stripped of all external reference.[1] When read thus, it reveals a woman speaker (so identified by the form of the adjectives *reotugu* and *seoce*) whose emotions range from uncertainty and bewilderment, to longing, to horrified realization and despair. In the first of the two sections below I shall apply to this exemplary text the techniques of stylistics[2] as Alain Renoir did those of New Criticism, examining the physical appearance of the poem in the manuscript, the variations of syntactic and lexical forms, and the speaker's emerging realization. This kind of analysis can give us a great deal of information about the internal tensions in the poem and the speaker's point of view, but *Wulf and Eadwacer* provides an exemplary text also for another kind of criticism usually felt to be antithetical to practical criticism; because of our cultural predisposition to regard poems of passion as "naturally" concerned with a certain type of relationship, we must practice historical criticism to discover what meaning this poem might have had within its own cultural context. After the essential nature of the drama has been established, therefore, I shall offer in the second section analogues within the Anglo-Saxon poetic corpus for the normal, human, and recurrent drama that the poem describes. I shall conclude with some suggestions about the significance of the manuscript context in which it appears.

I. *Strategy: The Text*

> Leodum is minum   swylce him mon lác gife
> willað hy hine aþecgan   gif he on þreat cymeð
> ungelic is ús·
> wulf is on iege   ic on oþerre
> 5 fæst is þæt eglond   fenne biworpen
> sindon wæl reowe   weras þær on ige
> willað hy hine aþecgan   gif he on þreat cymeð
> ungelice is us /
> wulfes ic mines widlastum   wenum dogode
> 10 þoñ hit wæs renig weder   ond ic reo tugu sæt·
> þoñ mec se beadu cafa   bogum bilegde
> wæs me wyn to þon   wæs me hwæþre eac lað·
> wulf min wulf   wena me þine
> seoce gedydon   þine seld cymas
> 15 murnende mód   nales mete liste
> gehyrest þu ead wacer   uncerne earne hwelp
> bireð wulf to wuda
> þæt mon eaþe tosliteð   þætte næfre gesomnad wæs
> uncer giedd geador   :

The text of the poem reproduced here appears on folios 100b–101a of the *Exeter Book,* following the poem called *Deor* and preceding the first group of riddles. It is marked off from *Deor* and the riddles by spacing, a large initial capital, and final end-marks. I have divided the continuously written text into verse-lines but have otherwise reproduced the manuscript forms in modern orthography. Other graphic suprasegmentals are three vowel marks, over *lac,* the first *us,* and *mod,* and three points, following lines 3, 10, and 12. Line 8, after which one might expect a point in conformity with line 3, terminates a manuscript line, which I have indicated with a slash. In any case the scribe's inconsistency is demonstrated by his vowel mark only over *us* in line 3, not in line 8, and by his variant spellings of *ungelic(e)*—unless this is intentional. In *Deor* the refrain *þæs ofereode þisses swa mæg* is set off from the rest of the text by a preceding point and following end-marks; the point occurring after *ungelic is us* in *Wulf and Eadwacer* suggests that the scribe felt that this truncated line should be set off from what follows, but notably not in so formal a manner as the *Deor* refrain. The other two points in the text may be interpreted in two ways; either they conclude the two descriptive preterit sentences of lines 9–10 and 11–12, or else they have the function of parentheses, setting apart lines 11 and 12 from the rest of the poem: "When the brave warrior laid boughs about me, it was joy to me to a degree, it was, however, also unpleasant to me."

Such physical passivity combined with strong emotional ambivalence is a keynote of the poem, recurrent throughout, but lines 11 and 12 are also representative of the enigmatic mode of the poem: We do not know the identity of the warrior, and the "boughs" may represent branches, embracing arms, or children. Even in their most unfigurative sense, as branches, the *bogum* may be representative of the wattling or logs of a house or of cage bars, or even of a home conceived of as cage. (Each of these alternatives has been suggested by previous commentators.) Such mystification reinforces the main tension of the poem, which lies between the crescendo of longing for Wulf in the first part (lines 1–12), and the modulation toward resentment and possibly fear in the second part, where Wulf is finally recognized as a wolf indeed.

Alain Renoir, whose article on *Wulf and Eadwacer* is the only one that I have found really rewarding, argues cogently that the tension between longing and the sense of separation is the thematic device that renders *Wulf and Eadwacer* lyrically coherent even when it is not wholly understood.[3] His analysis of these tensions is very useful indeed, but implies a static (if ambivalent) frame of mind for the speaker. What gives force to the passive speaker's strong and ambivalent attitudes is the change in her perception, when she stops fearing danger for Wulf and sees Wulf himself as dangerous.

This transition of understanding about Wulf is presented from an entirely subjective and highly emotional point of view and is dramatically telescoped into nineteen lines of varied forms of discourse. In addition there is extraordinary syntactic variety in this brief poem, with lines dominated by tmesis and inversion juxtaposed with lines in which the syntax is emotively simple and colloquial, syntax typical of the Chronicles rather than of poetry. The variation of syntactic and discursive forms helps to dramatize the speaker's conflicting and shifting attitudes.

The simplest line in the poem, and the most visual as well, is that iconic stasis of the speaker at the center of the poem, line 10 (in which the adjective identifies her sex):

> *þonne hit wæs renig weder   ond ic reotugu sæt*
> ([Then/When] it was rainy weather   and I sat weeping)

In this line the balance of inner and outer weather reflects that of inner and outer experience throughout the poem. Such balanced lines on the whole, however, yoke notions of conflict or separation:

wulf is on iege   ic on oþerre   (4)
(Wulf is on one island   I on another)

wæs me wyn to þon   wæs me hwæþre eac lað   (12)
(it was to me joy to a degree   it was to me however also horrible)

þæt mon eaþe toslite∂   þætte næfre gesomnad wæs   (18)
(one may easily rend asunder   what never was joined)

The figure of tmesis (separation of a phrasal unit by the intervention of one or more words) is used with similar effect, yet this figure itself paradoxically conflicts with its context, which in each case incorporates a sense of belonging: *leodum is minum* (1), *wulfes ic mines* (9), *wena me þine* (13); in these three half-lines the first person pronoun occurs either as a separated or separating element.

The image of the woman speaker sitting and weeping may be seen as a fulcrum around which the poem as a whole is balanced. First of all she proclaims that an unnamed person is a *lac* for her people, and wonders how they will receive him; although it is possible to take line 2 as another affirmative statement (they *will* do such and such), its context seems to call either for question or for conjecture about the future. *Us*, line 3, appears to link the speaker with "my people" (not with "him," because it is not the dual form), and then in the next line Wulf is first named and the unlike situations of *wulf* and *ic* are described. But the repetition of line 2 as line 7 suggests that "my people" are the savages on *that* island (Wulf's), although a vocal change in stress, *Willa∂ hy hine aþecgan?*, could indicate a change of subject; in any case there is now a clear indication that Wulf is in danger, and the question of his reception is a matter rather for concern than doubt.

After line 8 there is a new mode of discourse. The speaker has been describing the present situation and conjecturing about the future; now the verb forms move into the preterit. Again, following *ungelic(e) is us*, there is a contrast between *wulf* and *ic*, but this time in terms of stance rather than of physical situation: his far-ranging is in hopes or aspirations, whereas her stasis is associated with despair: rain and weeping. (That they are his hopes, not an instrumental, her hopes, with *dogode*, is borne out by *wena . . . þine* in line 13b, which is grammatically parallel to *þine seldcymas*, 14b.) Even in emotional stance Wulf is presented as active and the speaker as passive. The contrast is reminiscent of *Exeter Book* riddles 75 and 76, which some editors have suggested should be considered a single riddle:

Ic swiftne geseah   on swaþe feran

> (Runes read backwards: HLND).
> Ic ane geseah   idese sittan.
>
> (I saw swift on the track go
> [HUND "hound" or HæLeND "saviour"].
> I saw a lady sit alone.)

And yet, after the lady of *Wulf and Eadwacer* reminisces in line 10 about sitting alone, her present feelings do not seem so simply oriented toward a longing for Wulf as previously. When she has "boughs" about her, whatever they are, they serve as a constraint in comparison with the *widlastum wenum* "wide-ranging hopes" of Wulf in line 9, and the repetition of *þonne* in lines 10 and 11 and of *wæs me* twice in line 12 heightens the effect of the emotional tension created by this restraint. While these four central lines are not necessarily in a cause-and-effect relationship, their sequence is significant at the emotional level of the poem, where the *widlastum/sæt* contrast is followed by the *wyn/lað* ambivalence. The pointing of the manuscript suggests some such sense as the following, reading each *þonne* as "when" rather than as a when-then sequence:

> 9   I *dogode* my Wulf's wide-ranging hopes
> (or wide-ranging with hopes)
> when it was rainy weather and I sat weeping;
> when the one brave in battle laid boughs about me,
> it was joy to me, somewhat, but horrible, too.

The tense language itself prepares one to expect such an outburst as what follows, first the lament to Wulf about the past, then the sudden alert to Eadwacer about the present, both from a point of view of helpless stasis. In contrast to the speaker's stasis, all movement in this poem is associated with Wulf. The tone of lines 13–15 is wistful, although the substance is an accusation; these lines comprise the single long sentence in the poem. Here the speaker only sees Wulf as neglectful. The sudden sharp address to Eadwacer, announcing Wulf as an active danger to her son (if we may thus interpret "our whelp" at line 16), comes as a surprise in the poem and is presented as a revelation to the speaker as well—a new, inimical view of Wulf for which she was not prepared. The dry, even icy, gnomic statement at the end of the poem fittingly concludes the outburst and also sums up the total "inner" view of the poem from the emotional stance of the speaker.

Yet the final short line, *uncer giedd geador* "the riddle of us two together," remains in a sort of suspended opposition to the misery of *ungelic is us* "it is unlike for us [all]," and takes us back to the *leodum is minum* "to my people it is . . ." at the beginning—but with an ironic reversal that has resolved the ambiguity of *lac* in line 1, the first of a series of words of multiple meaning. *Lac* has a spectrum of meanings ranging from friendly to hostile; the root idea, according to Bosworth-Toller, "seems to be that of motion" (p. 603). The lexicographers list the meanings in this order: battle, struggle; an offering, sacrifice, oblation; a gift, present, grace, favor, service, message; medicine. "*He,*" later revealed to be Wulf, is like a *lac* given to the speaker's people; as it emerges that this is a matter for concern (what will *wælreowe weras* do with such a *lac*?), the sense of *lac* tends toward "sacrifice." The realization to which the speaker comes at the end of the poem is that "my Wulf," who seemed threatened by "my people," is the sacrificer and not the victim.

With this reversal of what the *lac* is comes a demand for renewed attention to the obscure diction throughout the poem and a line-by-line reading. As has been seen, the clue to the dramatic structure of *Wulf and Eadwacer* is offered us by the first line, *Leodum is minum swylce him mon lac gife* "to my people it is as though one gave them a *lac*," in which the word *lac* is not only ambiguous but misleading. The placing of the phrase *leodum is minum* at the beginning of the poem, together with the rhetorical figure of tmesis in which *leodum* and *minum* are linked by the copula *is* (even though *is* functions grammatically only as a link to what follows), stresses the significance of "my people" to the speaker, and hence the importance of someone giving them a *lac*. Both the dramatic and linguistic aspects of the riddle of the poem would seem to rest on the ambivalence of this gesture, whether it is friendly or hostile, and toward whom.

The second line does not help greatly, because the response of *leodum minum* is now also presented ambiguously: *willað hy hine aþecgan gif he on þreat cymeð* "will they/they will *aþecgan* him if he comes on *þreat.*" Whereas there is ample documentation for the various meanings of *lac* and its ambiguity rests on this range of meanings, lexicographers have displayed less interest in *aþecgan*, the root meaning of which seems to be "receive," and the association often with food. There is no reason to believe that the response of an Anglo-Saxon to these two words would be much different from ours: *lac*—friendly or inimical? *(embarras de richesses): aþecgan*—friendly or inimical? (insufficient evidence). Even line 6 does not clarify the meaning of *aþecgan* unless we are certain about Wulf's own nature; if Wulf is also a *wælreow wer* "slaughter-fierce man," as his name implies (the wolf is traditionally described as "ravenous"; see Genesis 49:27), then *aþecgan* may refer, after all, to a friendly reception as soul-brother comes to brother. On the other hand, the very presence of Wulf may evoke the "ravenous" associations of *apecgan*. Indeed, the separation described in line 4, *wulf is on iege ic on operre,* followed by the description of the unpleasant location of *pæt egland* (which must be Wulf's), indicates a worried speaker. Both the fen landscape and the *wælreowe weras* of line 6 are inimical by association; hence *apecgan* in line 7 probably has negative connotations. Or at least the worried speaker thinks it may.

In *preat* (lines 2 and 7) there is a range of meanings similar to that in *lac.* The word means "throng" or "press of numbers," but it can also mean "threat" on the one hand, and "host" as in "host of angels" *(engla preat)* on the other. In addition the syntax is obscure here: is "he" coming into or with a *preat?* Again the ambiguity lies in whether the nuance of the word is that of assurance or—threat.

By the time we have reached line 7 two things are certain: the speaker stands in relationship to a group of people to whom someone has done something that either does or does not seem inimical, and to which they will respond, probably in kind; and Wulf and the speaker are physically or figuratively separated on different islands, his surrounded by fen and inhabited by fierce beings. After lines 4–6 the *hine* of *hine apecgan* refers clearly to the antecedent *Wulf* (will they receive or devour *him?*), but is he the *mon* or the *lac* of line 1, the giver or the gift (sacrifice, hostage, fight, etc.)?

Also, by the time we have reached line 7 we have been introduced to the reticent mode of the poem, in which reference becomes clarified by context and aggregation, and ambiguities apparently work themselves out. The first *ungelic is us* refers to the speaker and some indefinite others: her people, the giver(s), or possibly the *lac* itself. By line 8 the antecedents of this repeated phrase have been reduced to *hy* and *hine* of line 7, with *hine* referring clearly to Wulf. This would seem to link the *wælreowe weras* of line 6, antecedent of *hy* in line 7, to the *leodum minum,* antecedent of the identical *hy* in line 2— unless the second *hy* is stressed by a lifting of the voice denoting difference rather than identity. The referent of *us* continues to be unclear, only slightly clarified by the fact that *that* island, not this one, is a dangerous trap; in this respect (the situation) "is unlike for us." The speaker does not feel any danger to herself.

Taking *ungelic is us* as an introduction to what follows, one sees that after each occurrence of the phrase the stance of the speaker and Wulf is described as being different: he is on one island, she on another; he is in some sense wide-ranging, she sits. While we cannot be sure of the relationship between *leodum minum* and Wulf, or whether or not this relationship is the same as that between the *wælreowe weras* and Wulf, we can be sure of this dissimilarity of stance between Wulf and the speaker.

Lines 9 and 10 (Wulf wide-ranging and the speaker stationary) seem to offer us something more, though again the information apparently offered is half-suppressed by the tantalizing word *dogode*. Wulf, who was first represented neutrally as separate from the speaker and the object of an uncertain response from my people, is now *my* Wulf. Moreover, the tmesis *Wulfes ic mines* has sufficient similarity to that which opens the poem (even though the "copula" between the possessive pronoun and its subject is now *ic* not *is*) to suggest that "my people" and "my Wulf" should be regarded as in some sort of emotional balance in the speaker's mind. But more important, the possessive attitude toward Wulf reinforces the concern in the antecedent lines: on *my* Wulf's island there are *wælreowe weras*. It does not seem a promising situation. It appears that it is Wulf's hopes (aspirations? But the poet does not say *ofer-wenum*) that are drawing him into such indeterminate situations. The speaker in her stasis, speaking now as though such concern has come to obsess her habitually, shifts to the preterit: she *dogode* those hopes.

Dogode does not occur elsewhere in surviving Old English texts, hence it has been emended by some editors to *hogode*, from *hogian* "to care for, think about, reflect." Others, preferring to retain the manuscript reading, suggest meanings for *dogian* from its context in the poem; Schücking suggests "suffer, endure," and Holthausen suggests "wait for impatiently" (German *harren*), taking the hopes of line 9 as her hopes ("I *dogode* my Wulf with wide-ranging hopes"), which the parallelism of lines 13b and 14b, "your hopes, your rare visits," renders unlikely. Most recently Scots dialect *dow* "fade, diminish" has been suggested as a cognate for *dogian*, and indeed "I pined for my Wulf with wide-ranging hopes" makes an attractive line. But again I would argue that the hopes are his and the dative object of *dogode*. In a poem about a person named Wulf, in which there occurs the figurative word *whelp* to describe the speaker's child, it seems to me one should at least consider that the source of the derived verb *dogian* might be *docge*, "dog," denoting some kind of traditional canine behavior. In allegory and iconography the dog traditionally represents loyalty and perseverance, occasionally servility; medieval ladies are depicted on their tombs with little dogs at their feet to illustrate the attributes of constancy and devotion (not the fact that they had a pet dog). This association in *dogode* is reinforced by *widlastum* "wide-ranging," in which occurs the word *last*, "footprint": although she is the lady sitting alone, the speaker is simultaneously the hound swift on the track. I do not like to translate *dogode* as "dogged" in this reading because the connotations do not seem right; I prefer to lose the wordplay and translate simply "followed." *Wenum,* coming as it does in a half-line separate from *widlastum,* is thus suspended delicately between the devoted speaker and her Wulf: "I followed my Wulf's wide-ranging (hopes) (in my hopes)," in the mode of syntactic ambivalence so typical of this poem.

The other *hapax legomonon* is *earne* (line 16), which I shall discuss at another time; my understanding of this word is not relevant to this argument, but I prefer to translate it "unfortunate" rather than "cowardly." The remaining three words that are heavily ambiguous, *bogum* "boughs" (line 11), *wuda* "wood" (line 17) and *giedd* "song" or "riddle" (line 19), present no problems for translation, only for interpretation.

To conclude, the ambiguities in the diction of *Wulf and Eadwacer* are of three kinds: words of clear but ambivalent meaning *(lac, þreat),* words of uncertain meaning *(aþecgan, dogode,* and later *earne),* and words that translate readily into modern English but may be complicated by a figurative meaning, like the name *Wulf* itself, and *hwelp, bogum, wudu, giedd.* There is also syntactic ambiguity such as the uncertainty of pronoun reference, the precise subject and object of *ungelic* (*what* "is unlike for us" and to whom does *us* refer?), and the lesser but equally strategic problem of whether "he" may come into or with a *þreat.*

The way in which the poem has developed in the first ten lines, through reticence followed by a gradual and retrospective revelation, suggests that certainly the ambivalence, and probably the use of unfamiliar words as well, was contrived with the specific intention of making the poem enigmatic, if not precisely a riddle. But much of the uncertainty is resolved within the context of the poem itself, with no outside reference needed as a gloss. This dramatic reticence is rather like the rhetorical figure of suspension used so effectively by the *Beowulf* poet. For example, when Beowulf and his men and a group of Danish warriors go out to seek Grendel's mother in her lair, they all know that the hall-companion of the Danes, Æshere, has been carried away in the night. But the form of the verse expresses their repugnance and shock when they discover precisely what happened to him:

```
1417                    Denum eallum wæs,
        winum Scyldinga   weorce on mode
        to geþolianne,   ðegne monegum,
        oncyð eorla gehwæm,   syðþan Æscheres
        on þam holmclife   hafelan metton.
```

> (To all of the Danes it was,
> to the friends of the Shieldings, difficult for the heart
> to bear, to many a thane,
> a strange horror, to each of the earls, when Æshere's
> (on that seacliff) head they encountered.)

A similar suspense is operating in *Wulf and Eadwacer,* but it is here being used as a device to give structure and meaning to the poem as a whole. A further similarity to the *Beowulf* sentence is that our dramatic point of view is that of the protagonist; our understanding of the situation emerges with hers. In a sense the primary message of the poem is its strategy of awakening awareness.

II. *The Situation and Its Anglo-Saxon Context*

And now, for the first time, I am going to examine more closely what the situation might be that the syntax and lexis refer to. In *Wulf and Eadwacer* a woman finds herself in a situation typical of Old English poetry, torn between conflicting loyalties. Many commentators see this particular situation as a sexual triangle, with Wulf the woman's lover and Eadwacer her husband. If so, then *Wulf and Eadwacer* is not typical, because most Old English loyalty crises occur within the family group. In *Beowulf,* for example, there are three major crises of this kind: Hildeburh sees her brother and her son slain on opposing sides in the fight at Finnsburg, Wealhtheow seeks to bind peace more firmly between her sons and their uncle Hrothulf, and the Geatish king Hrethel dies of remorse when he cannot take vengeance upon the murderer of his son Herebald, because the slayer is his other son and heir to the throne, and the homicide was apparently an accident. In *Wulf and Eadwacer,* as in these dramas, there need be no actors outside the family group.

One of the great maverick statements of literary scholarship is C. S. Lewis's claim that romantic passion as a theme of serious imaginative literature had its beginning in eleventh-century Provence, to which he adds:

> It seems—or it seemed to us till lately—a natural thing that love (under certain conditions) should be regarded as a noble and ennobling passion: it is only if we imagine ourselves trying to explain this doctrine to Aristotle, Virgil, St. Paul, or the author of *Beowulf,* that we become aware how far from natural it is.[4]

This is of course an extreme statement, but it is nevertheless true that romantic or sexual love was not the literary commonplace before the twelfth century that it has been since; other loves took precedence. For example, during the long years that Odysseus spends trying to get home to his beloved Penelope, she has been holding off her suitors with a trick, the paradigm of the faithful wife, but it is his mother who has actually died of sorrow at his absence, as she explains when he meets her dead spirit in Hades:

> Not that the keen-eyed huntress with her shafts
> had marked me down and shot to kill me; not
> that illness overtook me—no true illness
> wasting the body to undo the spirit;
> only my loneliness for you, Odysseus,
> for your kind heart and counsel, gentle Odysseus,
> took my own life away.
>
> (*Odyssey*, bk. 11, ll. 166–72,
> Fitzgerald translation)

Our cultural assumption is that if someone in literature is longing for someone else, it is likely to be a case of romantic or erotic love. But this is not an assumption that an earlier audience would share. The Anglo-Saxons seemed to associate love with devotion rather than sexual passion. The situation in *Wulf and Eadwacer* is far more typically Anglo-Saxon than as usually interpreted, if the speaker is understood to be the mother of the person she addresses as Wulf, as well as of the "whelp" of line 16. Once we accept this as the emotional relationship an Anglo-Saxon would more typically expect, and relinquish our own romantic preference for a story about lovers, various elements in the poem can be found to have analogues elsewhere in Old English.

There are two vivid vignettes in Old English verse about a mother who mourns the hard destiny of her son. In both there are verbal and episodic parallels to *Wulf and Eadwacer;* in both the mother's lack of control *(geweald)* is emphasized. The first passage occurs in a reply by Solomon to a question by Saturn as to why two twins may lead totally different lives (this is a standard *topos* used as an argument against the claims of astrology):

> Modor ne rædað,   ðonne heo magan cenneð,
> hu him weorðe geond worold   widsið sceapen.
> Oft heo to bealwe   bearn afedeð,
> seolfre to sorge,   siððan dreogeð
> his earfoðu   orlegstunde.
> Heo ðæs afran sceall   oft and gelome
> grimme greotan,   ðonne he geong færeð,
> hafað wilde mod,   werige heortan

sefan sorgfullne. . . .
Forðan nah seo modor geweald,   ðonne heo magan cenneð,
bearnes blædes,   ac sceall on gebyrd faran
an æfter anum;   ðæt is eald gesceaft.

(Solomon and Saturn, 372–86)[5]

(A mother does not know, when she bears a son,
how his wide journey through the world will be ordained for him.
Often she brings up a child to woe,
to her own sorrow, and then [she] endures
his hardship at its destined hour.
Often and again for that son she must
weep painfully, when he goes forth young,
has a wild spirit, a despairing heart,
a sorrowful mind. . . .
So the mother has no control, when she bears a son,
over her child's flourishing, but she must follow after her
     offspring
the one after the other; that is ancient destiny.)

The parental helplessness in this passage recalls that of "The Father's
Lament" in *Beowulf*, and it offers a context for the misery and helplessness of the mother in *Wulf and Eadwacer*. The other vignette occurs in *The Fortunes of Men* and offers parallels of metaphor as well as
mood and situation:

      Ful oft þæt gegongeð,   mid godes meahtum,
þætte wer ond wif   in woruld cennað
bearn mid gebyrdum   ond mid bleom gyrwað,
tennaþ ond tætaþ,   oþþæt seo tid cymeð,
gegæð gearrimum,   þæt þa geongan leomu,
liffæstan leoþu,   geloden weorþað.
Fergað swa ond feþað   fæder ond modor,
giefað ond gierwaþ.   God ana wat
hwæt him weaxendum   winter bringað!
      Sumum þæt gegongeð   on geoguðfeore
þæt se endestæf   earfeðmæcgum
wealic weorþeð.   Sceal hine wulf etan,
har hæðstapa;   hinsiþ þonne
modor bimurneð.   Ne bið swylc monnes geweald!

(The Fortunes of Men, 1–14, *Exeter Book)*

      (Full often it happens, with the might of God,
that a man and a woman   bear into the world
sons as offspring, and dress them brightly;
cheer them and cherish them, until that time comes
with the passing years   that those young limbs,
vigorous sprouts, begin to branch out.
The father and mother   thus train them and ripen them,
give to them and gear them.   God alone knows

what winter will bring them   in their burgeoning!
  To one it befalls   in the prime of his life
that the final end   to his suffering
occurs woefully: the wolf will eat him,
that hoary heath-stepper.   Then the mother
bemoans his return.   Such is not under a person's control!)

Into this pattern of a mother's lack of control over her son's adolescence and her suffering on account of his wildness and aberrant ways, *Wulf and Eadwacer* introduces definite story elements. Interpreting the relationships as similar to those in *The Fortunes of Men*, in our poem the mother is separated from her son Wulf, worries about his safety, about whom he may meet, and about where his aspirations are leading him, and she "follows" *an æfter anum*, in the sense that her maternal powerlessness no longer allows her to direct him: for that is (as Solomon tells us) the "ancient destiny" of mothers.

But when *se beaducafa* laid "boughs" about her, she found this both pleasing and distasteful. The *beaducafa*, "brave warrier," is probably her husband, who embraces her, imprisons her, or gives her children, depending upon how one interprets "boughs." Lines 5–6 of *The Fortunes of Men* quoted above suggest that the figurative reference is to children, traditionally both a delight and a sorrow to their parents (cf. Genesis 35 : 18). Now she addresses Wulf directly, but in such a way that his presence need not be assumed: "Wulf, my Wulf. . . ." One can imagine the mother shaking her head in dejection as she complains to her favorite son (in his absence) about how his absence hurts her. But the awakening from her *murnende mod* is sudden and sharp as she discovers that Wulf has returned after all, to no good purpose. She turns now to her husband, addressing him (ironically, it has been suggested) as "guardian of happiness," to tell him that the wolf-son is carrying off the whelp-son to the "wood." She concludes with a general statement of despair that is, as Alain Renoir has pointed out, a logical paradox:

Easily sundered, what never was whole . . .

yet that may be understood dramatically in the context of a mother's lament for her scattered and discordant family.

It was a Germanic custom to try to ensure peace between feuding tribes, to "settle the feud," by arranging a marriage between the daughter of one ruler and the son of the other; when a son was born of that union he would be sent at about the age of seven to be brought up by the mother's people. Thus bonds of loyalty would be forged to combat the feud. Sometimes this worked, but often it did not, and the mother involved would be helpless as the tragedy folded in upon her. Within this context the opening lines of the poem now suggest the apprehension that such a mother as "peace-weaver" might well feel when sending her son away to fulfil his destiny in her native land:

> Leodum is minum   swylce him mon lac gife;
> willað hy hine aþecgan,   gif he on þreat cymeð?

If this typical situation is seen as the background of the poem, then the physical separation is literal, along with the speaker's fears that her Wulf might fall in with *wælreowe weras,* persons still eager to resume vengeance and warfare, to become either their victim or their comrade-in-arms. She fears, I think, the first, her son being victimized; but in the event it is the latter, his collusion with the enemy, that develops.

Despite some specific difficulties with textual meaning, the story as I have offered it seems simple and clear. But one eighth-century Latin fabulist warns at the end of his poem, "Seek valiantly to ascertain what this fable may mean," and this homiletic tendency is demonstrated in the poems with which *Wulf and Eadwacer* is grouped in the *Exeter Book;* it is the last of three dramatic monologues sandwiched between the bestiary poems and the riddles. The first of these three poems is spoken by the soul to the body, by the principle of spirituality to the principle of carnality; the second is spoken by a protagonist with the generalized animal-name Deor, who uses the events of myth (or ancient "history") as a consoling analogy for personal misfortune, probably following Boethius[6]; the third, *Wulf and Eadwacer,* is, like the first two, a lament about personal misfortune, in which elements of bestiary allusion and riddle obtrude to lure the reader beyond the simple drama of the peace-weaver "to ascertain what this fable may mean." I agree with Alain Renoir that the poem can stand alone, and believe that the poet, like the *Beowulf* poet, had in mind a genre that would enable it to do so, while yet offering an extension of that surface meaning (*not* a substitution for that meaning, as in allegory). The anthologist, recognizing this generic tendency, placed the poem with two other dramatic laments for personal loss, but simultaneously made *Wulf and Eadwacer* "the first of the riddles."[7]

Whereas the mode of the bestiary poems is descriptive with an allegorical *significatio,* and that of the riddles of course enigmatic with the solution inherent in the description, the mode of these three lamentations is ironic with the solution prophetic; in all three of these poems the "solution" lies hidden in the future, and it is a solution that resolves a dynamic and tragic human situation rather than solving a static intellectual puzzle. Of course it will be apparent to the reader that I think I know what that solution is, what well-known drama *Wulf and Eadwacer* is a part of. But it is not Anglo-Saxon, and the situation in the poem is. *Ælces monnes lif bið sumes monnes lar* ("Each man's life is some man's lesson"), says *Distichs* 41, and it is with the life, not the lesson, in the poem that I am concerned in this paper. Indeed, having somewhat clarified the relationships in the speaker's life through analogies in other poems, I feel it is only fair that I should leave the reader, as the poet does, to baffle toward the greater story context, at least for a time. (In a later paper I shall offer suggestions about that as well.) But that context is not needed for an appreciation of the immediate drama of the poem. The situation in the lyric is sufficient to move us, and requires no further meaning once we recognize the speaker to be a mother. Even to the theme of the errant son leading the other son astray (one possible interpretation of ll. 16–17), *Wulf and Eadwacer* depicts a drama constantly being reenacted in real life: the "ancient destiny" of a mother, today as well as in former times, who must mourn for the children far-ranging from her side.[8]

NOTES

1. Alain Renoir, "*Wulf and Eadwacer:* a Non-interpretation," in *Franciplegius: Medieval and Linguistic Studies in Honor of Francis Peabody Magoun, Jr.,* ed. Jess B. Bessinger, Jr., and Robert P. Creed (New York: New York University Press, 1965), pp. 147–63.

2. I was first introduced to these techniques by Joan Lord Hall, now at the University of Colorado at Boulder; since we used this text it is hard for me now to unravel my insights from hers, and I should like to make proper acknowledgment here both for the theory and its particular application.

3. Renoir, "Wulf and Eadwacer," pp. 147–63.

4. C. S. Lewis, *The Allegory of Love: A Study in Medieval Tradition* (New York: Oxford University Press, 1958), p. 3. My thanks to Peter Ridgewell for reminding me of this passage.

5. This passage came to my attention in T. A. Shippey's thoughtful book, *Old English Verse* (London: Hutchinson University Library, 1972), p. 65; my interpretation is minimally different from his.

6. W. F. Bolton, "Boethius, Alfred, and *Deor* Again," *MP* 69 (1972): 222–27; cf. James L. Boren, "The Design of the Old English *Deor*," *Anglo-Saxon Poetry: Essays in Appreciation for John C. McGallaird,* ed. Lewis E. Nicholson and Delores Warwick Frese (Notre Dame, Ind.: University of Notre Dame Press, 1975), p. 270.

7. Thus it was described by those who first commented upon it, beginning with Heinrich Leo (*Quae de se ipso Cynevulfus . . . poeta Anglosaxonicus tradiderit* [Halle, 1857]), who forced runic names out of the text of *Wulf and Eadwacer* on the basis of which he ascribed this poem and the following series of riddles to the authorship of Cynewulf. His efforts are aptly described by Craig Williamson as "unprincipled in method and unsupported by any similar use of mutated runic names anywhere in Old English" (*The*

Old English Riddles of the Exeter Book [Chapel Hill: The University of North Carolina Press, 1977], p. [5]). Despite the dismissal of this particular commentator's conclusions, I think Leo was right in thinking that the manuscript location of *Wulf and Eadwacer* was not fortuitous.

8. After writing this article it has come to my attention that Dolores Warwick Frese of the University of Notre Dame has delivered a paper arguing independently for a reinterpretation of *Wulf and Eadwacer* along the lines that I suggest here. A summary of her article appears in *The Old English Newsletter* 15 (1982), pp. 46–47.

Wulf and Eadwacer:
Hints for Reading from *Beowulf* and Anthropology

Janemarie Luecke

Interpretations of the Old English poem *Wulf and Eadwacer* have continued to be offered in spite of at least two caveats warning of the dangers of single interpretations: that by Neil D. Isaacs in his 1968 volume, *Structural Principles in Old English Poetry,* and another by Alain Renoir in the 1965 *Franciplegius* volume. A few of the readings published since allow the ambiguities of alternate translations of key words to stand; I find Arnold Davidson's (1975) and Ruth P. M. Lehmann's (1969) the most helpful of these. However, of those critics who read some kind of a personal love relationship into the poem (as opposed to those who see it as a riddle, charm, rune, or charade) most assume that Eadwacer is the husband and Wulf the lover, regardless of whether there are two or three people involved. One of the more recent critics, John M. Fanagan (1976) who provides a sufficiently exhaustive review of the criticism to obviate repetition here, not only reasserts this assumption but concludes that, regardless of a choice of other translations of words in other combinations, no interpretation can go far wrong "if we stay within the bounds of the human emotions depicted therein" (p. 136).

In the context of his own interpretation, Fanagan's bounds are the limits of a love triangle—the woman/husband/lover plot nurtured in a patriarchal scheme of history. The patriarchal view assumes, with probably the majority of anthropologists, that in all known civilizations the husband has always been the dominant figure in a father-family and the hunter-provider for its welfare. However, research in the last century has provided data about matrilineal, matrilocal, and matriclan family arrangements in other cultures, and has suggested

190

that such groupings may have preceded the father-family model in our culture as well, and that dramatic tension probably accompanied the shifts from one societal arrangement to another. Although there is no way to document the earliest family arrangements among the northern European peoples prior to, during, and immediately after their emigration across western Europe, the possibility of other than nuclear or father-family arrangements is certainly suggested in the northern myths and sagas (as it is in those of the Mediterranean area also) and traces can be found in *Beowulf*. Hence critical interest demands that such anthropological evidence be utilized as may illuminate these traces, and thus provide a broader frame of reference within which to read our earliest poetry. And if the utilization is done with the proper objectivity and healthy doubt, it is possible to suggest entirely new readings of such a poem as *Wulf and Eadwacer* without at the same time imposing a single interpretation and eliminating all previous ones.

Three anthropological ideas that can affect the reading of *Wulf and Eadwacer* are the matrilineal and matrilocal society or matriclan, exogamy, and totemism. Vestiges of the first two remain in *Beowulf*. By alluding to these references in view of the studies of anthropologists, I will here suggest two or three hypothetical situations that could have prompted *Wulf and Eadwacer*, propose new readings for key words, and then conclude by offering a translation.

The first element, matriclan, has elements most familiar to Old English readers, chiefly the element of the importance of the maternal uncle. Tacitus said of the Germanic people: "The sons of sisters are as highly honored by their uncles as by their fathers. Some even go so far as to regard this tie of blood as peculiarly close and sacred. . . . However, a man's heirs and successors are his own children" (par. 20). Tacitus was writing his observations of a strange people without the benefit of reference to cultures other than his own. Anthropologists of the last hundred years have amassed data from large numbers of cultures, in various stages from the primitive, that show the same characteristics as did the Germanic. Ruth Benedict, for example, wrote of the Zuni Indians that "the most strongly institutionalized social bond" is the matrilineal blood bond, which is shared not by man and wife but by the woman and her kin. Most recently, Evelyn Kessler (1976) defined an avuncular household (that is, one that resides with the mother's brother) as "one of the patterns in a matrilineal culture" (p. 76). She quotes from a study of the Ashanti tribe in Africa (Basehart, 1962) and says that "authority is delegated to brothers; the highest authority rests with the oldest living mother's brother, who is not in constant residence, but probably lives at least part of the time with his wife" (pp. 59–60).

The social grouping operating in *Beowulf*, of course, is not matrilocal as described by Benedict and Kessler. If it was earlier, then there has been a shift to the father-family. However, the kin-clan bond (including the females) is still extremely strong in the poem's story, perhaps more so on the Scandinavian peninsula than in Daneland since we hear nothing of Hrothgar's sister—the hypothetical wife of Onela—nor of her sons in reference to Hrothgar, who under the earlier attitude should have been his closest bonded kin. Hence, if there was an earlier time when women were the authority figures in the clan, that time has long passed. The time of the brother's ownership and authority over his sister and her children was probably passing, and the father-family (patriarchy) is certainly a fact of Wealtheow's life with Hrothgar, although her situation might be read differently if we knew for certain that she was a Welsh captive or hostage who might be retaken by her brother and clan in an ongoing feud.

Social arrangements in Geatland, on the other hand, seem less advanced toward patriarchy—more in a state of confused lineal succession—than in Daneland. For although Beowulf was taken back into his mother's tribe at the age of seven, nevertheless it was his maternal grand*father* (who would have been more concerned about his sister's children in a true matriclan) who took him from his father: "Ic wæs syfanwintre / þa mec sinca baldor / freawine folca / æt minum fæder genam" (2428–29). Furthermore, nothing is said about his mother's residence; hence it is impossible to conjecture whether it was with her brothers or with her husband—the latter would have been doubtful after Ecgtheow was exiled—or whether she was dead. Nevertheless, there is also no mention of brothers' sons in Geatland until Heardred appears on Hygelac's death; whereas in Hrothgar's Danish hall they pose a threat. And Hygelac's wife (although she is in her husband's residence) has the power to offer Beowulf (the maternal nephew) the kingdom on her husband's death. In the earliest oral renditions of the narrative pieces that became *Beowulf* as we have it, scops may not have found it necessary to explain her reasons for doing so as does our poet in lines 2370b–72a: "Bearne ne truwode, / þæt he wiþ ælfylcum / eþelstolas / healdan cuþe." At the least, one may recognize traces of an earlier clan arrangement where the sister's son is the logical inheritor. However, the traces are dimmed by the fact that Hrethel is a patriarchal father-figure.

Nonetheless, the absent figure of Beowulf's mother can suggest a tantalizing hypothesis for the persona in *Wulf and Eadwacer*, or can provide clues for reading the poem. One clue is to the interpretation of *eadwacer* and *beaducafa,* for both terms in her case would refer to her maternal uncle or brother, thus providing a reading that can make sense out of the conflicting emotions expressed in line 12: "wæs me wyn to þon, / wæs me hwæþre eac laþ." For in *Beowulf* the tribal or clan bond (Ecgtheow belongs to a different clan, about which more below) is still extremely strong; indeed there is a question as to whether it or the husband-wife bond is the stronger. An inference on this point may be made from the Finn episode in *Beowulf.* The emotional position of Hildeburh, Hoc's daughter, must be in tension in spite of the scop's narrative simplification in lines 1157b–59a: "Hie on sælade / drihtlice wif / to Denum feredon, / læddon to leodum." There is an underlying implication here that "her people" are still the Danes, and hence there is a triumph, a joy *(wyn)* in her being returned to them. At the same time, I venture to suggest, after twenty years with a husband the event may also have been *laþ* to Hildeburh. But the importance of her apparently primary tie to her brother and his close bond to her son—his maternal nephew—are emphasized both in lines 1070–74 and in 1114–17, which tell of her loss of dear ones (brother and son) and her ordering them placed together on the funeral pyre. The poet does not take the time to ascribe any kind of sorrow to her on the slaughter of her husband.

In view of such ambiguity we can only acknowledge the operation of dual elements in the composition of the poem *Beowulf* as we have received it: the element of lived experience and the element of the transmission of oral poetry. The element of lived experience is a dual one also, since the scops probably included something of their own lived experience as well as their memory of an earlier lived experience on the continent, which was maintained in both their oral history and their oral poetic formulas.

One of the historians who draws from legal and civil records to write of that lived experience in Anglo-Saxon England is Dorothy Whitelock (1952). She speaks of women's kinship bonds (p. 45) and later of their divorce and marriage rights (pp. 150–52). Again, recent anthropologists supply information from their studies of contemporary preliterate societies that explain why Anglo-Saxon women enjoyed a status and power that was not to be seen again in Western Europe for a thousand years. Lamphere (1974) does so by contrasting tribal women to peasant women. She says of tribal society: "First, since a woman usually retains ties with her own kin, she may use the support of her male relatives against her husband, or sever the marriage tie altogether. Second, women's access to land or cash may make possible the formation of extra-domestic women's groups, which have economic functions and which wield considerable political power" (p. 109). The women seen in *Beowulf* and other Old English poems, however, are not given sufficiently large roles that we may relate them to Lamphere's statement. However, what is suggested there about the instability of the marriage bond is reflected in the poetry. Boulding (1976) writes that "marriage is never as central to the organization of economic and social life in a matrilineal society as it is in a patrilineal one," and cites examples from the studies collected in Schneider and Gough (1962) showing the prevalance of divorce and a casual attitude toward marriage in contemporary primitive societies that have a matrilineal social structure (pp. 143–45).

Such studies need not disprove the observation of Tacitus concerning the moral fiber of the Germanic peoples; but they do provide sociological data explaining why the political marriages recorded in the poetry could be arranged so arbitrarily, and broken so peremptorily. The instability of marriage in the matrilineal society (as examined in Mair, 1972) may be one of the reasons why societies, according to Murdock (1949), have always moved from matriliny to patriliny and not vice versa. Another factor is the instability of the matrilineal social organization itself, which seemed to accommodate only the small-scale agro-village in political and economic terms. Oppong (1974) describes the conditions for the change from matriliny to patriliny: "Considerable evidence from all over the world has been amassed to demonstrate that, wherever agricultural communities with matrilineage organization become involved in market systems with consequent migration, spread of private property ownership and private accumulation of wealth, the conjugal family emerges as the key kinship group with regard to residence, economic cooperation, legal responsibility and socialization. Inheritance, however, is noted as tending to lag behind in this change process" (p. 157). Inheritance, of course, has to do with family bonds, which are always slow to change.

What also lags behind to a considerable degree is the poetry, which is transmitted orally. It lags perhaps primarily for the reasons that the scops may have been trained into a poetic-formula system that did not easily admit change in the handling of cultural themes, and they may also have tended to idealize the past and to conserve its values. Hence, even if Anglo-Saxon society was thoroughly patriarchal in practice by the time *Beowulf* was written down, the poem could still reflect earlier cultural values. But the change would eventually occur in the poetry also, either in the definition of the relationship of the male and female characters or in the interpretation of that relationship. Reed (1975) summarizes previous scholarship when she says of the cultural changeover and its gradual reflection in the poetry: "The family makes its appearance at the turning point from savagery to barbarism. The emergence is reflected in the legends of Isis, the barbarian goddess, who is described in seemingly contradictory terms as both the sister of Osiris and the wife of Osiris. It would be incorrect to view this as a sister-brother marriage; rather it represents a telescoped version of the historical changeover from the sister-brother clan partnership to the husband-wife family partnership" (pp. 338–39).

Franz Bauml (1975) elaborated on the same subject but dealt with the Northern epics. He says: "I do suggest that the common distinction between the Norse and the German traditions—that is, the transformation of Kriemhild as fury avenging the murder of her brothers on her husband to Kriemhild as fury avenging the murder of her first husband on her brothers—I do suggest that this distinction is not one between Norse and German, or pagan and Christian, but rather between preliterate and disadvantaged literate. The former is an affair of state, and can only be perceived as an affair of state. Kriemhild, on this level, perpetuates tribal social order. The latter can be perceived as an exemplum of the faithfulness of wife to husband" (p. 31).

An understanding of matriliny, then, provides insights for recognizing certain references in the early sagas and in *Beowulf* as indicative of the poems' origins in earlier social groupings with different cultural patterns and values. If the poem *Wulf and Eadwacer* came to England from the continent through oral transmission, its link to a matrilineal situation is both clearer and more dramatic than is *Beowulf*'s, for it probably voices the experience of a woman whose marriage has been dissolved by her brother or maternal uncle (Eadwacer) since the clan interests supersede any kind of mating or marriage bond. However, the evident love of the female speaker for Wulf and the implication that she could be living with him if not prevented by Eadwacer probably places the poem's origin in a transitional period away from matriliny.

The second anthropological idea—the system of exogamy—provides one of the bases for the instability of marriage in the matrilineal society and for the heightened tension in the poem. This system demanded that a woman or man procure a mate from another group or tribe. Exogamy begins with the incest taboo of very early peoples, and then seems to continue as a political maneuver for furthering the alliance between hostile groups (Kessler 1976:158–59). Probably the society of *Beowulf* represents the later stage, for we have no way of knowing whether the exogamous rule bound only royal sons and daughters or every member of the clans. We know for certain only that Beowulf's mother, Hrothgar, Hildeburh, and Freawaru have mates from other clans or tribes. There is no way of ascertaining the same about Hygelac because of the likeness of Hygd's name to his family's. And the Eofor to whom Hygelac awarded his daughter may or may not have been a member of Hygelac's *mægth*. Klaeber glosses his name as a Geat, but there may have been an earlier alliance that had bound earlier exogamous clans.

Such alliances seem to have been the goal at one stage of political development. Tylor (1931), for example, describes the exogamous rule as "an institution which resists the tendency of uncultured populations to disintegrate, cementing them into nations capable of living together in peace and holding together in war till they reach the period of higher military and political organization" (p. 471). Rosaldo (1974) more recently studied present-day people and writes of them: "The Mae Enga of the Western Highlands say that they 'marry their enemies'; women are pawns in a tenuous political alliance" (p. 32). We assume from *Beowulf* that Germanic women are used in this same kind of role; they were given in marriage as the "peace-weavers" between warring Germanic tribes. As such, we may see the practice already somewhat late in its history, when the flourishing clans such as Hrothgar's Danes had already achieved some political strength by several generations of such alliances. Probably in the earliest savage stages, the people of one tribe considered members of any other tribe or totem not only as enemies but actually as nonhuman. Hence, as Briffault (1927) suggested, "For a lover [mate] to pay a stealthy visit in the night to a female of a strange group is thus almost impracticable; and unless there exists some friendly understanding between the two groups, it is equally impossible in the daytime" (p. 561).

Beowulf's mother certainly was not in such a situation as Briffault suggests, but she could have been in one that succeeded it. We can only accept the scop's word that Ecgtheow, her mate, has aroused a feud by slaying a member of the Wylfing tribe (lines 459–62). Actually, in the early stages of exogamy, when the male mate resided, occasionally at least, in his wife's community, he was always the outsider; hence he could be held responsible for any deaths or accidental injuries that occurred, and would be expelled as a result. For as long as the matriclan relationship was indissoluble, the matrimonial tie was easily and repeatedly torn apart. Regardless of the circumstances surrounding Ecgtheow's guilt, the one fact that the scop does give is that his mate's people "for herebrogan /[hine] habban ne mihte" (l. 462); that is, Beowulf's people would not risk war for an outsider (even though the outsider is Beowulf's father) as they would do unhesitatingly for a member of the *mægth.* And I use the phrase *Beowulf's people* here purposefully, since, according to Reed (1975), "his membership in his mother's clan is indissoluble whereas that with his father's clan is limited, and could end if the marriage was dissolved" (p. 378). She quotes from Malinowski (1929): "As soon as the [boy] child begins to grow up . . . certain complications arise, and change the meaning of *tama* for him. He learns that he is not of the same clan as his *tama,* that his totemic appellation is different, and that it is identical with that of his mother. . . . Another man appears on the horizon, and is called by the child *kadagu* ('my mother's brother'). . . . the child also learns that the place where his *kada* (mother's brother) resides is also his" (p. 6). However, the system is no longer uncomplicated in the social structure seen in *Beowulf* as we have received that poem. Hrothgar assumes that Beowulf feels a filial debt for Hrothgar's kindness to his father; Beowulf is frequently apposited as the *bearn Ecgtheowes,* and tribal alliances have become confusing by the time we try to place Wiglaf of the Wægmundings within Beowulf's kin-clan.

Like the hypothetical mother of Beowulf, any conjectured female persona in *Wulf and Eadwacer* might very logically have been a victim of an exogamous pairing with a member of a hostile tribe, this one perhaps identified by the Wulf totem. Her own clan (probably particularized in her brother, the *eadwacer* for the clan) may have either *læddon* [her] *to leodum* (like Hildeburh) when her son was still a child, or the *eadwacer* "genam" the child and her with it (as Hrethel did Beowulf) at the same time that Wulf was expelled for whatever reason. Or, Wulf, while spending conjugal time in his mate's tribe, may have killed someone for whom her tribe would neither pay wergeld nor suffer the threat of a vengeance attack for harboring the killer; hence, he was exiled—as was Ecgtheow—and threatened with death if he tried to return. Three words in the poem reinforce such readings: *Wulf, hwelp,* and *apecgan.* All three may be linked to a practice of totemism, which linkage would suggest the poem's origins in early prehistory.

Although Lévi-Strauss in 1961 succeeded in deflecting the energies spent on the subject of totemism, he did not erase the possibility of a pervasive influence of the totem in prehistory. If totemism was a reality in the savage stages of the northern European peoples who were ancestors to the Angles and Saxons, it was probably a system by which a tribe established an affinity with one species of animal. All members of that totem (human and animal) thus became tabooed: one could not hunt, kill, eat, or mate with any other member of one's own totem. People and animals of other totems, on the other hand, were fair game.

Apecgan may be the most significant word in *Wulf and Eadwacer* to link it to totemism. Scholars now pretty much agree that the word may be translated in one or all of the following ways: take in/receive/consume/devour/oppress/relieve/assume protection of. What I have not found in any published work on the poem is the relation of these apparently contradictory meanings to the fact that in the languages of many primitive peoples the same term is used for both eating (among cannibals this includes eating humans) and sexual intercourse. For example, Margaret Mead (1935:83) records a series of aphorisms from the Arapesh:

> Your own mother
> Your own sister,
> Your own pigs,
> Your own yams that you have piled up,
> You may not eat.
> Other people's mothers,
> Other people's sisters,
> Other people's pigs,
> Other people's yams that they have piled up,
> You may eat.

Today the Arapesh have done what the monks probably did with Germanic poetry: they interpret the words allegorically. Hence for the Arapesh the aphorisms embody chiefly their ideal of unselfishness rather than conveying a totemic taboo against eating or mating with their own. At the same time, however, the series demonstrates the use of the same word for eating and mating. If we allow the word *apecgan* in *Wulf and Eadwacer* to retain all of its meanings in the same way as in the above aphorisms, and accept "devour" or "take in" to include sexual intercourse, then I think we have the best possibility for making sense out of the refrain while still allowing ambivalence. For to the female singer's people, *apecgan* in regard to Wulf may signify to eat, devour, or consume. But, "*Ungelic is us!*" In regard to her and Wulf, *apecgan* can mean to mate. And still later, as with the Arapesh, *apecgan* may signify simple hospitality or be used allegorically.

The use of the word *hwelp* for what is usually understood as a child reinforces a totemic situation. The simplest reading would identify the *hwelp* as the child of Wulf—belonging to the Wulf totem—and this could be the woman's way of saying that she is defending his father-rights. However, a more ambiguous reading would be more sensitive to the long process involved in the move from matriclan to father-family. For *hwelp* in Old English may be the young of any wild beast. Hence it can refer to the child (even though of Wulf's paternity) as belonging to her own clan, and thus to her brother or uncle *(ead-wacer)*, just as Beowulf belonged to Hrethel and Hygelac. Such a reading reflects Malinowski's description of the Melanesians as seen above. Viewed in this light the poem can be read to express some of the tension and pain suffered by those caught in the shifting societal pattern, especially by a woman in an early stage of change who was caught between a passionate relationship with a mate from an outside, hostile tribe and a brother who still had ultimate power over her.

My suggestions for the interpretations of the three words just discussed are not dependent on the existence of totemism, for the scop's use of the words may be simply metaphorical. However, the usage is highly suggestive of a totemic culture—if such cultures actually existed.

Closely linked to the words *hwelp* and *wulf* in lines 17 and 18 is the word *toslitep* in line 19 of the poem. *Toslitep* can be linked also to the changeover from matriclan to patriarchy. Although less clearly supported in recent studies, Lippert (1886) and Layard (1931) described the sacrifice of the first-born son as the ritual-resolution of the dilemma as to whom the children belonged—to the mother's brother or to the father. Reed (1975) summarizes the transition as follows:

> On the one hand, the mother's brother could not easily relinquish his inherited "blood bond" to his sister and sister's children. On the other hand, the father could not easily shed his inherited "blood debt," carried over from the epoch of cannibalism and blood revenge. . . . Apparently there was no other way to sever the Gordion knot of the matrilineal blood line that created the divided two-father family. The very form of the sacrifice is symbolical; it is sometimes called the "partitioning" of the child. (p. 399)

Since the father was the one to perform the sacrifice, the words in *Wulf and Eadwacer* are fitting: "Uncerne earne / bireþ wulf to wuda / þæt mon eaþe toslíteþ / þætte næfre gesomnad wæs." Such a reading would support the choice of *lac* in the first line to mean "sacrifice," and would thus suggest that the poem may have been occasioned by the father's returning to sacrifice his child.

What the female scop intended with *gesomnad* must remain more ambivalent than even the preceding terms; and in any reading of the poem as a human relationship, *giedd* in the final line may be either a clear metaphor or may mean a story in the sense of history. For to the female persona who is passionately in love with the father of her child and hence a proponent of the new order of father-family, the old "story" of brother's right never signified a physical union. As such, she would be a polar opposite to the Greek Antigone, who risked her life to preserve the traditional order. On the other hand, *giedd* may be (to the one caught in the transition) the awful riddle begging for an answer as to who is the rightful partner in the dual *uncerne* and *uncer* in either line 17 or 19 or both.

By the time this poem was written down, if child sacrifice was practiced by the northern European people, it had long since given way first, perhaps, to the use of a sacrificial animal (which prompts a suggestion that *hwelp* may be the sacrificial animal instead of the child) and then to the custom of the prized first-born son. However, *tosliteþ* might still be retained in the poem to symbolize the vestiges of the transition. For, as we noted above, Beowulf too was seized *(genam)* from his father by his maternal kin. For that matter, Beowulf bears another resemblance to the *hwelp* who was *earne* (slow/cowardly/vile/useless). When Beowulf was a child, as the scop tells us in lines 2183–88, he was long *hean* (which is glossed as abject/humiliated/wretched/despised), and was suspected of being *sleac* (slow/slothful/lazy) and *unfrom* (inactive/feeble/un-bold/un-brave).

Reading *Wulf and Eadwacer* with the wider lens that such anthropological hints and references to *Beowulf* provide can be a fresh experience. However, doing so does not much alter a simple translation, if one needs a translation. I much prefer retaining the poem in Old English even with undergraduates, and then providing interpretative material. But for the sake of illustrating the poetic ambiguities that will remain in any acceptable translation, I offer the following as expressing the interpretation I have suggested in this paper. (I assume with Ruth Lehmann [1969] two lines lost at the beginning of the poem.)

> . . . .
> . . . .
> is to my people   as if one give them game.
> Will they devour him,   if he comes in need?
>   It is different with us!
>
> Wulf is on one island,   I on another;
> Fast is that island,   wrapped around by fens.
> Slaughter-rough are the men   on the island there.
> Will they devour him   if he comes in need?
>   It is different with us!
>
> Of my Wulf's wide-trackings   I suffered in hopes.
> When it was rainy weather   and I sat weeping

then the battle-ready one   laid arms around me;
That was somewhat a joy to me;   it was nevertheless loathed.

Wulf, my Wulf,   hopes for thee
make me sick,   thy seldom coming,
a mourning heart,   not at all lack of food.

Hearest thou, homewatcher!   The wretched hwelp of ours
    Wulf bears to the woods.
One easily tears that apart   which was never joined,
    Our riddle together.

Such a translation clearly allows for other interpretations; hence
the one I have suggested will not replace others proposed. My reading implying a matrilineal culture would represent perhaps the earliest origin of the poem. In the transition to a patriarchal society, the
relationship of a female speaker in the poem to Wulf and to Eadwacer
would have shifted for the listeners as did that of Isis to Osiris. However, because the poem is such a brief lyrical fragment, such a shift is
not so clearly stated as in the sagas. Finally, the monk who wrote down
the *Wulf and Eadwacer,* whether that was as early as the seventh century or as late as the end of the tenth, almost certainly represented
another cultural step and heard the poem allegorically (as recent
critics have suggested) giving both anagogical and eschatological interpretations. Doing so would bring the poem sufficiently into conformity with the then current Christian values to justify his recording
it at all. Hence no one interpretation of the poem can be considered
today as the single accurate one. Probably each represents a moment,
or an epoch, in the dramatic and traumatic sociological upheavals
experienced by the preliterate and then literate peoples who became
our Western European Church and society.

WORKS CITED

I. Works on *Beowulf* and *Wulf and Eadwacer:*

Davidson, Arnold. "Interpreting *Wulf and Eadwacer.*" *Annuale
Medievale* 16 (1975): 23–32.
Fanagan, John M. "*Wulf and Eadwacer:* A Solution to the Critic's Rid-
dle." *Neophilologus* 60 (1976): 130–37.
Isaacs, Neil D. *Structural Principles in Old English Poetry.* Knoxville:
University of Tennessee Press, 1968.
Klaeber, F. *Beowulf and the Fight at Finnsburg.* 3d ed. Boston: D. C.
Heath, 1950.

Lehmann, Ruth P. M. "The Metrics and Structure of 'Wulf and Ead-wacer,'" *Philological Quarterly* 48 (1969):151–65.

Renoir, Alain. *"Wulf and Eadwacer:* A Noninterpretation." *Franciplegius: Medieval and Linguistic Studies in Honor of Francis Peabody Magoun, Jr.* Edited by Jess B. Bessinger, Jr., and Robert P. Creed. New York: New York University Press, 1965, pp. 147–63.

II. Works in Sociology and Anthropology:

Basehart, Harry W. "Ashanti." *Matrilineal Kinship.* Edited by David M. Schneider and Kathleen Gough. Berkeley: University of California Press, 1962, pp. 270–79.

Bauml, Franz H. "Transformations of the Heroine: From Epic Heard to Epic Read." *The Role of Woman in the Middle Ages.* Edited by Rosmarie Thee Morewedge. Albany: State University of New York Press, 1975, pp. 23–40.

Benedict, Ruth. *Patterns of Culture.* 1932; reprint ed. New York: New American Library, 1959.

Boulding, Elise. *The Underside of History: A View of Women through Time.* Boulder: Westview Press, 1976.

Briffault, Robert. *The Mothers: A Study of the Origins of Sentiments and Institutions.* 1927; reprint ed. New York: Macmillan, 1952.

Kessler, Evelyn. *Woman: An Anthropological View.* New York: Holt, Rinehart and Winston, 1976.

Lamphere, Louise. "Women in Domestic Groups." *Women, Culture and Society.* Stanford: Stanford University Press, 1974.

Layard, John. *Stone Men of Malehula.* London: Chatto and Windus, 1941.

Lévi-Strauss, Claude. *Totemism.* Boston: Beacon, 1962.

Lippert, Julius. *The Evolution of Culture.* 1886; reprint ed. New York: Macmillan, 1931.

Mair, Lucy. *Marriage.* New York: Universe, 1972.

Malinowski, Bronislaw. *The Sexual Life of Savages in North-Western Melanesia.* New York: Harcourt Brace, 1929.

Mead, Margaret. *Sex and Temperament in Three Primitive Societies.* New York: William Morrow, 1935.

Murdock, George. *Social Structure.* New York: Macmillan, 1949.

Oppong, Christine. *Marriage Among a Matrilineal Elite: A Family Study of Ghanaian Senior Civil Servants. Cambridge Studies in Social Anthropology,* 8. Cambridge: Cambridge University Press, 1974.

Reed, Evelyn. *Woman's Evolution: From Matriarchal Clan to Patriarchal Family.* New York: Pathfinder Press, 1975.

Rosaldo, Michelle. "Woman, Culture and Society: A Theoretical Overview." *Woman, Culture and Society.* Edited by Michelle Rosaldo and Louise Lamphere. Stanford: Stanford University Press, 1974.

Schneider, David M. and Kathleen Gough, eds. *Matrilineal Kinship.* Berkeley: University of California Press, 1962. Pertinent articles: David F. Aberle, "Navaho," pp. 96–201, and "Matrilineal Descent in Crosscultural Perspectives," pp. 655–730. Elizabeth Colson, "Plateau Tonga," pp. 36–95. George H. Fathauer, "Trobriand," pp. 234–69. Kathleen Gough, "Nayar: Central Kerala," pp. 298–384; and "Nayar: North Kerala," pp. 385–404.

Tylor, Edward Burnett. "On a Method of Investigating the Development of Institution." *Source Book in Anthropology.* Edited by A. L. Kroeber and T. T. Waterman. New York: Harcourt Brace, 1931.

Whitelock, Dorothy. *The Beginnings of English Society.* 1952; reprint ed. Harmondsworth, England: Penguin Books, 1972.

Deor, Wulf and Eadwacer, and The Soul's Address: How and Where the Old English Exeter Book Riddles Begin

James E. Anderson

I. *An Imposter's Peril*

Of the eight Exeter Book poems that we call elegies, the two brief-est—*Deor* and *Wulf and Eadwacer* (fols. 100a–101a)—are in many ways also the most obscure. The forty-two poetic lines of *Deor* seem to tell the full story of a dispossessed minstrel's lament; yet an echo of Boethian consolation seems to jar against the famous heroic stories on the minstrel's mind. As a whole, therefore, his song has a puzzling dual effect. His old heroic tales themselves also present some curious difficulties of vocabulary, names, images, and MS readings. The opening line of the poem, about Weland the Smith, is strangely ab-rupt. The third stanza tells a story whose very identity is uncertain. Worst of all, perhaps, we cannot solve these problems by obvious comparisons, since no minstrel called Deor appears anywhere else in Germanic literature.

The next nineteen lines of poetry in the MS, generally called *Wulf and Eadwacer* from what seem to be two men's names in the text, only magnify the uncertainties of *Deor*. The feminine nominal appositive in *ic reotugu* "I, the sad one" (l. 10) confirms that a woman is speaking. The sudden outburst *Gehyrest þu, eadwacer* at l. 16, along with the shift to direct address and bitter tone and the question whether *eadwacer* and *wulf* (l. 17) are proper names, might almost imply a different speaker or even a separate poem. For the unity of these nineteen lines, then, we rely heavily on the implicit word of the scribe, who copied them without a break at l. 16. Moreover, since the word *ead-*

wacer has plausibly been read as an epithet rather than a name, the number of male figures in the poem and also the title *Wulf and Eadwacer* are open to some debate.[1] The speaker's tone has been variously assumed or described as respectful, ironic, sarcastic, jocular, bitterly resigned.[2] But if the last lines end the story bitterly, the first line seems to put the reader even more awkwardly *in medias res* than does the beginning of *Deor*. From these shadowy appearances, *Wulf and Eadwacer* might be either fragmentary or complete, heroic or elegiac, or perhaps a woman's song taken as a set-piece from a longer heroic work.[3] It has an unusual concentration of hapax legomena, rare words, and obscure images, far more even than *Deor*. Its crude or irregular verse and alliteration so perplexed its first modern editor, Benjamin Thorpe, that he chose merely to print the untranslated words, of which he could neither "make . . . sense, nor . . . arrange the verses."[4] Long since arranged, the verses have received aesthetic judgments at opposite extremes. Schücking once described the half-line *Wulf, min Wulf* (l. 13a) as a dramatic outcry of unmatched intensity; but another German scholar—in an annoyed tone of voice—has called the same words "meinetwegen ein Unvers!"[5] Finally, if Deor's name is unfortunately unique, the woman who follows him is utterly anonymous. Every question raised in *Deor* becomes in *Wulf and Eadwacer* an agony of scholarly doubt.

In 1962 P. J. Frankis conjectured that some of our doubt might come from reading the two poems separately.[6] Except for a charm or two whose refrains stem from reiterative magic, *Deor* and *Wulf and Eadwacer* are, as Frankis noted, our only two surviving Old English poems with purely literary refrains. Frankis therefore guessed that they had been deliberately placed together in the Exeter Book, and supported his guess with a suggestion of cross-textual wordplay on *deor* "beast" and *wulf*. From both texts together he deduced a hypothetical narrative, a story of thwarted love, abduction of a woman, and ensuing conflict. Even though they were not tested against every detail of the two poems, his conjectures were, I think, very nearly right. Pursued to their limits, however, Frankis's ideas suggest not his rather perfumed tragedy of wasted love, but a double riddle based on a famous Germanic abduction story, and full of the old heroic reek of blood and death. But the same wordplay that Frankis detected also extends beyond *Deor* and *Wulf and Eadwacer* into the preceding poem in the Exeter Book, *The Soul's Address to the Body*. From their many plays on words and themes, these three texts appear to be a long triple riddle that equates heroic abduction with spiritual death and exposes pagan heroism as bitterly unheroic in the end. In that event, the

Exeter Book riddles would not begin with *Wulf and Eadwacer,* as was once widely believed, nor even with *Deor.* Indeed, the Exeter Book scribe himself seems to have conspired in the real beginning, at *The Soul's Address* on fol. 98a.

To begin with, *Deor* and *Wulf and Eadwacer* share more than the simple fact of their refrains. Beneath the apparent vagueness of both refrains lies elusive rhetoric—the kind of language that defies guesses and paraphrases but seems to repay close thought. In *Deor,* the refrain *þæs ofereode, þisses swa mæg* contains both uncertain pronoun reference and double meaning in the verb. *Ofereode* means not only "passed away," as it is often translated, but also "went on, transferred," especially with genitive objects such as *þæs* and *þisses.*[7] Because these pronouns are objects rather than subjects, the line seems best rendered in the passive voice: "That was moved on, so this can be, too." The shift in tense from *ofereode* to *mæg* also hints of playfulness rather than merely clumsiness in the thought. In one sense "that" becomes the story of each stanza that has just "passed by" before the refrain, and "this" becomes the next story, to which the argument of the poem can "move on." In the last line of *Deor,* "that" looks backward to Deor's complaint of his own dispossession, while "this" seems to squint ahead at *Wulf and Eadwacer,* whose refrain insists on unlikeness. Together, then, the two refrains have the aura of a riddler's wit, the same deceptive habit of mind that contrived more obvious double riddles elsewhere in the Exeter Book.

In Riddle 42, for example, a passage of scrambled rune-names gives the anagrammatic solution *hana* "cock" and *hæn* "hen." The remainder of the text, however, plays on widely distributed folklore motifs of the cock and hen as both fleshly and spiritual marriage partners.[8] The riddlic word *orþoncbendum* "skillful bonds of thought" then links the copulating cock and hen in the implicit farmyard of Riddle 42 to the nobler marriage of "body and soul," figuratively confined *in geardum*—that is, within the nature of Man—in Riddle 43. The scribe seems to have acknowledged the joint themes with a sly graphic trick of his own: he copied both riddles as one text, but also "separated" them by a bold raised point and a somewhat elongated small capital in the middle of a MS line. For two later one-line fragments, Riddles 75 and 76, the cock and hen are again the probable solution. The swath-maker of Riddle 75 appears in runes as DNLH, feasibly deciphered as an inverted vowelless spelling of *HaeLeND* "Savior." The riddlic creature seems to be the cock, a frequent symbol of Christ, pecking his way through scattered corn. This answer is partly urged by Riddle 76, which presents a single image of *ane . . .*

idese sittan "a lone lady sitting." She might easily be a setting hen, perhaps made to stand for the brooding Church on earth.[9] These fairly certain paired riddles are good reasons for approaching *Deor* and *Wulf and Eadwacer* with a riddler's care.

To borrow a prominent motif from Riddles 42/43, a successful riddlic device is both lock and key to true meaning. Likewise, the ambiguous refrain of *Deor* both shows and conceals the true argument of the poem. At first the refrain connects the stanzas about Weland and Beadohild, which must be recognized as two sides of the same violent abduction story. The opening line of the poem says that Weland tried punishment on *him* "them," that is, the brothers of Beadohild. According to the old legend, Weland slaughtered them, and Deor mentions their death in the first line of stanza two. In further accord with the legend, Deor recalls that Weland's revenge was bloody: the puzzling phrase *be wurman* in l. 1 means "with purple," a poetic reference to blood that we know from Elizabethan speech.[10] But the rest of the first stanza shows Weland as victim, whom Niðhad cruelly hobbles with *swoncre seonobende* "thin chains of sinew," a riddlic—indeed a skaldlike—conceit on Weland's severed hamstrings. This phrase begins a strain of Scandinavian touches throughout *Deor* and *Wulf and Eadwacer:* the prominent mention in *Deor* 36 of the Jutish *Heodeningas*, for example, or the strong formal resemblance of *Wulf and Eadwacer* to the Norse *ljoðhattrstrophe*.[11] But Deor's other old stories are not interrelated at all in Germanic legend. They appear together only in *Deor*, presumably in some mutual connection with the singer's ambiguous refrain.

The first two stanzas of *Deor* allude to the suffering and revenge of a famous abductor and to the mental agony of his female victim. According to Frankis, *Deor* and *Wulf and Eadwacer* taken together also comprise an abduction story told alternately by a man and a woman. Deor the minstrel sketches old stories that somehow lead to a longer treatment of his own. All of these structural clues suggest that his refrain is bound in yet divorced from narrative time. The refrain would not only look back at what has just been told and ahead to what comes next, but would also draw timeless comparisons between each of Deor's old stories and his own trouble. In telling his own misfortunes, however, Deor becomes a man with a grudge and a case to argue, against both his lord and the *leoðcræftig monn* (l. 40) who has taken his wealth and position. He should be slanting the old stories to favor his own case in the sixth part of the poem. From these hypotheses *Deor* shows a hidden coherence built around the minstrel himself.

Stanza one implies that Deor has sought a revenge like Weland's, apparently for the reason given in stanza six: his *londryht* "right to hold land" has been taken from him and given to another singer. Since this grievance is so much less than Weland's, violent retribution would be unjust; yet stanza two insinuates just such an outrage— namely, that Deor has avenged himself on a woman just as Weland did. But if Deor means to glorify Weland's deeds, and therefore, by innuendo to exalt himself, then he would conveniently omit the more unheroic elements in the Weland story. In fact, he does not say, as the legend does, that Weland murdered his male enemies in their sleep; instead, the deaths of Beadohild's brothers are couched in riddlic language and told piecemeal across both stanzas. Stanza one gives five lines to Weland's suffering, but only the first line—by far the hard- est—to his crimes. Stanza two, again unlike the legend, focuses not upon the violation of a helpless woman but upon Beadohild's mental anguish afterwards. The rape itself is concealed in a passing euphem- ism about her pregnancy, and her agony is ascribed to other causes— the deaths of her brothers, her increasing size, and worry about how a vague "it" (*þæt*, l. 12) might end. Deor does not mention that Weland was the cause of all her grief.

As still further evidence for Frankis's argument, these omitted truths about Beadohild seem to appear from between the lines of the woman's narrative in *Wulf and Eadwacer*. In l. 11 the woman com- plains that [*se beaducafa*] *mec . . . bogum bilegde* "the bold fighter bore me down with his shoulders." But OE *bog* more precisely means "shoulderbone of an animal," and ModG *belegen* can still mean "to mount (for sexual intercourse)." These images of brutish lovemaking belong to the main wordplay in the poem, on *Wulf* as both man and animal. Like Beadohild, the woman seems to have endured forcible rape, the probable source of her *lað* "loathing, pain" (l. 12b). Para- doxically, however, she also remembers *wyn* "joy" (l. 12a), and genu- ine anxiety and longing for Wulf during his long absences and *seldcymas* "rare returnings" (l. 14). In the Beadohild stanza of *Deor* there is no corresponding joy except, perhaps, for Beadohild's un- born child, the source of her gravest anguish. Deor, who seems so absorbed in himself, could be expected to miss this paradox of motherly love, which might then be left for the woman of *Wulf and Eadwacer* to express. The point, I suspect, is that the two women share both the feelings and their cause, and that the mysterious *hwelp* of *Wulf and Eadwacer* 16 is a riddlic one—a child stolen while still in the womb of its abducted mother. Of several proposed emendations for MS *earne* (l. 16), *ear[m]ne* would probably best sustain a riddlic theme of maternal grief: by crying "poor whelp," this woman would seem to worry, like Beadohild, about the dark future of her child conceived in misfortune.[12] With grief and confusion to match Beadohild's, she might well intend sarcasm with the unique compound *beaducafa* "bold fighter" (l. 11). The word is applied to Wulf's bestial embraces, not his deeds, and probably insinuates that he is bold mainly at pressing women. Perhaps, in an utterly silent parallel with Weland, Wulf has also "boldly" committed stealthy murders before taking flight. Thus some of the harder words and images in *Wulf and Eadwacer* seem to veil unflattering correspondences with the story of Weland and Beadohild.

Deor, however, is also busy comparing himself to other famous avengers besides Weland. In stanza four, the minstrel relives the glory of Theodoric of Verona, who returned after long exile to the wealth and power he had lost. The clue to Theodoric's identity lurks in the words *ahte . . . mæringa burg,* not a reference to a place or tribe but a skaldic conceit on exile. OE *mæring,* found only this once in poetry, denotes a medicinal herb or flower, perhaps basil, in OE leechcraft. Accordingly, the declaration *Ðeodoric ahte þritig wintra mæringa burg* would mean "for thirty winters Theodoric held a fortress of basil-flowers," that is, dwelt in the open fields as an exile, in an ironic "stronghold" indeed.[13] These thirty years of exile, overcome at last, Deor illogically compares with his own lost wealth and standing, which he had held *fela wintra* "for many winters" (l. 38): the lexical echo of *wintra* is the riddlic key for this larger argument. Deor's hope, expressed in the refrain, that like Theodoric's his own exile will pass, would perhaps be Boethian if only it made good sense. But whereas the Theodoric of legend was unjustly exiled, the Weland and Beadohild stories and their probable analogies in *Wulf and Eadwacer* already suggest that Deor is hardly innocent of crime. The falsity of his comparison undermines the hope of his refrain.

Nevertheless, the refrain also "moves on" to stanza five and Eormanric, Theodoric's lord in legend though not in history. This legendary connection, which is not exploited in stanzas four and five, is perhaps a deliberately false trail. Indeed, stanza five is only superficially about Eormanric, the cruelest tyrant of Germanic song and story, in Deor's words a man of *wylfenne geþoht* and a *grim cyning* (ll. 22–23). The second half of the stanza is given to Deor's real purpose, not Eormanric himself but his oppressed subjects, who sat *sorgum gebunden* "bound in sorrows" (l. 24) and wished for the tyrant's downfall. Deor's ulterior motive for telling their side of the story is revealed, again with a sly lexical echo, as the minstrel begins his own complaint in stanza six. He, too, knows how a man *siteð sorgcearig* "sits full of sorrow" (l. 28) when his luck turns bad. By comparing himself to the persecuted Goths of old, Deor begs the other side of the question with a liberal dash of self-pity: his own lord, who has cruelly cast him out, is Eormanric's match in tyranny and injustice. The suggested parallel between Deor and the Goths, both secret malefactors of their lords, is cunningly left unwrought.

The obscure and much-discussed third stanza begins with the claim that "we . . . many have known" its legend; and the mention of sleeplessness and *sorglufu* "sorrowful love" (l. 16) implies a love story both tragic and famous. If this tale is as celebrated as all the others, MS *mæð hilde* (l. 14) probably does not contain the otherwise unknown and phonologically unlikely name *Mæðhild*.[14] But if the name is *Hild* instead, and if *Geates* (l. 15) hides a riddlic eponym *Geat* "Jute," spelled as in *Anno 449* of the Anglo-Saxon Chronicle, then the lines call to mind a widely told tale of abduction that Saxo Grammaticus knew as Jutish. This is the story of the eternal fight of the Heodenings. In four separate Scandinavian versions including Saxo's, Hild is stolen by Heoden and pursued by her angry father to an island supposedly either in the North Sea or in the Baltic.[15] Instead of making peace between Heoden and Hagena and their battle-poised armies, Hild falsely tells each general that his enemy will fight to the death. A prominent feature of the legend is a ring that Heoden offers as a bridal price in order to effect the truce, and perhaps Hild originally took offense at the cheap offer. But in the extant versions her treachery goes unexplained, and only redoubles her valkyrie mystery and power. Each night after the fighting she ranges the battlefield and rouses the slain with her magic, so that the warfare over her is forever resumed at daybreak. All the contested details of ll. 14–17 in *Deor* can be read as riddlic traces of this story.

If we may judge from spellings found in Anglo-Saxon law, the word *frige* (l. 15) is a variant plural of *freo* "freeman, soldier."[16] *Geates frige* would refer not to "Geat's love," as it is usually rendered, but rather to "the Jute's (i.e., Hagena's) troops"—a riddlic clue to the armies of the Heodening myth. If l. 14 is understood to name Hild, then MS *þæt mæð* could only designate the neuter OE cognate of OHG *mad*, MHG *mat* "mowing, harvest."[17] Probably, then, the poet intended another skaldic conceit here, this time on mowing. Hild's destructive "harvest" consists not of hay, but of Geat's men, who become *grundlease* "detached from the ground" like hay when it is mown. The metaphor implies a mental picture of Hild gathering up the slain like hay from their resting places. Abruptly shifting his metaphor, however, the poet expresses this reaping, in grammar more like OSax than OE, as "robbing them [i.e., the dead] of their sleep."[18] Behind the shift I suspect some riddlic wordplay, whereby the Anglo-Saxon reader was challenged to leap from *binom* "robbed" (l. 16) to the synonymous *bireafde,* then to an unspoken pun on *ripan* "to reap."

Probably because it was an abduction story belonging to Deor's own people, the *Heodeningas* (l. 36), and therefore closest to the riddlic center of his narrative, this middle stanza was also carefully infused with more riddlic obstacles than any other discrete part of *Deor.* But perhaps there is some even keener craftiness on Deor's part. As in stanza five, where he appears to insinuate that his lord is like Eormanric, so stanza three might attempt to pass blame on a woman who has acted like Hild. For the present, it would be hard to imagine how Deor's rival Heorrenda, or even the wittiest of Norse skalds, could be *leoðcræftigere* (l. 40) than the wily minstrel himself.

Woven among his artful old stories, Deor's real complaint appears to be his best-guarded secret, to be pieced together from what he does not say at least as much as from what he says. Like Weland, he has brooded over an injustice and apparently exacted bloody revenge for it. From stanza two, about Beadohild, we might guess that he has abducted and impregnated a woman, perhaps after also killing someone in her family. In stanza three he refers darkly to the most famous abduction story of his own people, a great mythical drama that he has perhaps hoped to restage. He seems here to have a dual purpose: to glorify his violent deeds while also excusing them as crimes, by the simple device of blaming others for provoking and betraying him. Stanza four suggests that, like Theodoric, he has been exiled. In stanza five he claims to resent his lord as justly as Eormanric's subjects resented their tyrant-king. Matched against the old legend, this last comparison is clearly overblown. Whereas Eormanric was cruel enough to have his own wife drawn apart by horses on mere suspicion of infidelity, Deor's only substantial complaint is that his own lord has seized his wealth and position and given them to another singer. His suffering, then, also falls far short of the imprisonment and maiming that Weland endured; and unlike Theodoric, he has probably caused his own exile. Even his attempt to discredit his rival as *leoðcræftig* seems only to recoil upon himself, for the word shows his own craftiness, especially at self-delusion, but involuntarily praises Heorrenda as "skillful in song." Instead of achieving a fame like Heoden's, he seems to become, like Unferþ in *Beowulf,* a braggart and would-be hero who cannot get his stories straight.

Like all such falseness, Deor's seems to begin in the refusal of wisdom. In ll. 31–34 he remembers, as Boethius also knew all too well, that the favor of this world is changeable. But rather than consolation, Deor's last refrain seems to imply a foolish hope built on the fickleness of princes: as his lord's disfavor came over him, so it can pass, too. In this quite un-Boethian self-deception he shows himself to be both a lesser hero than Heoden and a lesser minstrel than Heorrenda. Worse still, the other meaning of the double-edged refrain—its suggestion of onward movement into the next poem—stands to unmask Deor to the world. With Frankis I believe that *Wulf and Eadwacer* takes up the abducted bride's part of the story. From a love turned to bitterness or even hatred, she looks back to proclaim her unlikeness to Deor, whom she calls *Wulf* either in truth or in riddlic wordplay. *Ungelic(e) is us,* she says: "For us it is unlike." But the unwritten "it" of the OE will also prove to be a riddle that embraces far more than one unlikeness.

Most obviously, perhaps, the foolish braggadocio of *Deor* is unlike the bitter tone of *Wulf and Eadwacer.* Even as the minstrel flatters, excuses, pities, and deludes himself, the woman is contriving grim riddles of her own on his desperate plight. The stark reality is summed up in her final words, which Frankis recognized as a biting turn on the words of the marriage promise. *Uncer giedd geador* "our vow together," the woman declares, was never joined, and *mon eaþe tosliteð* "is easily rent asunder." Her use of *toslitan* "to rend, tear, or bite to pieces" extends a dominant theme of wolfish rapacity in the poem. With the entire thought the sense of her earlier lines agrees: their marriage in the wilderness has been only a precarious togetherness, full of pain and weeping and long periods of separation, and now subject to a violent end. This dramatic disparity between Deor's and the woman's tone also seems to have a technical cause, which the poet has hidden in the ambiguous word *giedd.* Besides, "vow, formal speech," *giedd* also means "song, poem," and thus carries the innuendo of two songs—that is, *Deor* and *Wulf and Eadwacer*—whose marriage has been an uneasy one at best. By inference the two poems themselves make a strange and unlikely pair, perhaps a union of heroic and elegiac song. No one, it seems, had ever joined them, until their tenuous partnership was made with a riddler's wit. Thus, I think, the woman's last lines twist the meaning of the unlikeness which she has already twice asserted in her refrain.

In the story created by the dual texts she is unlike Wulf, or Deor-Wulf, first because of her knowledge of his peril. Her song closes with a chilling hint of "easy" (*eaþe,* l. 18) separation by bestial violence, an echo of the explicit theme in the opening lines. In the puzzling first line she appears to see him as an easy victim of *leodum . . . minum,* that is, of members of her own family or clan. In this context the word *lac* most probably suggests that Wulf is an imminent "sacrifice."[19] The resulting image would be as skaldic as the conceits of *Deor,* since it calls to mind the heathen sacrifices of wolves and men together that so repulsed Adam of Bremen on his visit to the sacred groves of Old Uppsala. But far less remotely, I think, the line makes an ironic skaldic hit at Deor-Wulf, who cannot see for himself how much he resembles the impotent victims of Hild. The next line, which assumes special urgency as part of the refrain, also hints that Wulf's enemies have the advantage of surprise. The unique word *apecgan* probably adds some trenchant irony of its own. With its perfective prefix, its causative relationship to *picgan* "to consume food or drink," and its resemblance to the words *gepecgan* "to be consumed (by thirst)" and *ofpecgan* "to be slain (by the sword)." *apecgan* seems to mean not merely "kill," but "consume completely," or, in the context of word-play on *Wulf,* "eat up."[20] Taking *preat* to mean "troop, crowd (? of wolves)," I think l. 2 forebodes tragedy with a tinge of black humor: "They'll eat him up if he comes to the pack." While Deor absurdly hopes for reconciliation with his estranged lord, the woman sees her Wulf in danger of being chewed up himself. In the next line she might even be gloating a bit to be "unlike" him.

Wulf's bride sees his military situation, which is the riddlic matter of the next few lines, from a safe distance, for they are separated from one another on two islands. In l. 5 the woman knows that Wulf's island is *fæst* and *fenne biworpen,* "fast" and "surrounded by fen." Judging from the theme of impending slaughter in l. 1, however, *fæst* is probably a riddlic word, not "secure," as it is usually understood, but rather "made fast," sealed off against Wulf's escape. A picture then emerges of a man surrounded, caught between impassable marshes and men who are *wælreowe* (l. 6), perhaps not so much bloodthirsty in general as "eager for blood," specifically Wulf's. They now appear to be her own angry people, with whom she abruptly began her song. From all the riddlic clues the drama in the first lines of the poem seems clear: Wulf's angry pursuers have "unjoined" the lovers on two islands, stealthily encircled the unwatchful Wulf on one of them, and need only to play the waiting game to make their easy kill. Joined together with *Deor,* the situation so far would be full of ironic un-likenesses: Deor sings of Weland's imprisonment but seems not to know of his own entrapment; he thinks in terms of deeds known to many, yet he seems to be outnumbered and even alone. His predicament is not heroic, but miserable and desperate; and the woman's knowledge, compared with his ignorance, is terrible indeed.

The bride's suffering, as unlike Deor-Wulf's as Beadohild's misery was unlike Weland's, is recounted in the past tense in *Wulf and Eadwacer* 9–15. In some part her superior knowledge of the threat against her abductor proceeds from the very nature of a woman's lament, which can complain of suffering without heroic delusions—without, say, the Wanderer's fleeting impulse to keep his heroic silence (*Wanderer* 11b–14). In this middle passage the speaker recalls her exile with Wulf in the elegiac manner, with images of sadness in which even the "rainy weather" cooperates (l. 10), loneliness and sickness and uncertainty of Wulf's "rare visits" to her in the wilderness (ll. 13–15a), and her agony of joy and loathing at his rough embraces (ll. 11–12). *Nales meteliste* "no lack of meat at all" (l. 15b) at first suggests that her anguish has been psychological rather than physical, and seems to commend her abductor as a good forager and hunter, like his namesake the wolf. But I think the verse is really an indelicate riddle on her final parallel with Beadohild: from the carnal union with Wulf she still has "no lack of meat," for she now hides a *hwelp* in her womb and between the lines of her song. The faint sarcasm of a riddlic likeness to Beadohild would in some measure belie her elegiac voice.

If Wulf's bride could thus be closing her memories on a false note, it would especially behoove us to know how her sad reverie begins. But l.9 is arguably the most difficult of the entire poem, since its preterit verb *dogode* is a hapax legomenon of uncertain meaning. It is sometimes identified with OSax *adogian*, unfortunately also a hapax, which seems in its only recorded instance to mean "endure." The woman would then be saying *Wulfes ic mines widlastum . . . dogode* "I endured my Wulf's tracks of exile," an illogical way of introducing her own wandering unless she is purposely speaking in a riddle. Moreover, even in a poem of such unusual verse as *Wulf and Eadwacer*, the rare but regular b-verse of a short stem vowel *dogode* appears to eclipse the otherwise unknown versification that *dōgode*, from OE *(a-)dōgian*, would require. From the pervasive wordplay on *Wulf*, a *hwelp*, and carnivorous activity such as devouring, tearing, and carrying off meat, I think the disputed word is *dogode*, the preterit of OE *dogian* "to dog," with dative object grammar like its probable synonym *folgian* "to follow." The noun *docga* "dog" occurs only once in OE, as a gloss for L *canis* in a figure of speech about just such cruel and rapacious men as Wulf and his wolfish attackers.[21] From the noun, probably a pejorative word, the riddling poet of *Wulf and Eadwacer* might even have invented his verb. The inconsistent medial consonant of *docga/dogode* might derive from a Celtic origin, as parallel spellings of early ME *hocge, hoge* "hog," a confirmed Celtic loanword, would seem to attest.[22] The whole of l. 9 thus appears to say that the woman "dogged" Wulf's tracks in exile *wenum* "with thought," that is, deliberately or voluntarily. Her words suggest elopement, the typical behavior of women in Germanic abduction stories; yet in l. 11 her use of animal imagery hints of forcible rape.[23] Given the relative powerlessness of Germanic women even in the late times of codified law, we cannot presume that women's elopements were not also brutally forced; indeed, they probably often were.[24] But in *Wulf and Eadwacer* the speaker uses the word *wenum*, a hint of acquiescence, at least, in her own exile. She cries out *Wulf, min Wulf,* as to a lover whose long absences made her sick; and she remembers their life in exile as a time of mixed joy and pain. In a plain word, her argument somehow does not add up.

As before, this imbalance of theme in *Wulf and Eadwacer* should perhaps be weighed against some unresolved innuendo in *Deor*. One such possibility remains: the minstrel's elusive suggestion, near the heart of his scheme, of yet another woman as treacherous and ferocious as Hild. As with the Weland and Beadohild stories, the Hild stanza of *Deor* seems to answer a veiled duplicity in the lament of Wulf's captive bride. The duality is already reflected in the intuition of those many scholars who agree to name the poem *Wulf and Eadwacer* because it seems to address two different men. The two islands of l. 4 are a likely riddlic clue that *Wulf* and *eadwacer* are not the same person, and that the last lines of the poem, beginning with *Gehyrest þu, eadwacer?* (l. 16a), are not spoken to Wulf, who appears in third person in l. 17. I think they are said to one of the speaker's angry clan, someone called *wælreowe* in the earlier lines. The word *eadwacer* "wealth-watcher" seems to me to be a sarcastic epithet, immediately reversed by a reminder of the stolen *ear[m]ne hwelp* "poor whelp" who stands to disgrace the family. Her last lines would then incite *eadwacer* to make quick work of Wulf and of her own nonmarriage—in other words, to take the gift of easy slaughter depicted in her opening line. Pursued and caught by her vengeful family, she seems now to turn on Deor-Wulf with the treachery of Hild and the ferocity of Norse saga heroines who urge their menfolk on to bloody revenge. Small clues of her two-facedness even seem to occupy her refrain. The pronoun *us* in *ungelic is us* (l. 3) seems to designate Wulf and the bride herself: "For us [Wulf and me] it is unlike," the woman's arrogant presumption of her own safety. Even more vague and uncertain, the grammar of *ungelice is us* (l. 7) hints at plurality and perhaps a hidden shift of reference: "For us [*eadwacer* and me] the situation is unlike [all of Wulf's dangers]." Similarly, the woman would abandon her false outcry to Wulf (ll. 13–15) in order to divert *eadwacer*'s lust for vengeance from herself. The small and perhaps secret variation in her refrain should therefore be given in translation: "our outlook's unlike" (1. 3); "our outlook's not like this" (l. 7). Her entire song as I read it would be cunning indeed, much like the poem of the shifty minstrel whom she professes to be "unlike." But her riddle is even harder than Deor's, perhaps because she is even more ominously *leoðcræftig* than he.

Deor and *Wulf and Eadwacer* together appear to hide not one but four *leoðcræftige* singers: Heorrenda, the minstrel who calls himself Deor, the woman who calls him Wulf, but most of all the riddler who has joined these two unjoinable poems. The heroic source of his double riddle, for example, might seem hopelessly well-concealed; indeed, his confession that his song "was never joined" might mean that he composed his story himself from stereotypical features of good tales of abduction. But the skaldic touches in both poems suggest that he borrowed or even translated snatches of a known heroic story and "joined" them into a new form. The names *Heodeninga* and *Heorrenda*, which Deor connects intimately with himself, also imply that the riddler had a particular heroic story in mind. Deor's rival Heorrenda is almost certainly Horant, the skillful singer of the MHG poem *Kudrun*. Were it not so loaded with self-pity, Deor's word *leoðcræftig* would describe Horant perfectly. He comes as a stranger to Hagen's kingdom, enters the conspiracy to steal Hilde, and distracts the king from the plot with wonderful music. Charmed into carelessness, the fierce old king gives Horant rich gifts and a distinguished vassalage, perhaps the same *folgað tilne* "high office" and *londryht* which Deor complains of losing.[25] Although the Kudrun poet does not say that Hagen dismisses his own singer to make room for Horant, a gulled king as in *Kudrun* could perhaps be the missing motive for Deor's complaint and revenge. Possibly the poet of *Deor* and *Wulf and Eadwacer* used an otherwise unpreserved tale of Hagen's cheated minstrel, who bitterly resented Horant's success but hoped it would not last. Later events in *Kudrun* prove Horant's luck to be fleeting.

Although they were composed as much as three-and-a-half centuries apart, the English *Deor* and the German *Kudrun* might confirm one another even beyond their coincidence of names. In *Kudrun*, Hagen himself is carried off in infancy by an eagle that sets him down in the foreign kingdom he will grow up to rule. His tyrannical rule then generates two abductions, Hilde's and Kudrun's, from his own family. The eagle episode therefore seems to name abduction as the perpetual evil of Hagen's house. In Scandinavia his legendary inheritance was not an endless series of abductions, but a single abduction resulting in eternal strife. Deor alludes to this famous Northern version in stanza three, but in essence the clues of his own story markedly resemble the second abduction in *Kudrun*. He compares his

lord, who might be Hagen of the Heodenings, to the tyrant Eormanric; but to the embittered woman of *Wulf and Eadwacer,* who
seems to correspond partly to Kudrun, this bungling minstrel must
pay the whole debt of their failure together. Just as Deor proudly
links himself to the Heodenings and to the legend of Hild, so his bride
appears to borrow her lethal rhetoric from the Heodening cycle. She
pictures him as a cornered wolf, brought to bay on one of two islands,
whose memory the Kudrun poet might have preserved as two
names—*Wülpensand* and *Wülpenwert*—for the spot where the great
battle over Kudrun takes place. Furthermore, a woman of wolfish
mind occupies all three of our stories. In the Northern version the
rapacious woman is Hild, as Deor also knows. In *Kudrun,* Gerlind, the
mother of Hartmut, Kudrun's abductor, is several times called *die
wülpinne:* her prototype might originally have spoken those last savage and sarcastic taunts to a husband whom she calls *eadwacer.* In that
case the English riddler would have "joined" the speech of two different women into a single treacherous personality, for reasons that
emerge only after some reflection on *The Soul's Address.* This composite speaker of *Wulf and Eadwacer,* whom I would count among the
things that "never were joined," seems to taunt *eadwacer* and tease the
reader with a sly allusion to the greatness of Hagen: this time not an
eagle, but a mere skulking wolf, carries an infant away. A modern
reading of MS *earne hwelp* (*Wulf and Eadwacer* 16) as "eagle's hwelp"
might thus come very near the riddlic truth—a clumsy pun, I would
guess, on *earne* and *ear*[*m*]*ne* as a clue to the poet's source.[26] By riddlic
logic the speaker of *Wulf and Eadwacer,* assembled from prototypes of
Kudrun and Gerlind, would have been conceived to act with the
wylfenne geþoht of yet another Hild. I suspect that we have failed to
discover the names *Deor, Wulf,* and *Eadwacer* in known heroic sources
for the best of reasons: they simply are not there. To my mind our
riddler, like the shifty Deor himself, was partly retelling, partly in-
venting a heroic story from an eternal wellspring, the endless rapes of
the Heodenings. With his scrupulous logic, the riddler appears to me
to have understood his eternal source as the mother of his own invention. In this way his choice of heroic matter would have become the
grand clue to his method.

II. *The Spiritual Vision*

The riddler's method in *Deor* and *Wulf and Eadwacer* gives no visible
hint of his purpose. To turn the feats of old heroes into the invented
foolishness of invented imitators would be contagious madness unless
it had a point. To discover that point, I think, we must now look

backward in the Exeter Book, from the cross-textual punning on *deor, wulf, wylfenne geþoht,* and vicious bestiality of *Deor* and *Wulf and Eadwacer* to more of the same talk in the longer poem just before. Since it is not completely a soul-and-body poem, I prefer to call it *The Soul's Address.*

Unlike either *Deor* or *Wulf and Eadwacer, The Soul's Address* has no signs of double-talk or playfulness, and none of the more obvious devices of riddling. Its tone is serious, its ostensible purpose didactic, its main concern the relationship of body and soul. It is not a debate, for the soul rants after death at a vacant body that endures the abuse in silence. The main dramatic interest of the poem comes from the soul's monologue of eighty lines; yet the poem is not exactly a dramatic monologue, either. The soul's speech comes between sixteen introductory lines of grim warning and twenty-five closing lines of macabre graveyard imagery. The exordium is in a sense conventionally didactic, a moralizing plea in the third person for spiritual reflection in this life, before death comes. After death it will be too late to examine the state of the soul, whose reward will then be *swa wite swa wuldor* "either torment or glory," precisely according to what it has wrought in mortal life (ll. 7b–8). The poet speaks of eternity in threatening understatement: *Long bið siþþan* "It will be a long time after [death]" that the spirit receives its due from God Himself. Several lines (9–14) then paint dreadful images of the soul *gehþum hremig* "clamoring for relief." After seven nights' journey beyond death it will find the body, *butan ær wyrce ece Dryhten, ælmihtig God, ende worlde* "unless the eternal Lord, God almighty, should first bring about the end of the world." Thus the poet subordinates the theme of the imminent apocalypse, as if perhaps he were merely satisfying a convention of didactic poetry. Finally, the Exeter Book does not contain the fullest version of *The Soul's Address.* The same poem, despite numerous lexical and dialectal variations, appears with forty-four additional lines in the Vercelli Book. Outwardly, then, the Exeter Book text of this rather dry poem has comparatively little merit of its own. Expediently, if not justly, scholars have not given it very much separate attention.

The vocabulary of the opening lines, however, suggests that perhaps *The Soul's Address* should not be considered alone at all. The poet begins by urging *hæleþa æghwylc* "every man," with perhaps a play on "every hero," to prepare himself for the moment *þonne se deað cymeð* "when death will come." Death *asundrað þa sibbe, þa þe ær somud wæron, lic ond sawle* "will put asunder those kinsmen who before were joined, body and soul." The lexical parallels to *Wulf and Eadwacer* are striking enough to suggest thematic correspondences as well: death will come unexpected, even more surely than to the unwatchful Wulf *gif he on þreat cymeð* "if he comes upon the pack." It will sunder body from soul just as Wulf and his bride, who are *sib* in conjugal flesh, are separated on two islands and by the looming threat of the minstrel's death. Besides these smaller coincidences of word and theme, a touch of the same falsity and self-delusion found in *Deor* and *Wulf and Eadwacer* appears even before the soul begins its address. In a passing subordinate clause, the poet declares that the soul will again encounter the body *þa heo ær longe wæg* "which it once moved for a long time." These words appear to make the soul the governing principle that drives the body about in this life. The soul therefore ought to be mainly responsible for earthly conduct; yet it addresses the body with *cealdan reorde* "cold speech" (l. 15b). It calls out *grimlice* "grimly" to the flesh, *swa cearful* "as follows, filled with grief":

> Hwæt drug þu, dreorga?   To hwon dreahtest þu me,
> . . . lames gelicnes?   Lyt þu geþohtes
> to won þinre sawle sið   siþþan wurde,
> siþþan heo of lichoman   læded wære!
> Hwæt, wite þu me, werga!

> (Villain, what have you done? Why have you vexed me,
> . . . you clump like clay? Little you thought
> about what the state of your soul would become
> after it should be freed from the flesh!
> How you do worry me, you blasted wolf!)

> (ll. 17–22)

Unaware that the poet of the exordium has already stolen such thunder, the soul violently denies its spiritual custody and heaps names and dire accusations upon the body instead. As the governing creature whom the body could only follow through life, the soul inescapably curses itself even with its opening words. During the rest of its speech it tries mightily to escape, mentioning itself sometimes in the first person, other times in the third, writhing to avoid its own part in the blame. Its rhetorical antics broadly resemble the shifting pronouns and double-dealing argument of *Wulf and Eadwacer*. In the end, however, the soul is caught in its own guilt and snatched away to *secan helle grund* "seek the bottom of hell" (l. 98a), for its belated and false complaint does not divert the awful scrutiny of God.

The final forty-four lines of the Vercelli Book text show *se halga sawl* as it comforts the worm-riddled body with assurances of their glorious reunion. The Exeter Book *Soul's Address* does not include these lines. The great irony of the shorter version is that the soul speaks only for and to itself. Death has struck the body deaf and dumb; it cannot answer the soul's insults, accusations, or threats of damnation. Rave or dissemble as it will, the soul must encounter even with its rhetoric the spiritual facts of its own falseness and punishment. With tricky logic it tricks itself. Its reasoning crumbles, for example, just before it departs to hell (ll. 93b–96), where it addresses the body as *þu* but simultaneously lapses into dual pronouns. The argument is a classic study in duplicity:

> Ac hwæt do wit unc
> þonne he unc hafað geedbyrded   oþre siþe?
> Sculon wit þonne ætsomne   siþþan brucan
> swylcra yrmþa   swa þu unc ær scrife?

> (But what shall we do with ourselves
> when He has begotten us yet once again?
> Shall we then bear together just such torments
> as you would ordain for us?)

These hostile words are the soul's last. By l. 99a it is out of sight and mind, gone to seek the pit of hell. At l. 99b the poet turns to the earthly grave, where the helpless body lies in a different state. Here, then, the separate natures of body and soul implicitly belie the soul's parting thoughts.

Though the onslaught of the worms is luridly described, the corpse cannot feel its horrors, which will end when the greedy worms have divided and eaten it. The soul, on the other hand, will know its own agony forever. Thus the body's demolition by worms and the soul's punishment in hell are different in every way. In the soul's insulting words the body is *lames gelicnes* "the likeness of clay," an inferior being worthy only of contempt. Yet as the soul is the far higher creature, so the poet is silent about its inexpressible torments: *swa wite swa wuldor,* as he has said. Fear and awe of this indescribable punishment, the main dramatic effect of *The Soul's Address,* can only be suggested by fear and awe of the describable. In his own final words, therefore, the poet gives his gruesome meditations on the mortal flesh over to *men modsnotterra* "men of wiser mind," who will perceive his implied lesson. *The Soul's Address* most truly concerns the disaster of the soul that squanders its earthly life.

In *Deor* and *Wulf and Eadwacer* the minstrel and his bride face an analogous disaster. Deor does not seem to know the real danger, but the woman who has accompanied him now laments bitterly her chosen life of fear and pain. Suddenly their union was never really joined, and she and Deor-Wulf are as different as soul from body:

ungelic is us. Her argument, that she only "dogged" the wolf who carried off their whelp, is internally false, like the soul's attempt to blame the body for their tragedy. The woman's invective and the soul's name-calling are much alike: OE *wearg, werg,* the soul's bad name for the body in l. 16, means both "outlaw" and "wolf."[27] An anticipation of wordplay also occurs at *The Soul's Address* 77–78a, where the soul says that the body should far rather have been created *on westenne wildra deora þæt grimmeste* "the grimmest of wild beasts in the wilderness" than ever to have become a baptized man. The imagery of wolves and beasts, beginning with *werga/deora* in *The Soul's Address,* extends to *deor/wylfenne* in *Deor,* and culminates in the many resounding plays on *Wulf* and the frequent preying, rending, and eating in *Wulf and Eadwacer.* In *Deor* and *Wulf and Eadwacer* the would-be hero is exposed as the skulking outlaw-beast of the wood, and as the sacrificial criminal, both human and animal, of the pagan North. In the contrasting "English" poetry of *The Soul's Address,* the soul has outlawed itself from the spiritual heroism into which it was baptized. All of these analogies are signs of riddlic *orþoncbendum* which bind together *The Soul's Address, Deor,* and *Wulf and Eadwacer* into a secret poem of 182 lines.

The explicit idea of *orþoncbend,* which loosely means a secret connection, comes from the joined Riddles 42/43, which closely resemble our longer triple riddle in many ways. In only thirty-two lines the double riddle transforms the farmyard cock and hen into the body and soul as traveling companions through mortal life. In the threefold riddle, the earthly life is also a pilgrimage jointly undertaken by flesh and spirit, as the soul's arguments often imply and the woman in *Wulf and Eadwacer* obscurely states when she recalls following Wulf into exile. In Riddle 43 the soul and body travel as a noble guest and its lower *esne* "fellow," enclosed together *in geardum,* that is, in the figurative "yard" of Man. Together they can find bliss among numberless kindred in their home—that is, the angels and saints; or else they can find *care, gif se esne his hlaford hyreð yfle, frean on fore* "sorrow, if the fellow serves his lord evilly, his master on the journey" (ll. 8b–10a). Neither *The Soul's Address* nor Riddle 43 leaves any doubt about who must lead and who must serve. By comparison with Riddle 43, *The Soul's Address* seems grim and gloomy because it warns relentlessly against the evil journey but says little of the happier one. Yet the good journey is at least implied at the beginning and end of *The Soul's Address,* too. The poem begins *Huru, þæs behofaþ hæleþa æghwylc* "Indeed, every man truly needs" to examine deeply the state of his soul before death. By such reflection, every man can join the fraternity of *men modsnotterra* "men of wiser mind" in the last verses. They are, by implicit contrast with the fallen soul, the spiritual heroes in the poet's scheme. It is they who can guide the riddle-solver on his own journey. But the thoughtless soul that casts away its own redemption will endure worse torment than the worm-ravaged body, and worse pain and anguish than the false heroes of pagan legend.

The estranged body and soul in *The Soul's Address* and the "unlike" hero and heroine of *Deor* and *Wulf and Eadwacer* have similar miseries, described with the same themes or even in the same words. In *Wulf and Eadwacer* the speaker knows Wulf's enemies as *wælreowe* "eager for blood." They will eat Wulf alive, as the ironic refrain-word *apecgan* tells. The bestial innuendo of *toslited* (l. 18) reveals their intention to separate the lovers with wolfish savagery. In *The Soul's Address* this same word +*slitan* tells how grim and greedy beasts, here worms rather than wolves, will rend the dead body: *beslitan seonwum*, l. 57a; *seonowum beslitan*, l. 68a; *goman toslitene, seonwe beod asogene . . .* , ll. 104-5a. OE *asogene* "sucked dry, consumed" uses the same prefix as *apecgan* in *Wulf and Eadwacer,* and has virtually the same thematic effect. The grisly insistence on parted sinews corresponds with Weland's riddlic *seonobende*, that is, his severed hamstrings, in the gory first stanza of *Deor.*

Like Weland and the other heroes and heroines of Deor's old stories, and also like Wulf and his bride, the soul suffers both exile and imprisonment. Like the minstrel and the woman, too, it blames all its trouble on someone else. In various language all three poems seize on the themes of chains, hunger and thirst, and the captivity that brings such torments. The soul complains of being "knotted with hunger and shut in with the torments of hell" by the tyrannical body: *þu me . . . hungre gebunde ond gehæftnadest helle witum.* In ll. 36–38 the body is accused of being *wines sæd* "sated with wine," so that the soul *ofþyrsted wæs Godes lichoman, gæstes drinces* "consumed by thirst for God's body, the spirit's drink." But this charge is as false as Wulf's bride's efforts to blame him for a disastrous journey, which, as she admits, she freely undertook. Her confession that she was *nales meteliste* "not meatless at all" seems to be a bitter jest on coition and pregnancy in *Wulf and Eadwacer;* but in the larger riddle it also shatters the soul's flimsy alibis about spiritual thirst and starvation. Thus the soul, like the woman, speaks with cunning falsehood. Its adversary the body, if it could speak, might bring even more plainly ridiculous charges, like Deor's, against its lord. The riddler, however, does not need to exhaust this analogy, which demonstrates fallen human nature clearly enough as it is. The reader's imagination is wisely left to finish the job.

Although it might have been borrowed wholesale, or nearly so, to fit the riddler's plan, the matter of *Deor* and *Wulf and Eadwacer* was also picked for its insistence on the violence, agony, and sorrow of enslaved heroes. The tyrants Niðhad and Eormanric once bound their prisoners in woe and torment (*on nede legde, seonobende,* [*Deor* 4–5]; *sorgum gebunden,* [*Deor* 24]). Weland knew *sorge ond longaþ* and the miseries that belong to elegiac winter, *wintercealde wræce;* and the love of Hild and Heoden turned to *sorglufu* "sorrowful love." Deor himself seems oblivious to all the sorrow in the tales he has chosen; but of his own sorrow he sounds a bit more evasive, preferring to say that "one" *siteð sorgcearig, sælum bidæled* "sits in sorrow, cut off from the good times." There is a hint here of the soul's wily but illogical third-person reference to itself as *þin* (i.e., the body's) *sawl* (*The Soul's Address* 57). When the minstrel finally speaks in the first person (*Deor* 35ff.), he shows ignorance of the nonsense in his own complaint. It takes the woman, whose blindness seems more willful than Deor's, to show in spite of herself how closely their *renig weder* matches Weland's wintry torments, or how their *widlast* answers to Theodoric's "fortress" built only of meadow-flowers. As it reviles the body, the hypocritical soul pretends that its rightful submission to the flesh has ended in the "sorrow" so often found in *Deor*. It declares itself *synnum gesargad* "saddened by [the body's] sins" (ll. 61–62); and its taunt *ne sindon þine dreamas wiht* "your joys are not worth a thing" (l. 60) helps to confirm the irony of *Wulf and Eadwacer* 12: *wæs me wyn to þon, wæs me hwæþre eac lað* "it was thus far my pleasure, that it still was my pain." Like the woman, too, the soul feigns a longstanding wish for deliverance from its captor: *Hwæt ic uncres gedales gebad* "How I've longed for our separation" (l. 34). But like the earthly antagonists in the following two poems, the soul may dodge the blame as it will; it can escape neither its own guilt nor its terrible doom.

When it stops speaking, the soul is perched on the brink of hell, from which, as the poet now teaches, it *sceal . . . secan helle grund, nales heofondreamas, dædum gedrefed* "must seek the bottom of hell, not the least joy of heaven, vexed by its own deeds" (ll. 97–99a). Its lot is eternal banishment to *helle grund,* as shelterless at Theodoric's absent stronghold and as *grundleas* as the eternal victims of Hild's anger. The pit of hell and the earthly bed of worms now become the two loci for the unhappily parted soul and body, just as in *Wulf and Eadwacer* the doomed lovers are trapped on separate islands. Like the misguided minstrel and even more like his bride, the dissembling soul tries to glorify and excuse itself all at once *þonne se deað cymeð* "when death comes." But the intrigue of all three poems only ends in self-mockery and destruction. Like *Deor*, who hopes that his exile will end like Theodoric's, after *þritig wintra*, the soul has let itself be fooled by time: *Ðæt me þuhte ful oft þæt wære þritig þusend wintra to þinum deaðdæge* "time after time I thought it to be thirty thousand winters until your death-day."

From all these and many more analogies of word and theme grows an enormous riddlic comparison of wasted spiritual and heroic life. The final forty-four lines of the longer Vercelli Book *Soul's Address*, a portrait of *se halga sawl*, were almost certainly left out of the Exeter Book so that only a vision of fire and brimstone would remain. The Vercelli Book *Soul's Address* thus helps to confirm the riddler's description of his own method—not so much original writing as astonishingly clever joining of what had never before been joined. *Deor* and *Wulf and Eadwacer,* with their strong Scandinavian affinities, might have been borrowed and reworked into riddling at a time and place of uncommon access to Danish heroic poetry, and of especially bitter memory of Danish adventurism in England. Late ninth- or early tenth-century East Anglia would fit these hypothetical conditions especially well; and the words *fenne biworpen* "surrounded by fen" (*Wulf and Eadwacer* 5) might have been either a happy coincidence or a deliberate East Anglian touch. The viking raids and settlements there could have lent some personal conviction to the riddler's wit and made his tandem riddling a genuine object lesson on the contemplative hero.[28]

By general scholarly agreement, however, the Exeter Book was copied in southwest England in the late tenth century, quite far in place and time from postviking East Anglia. The visible meeting of minds between the poet, whoever and wherever he was, and the Exeter Book scribe are therefore rather remarkable—no less so if, as was probably the case, the scribe was merely copying the riddles from another MS that has been lost. The tandem riddles of the Exeter Book, such as the continuous "body-and-soul" Riddles 42/43 with their slight division in mid-line, show tantalizing signs of the scribe's complicity in, or at least faithfulness to, their game. Although the juncture of Riddles 42/43 has been called a mistake, it can also be defended as scribal response to the *orponcbendum*, or secret word-linkages, in the two texts.[29] Similarly, I think, the closing theme of *Wulf and Eadwacer,* the unlikely song that never was joined, reverberates all the way back to the boldly inscribed opening of *The Soul's*

Address. Several intermediate places, too, seem to witness the scribe's graphic cooperation in the design.

After the last word of *Physiologus*, on fol. 98a, comes a bold notation in minuscule: *FINIT,* the only instance of the word in the Exeter Book. A ruled MS line was then skipped to leave room for a large and sweeping initial *H,* gracefully if sparely ornamented, of about the same size and decoration as the *W* that begins *Deor* two folio pages later. Then the first on-verse of *The Soul's Address,* [*H*]*uru þæs behofaþ,* takes up the entire MS line in serifed block capitals more than twice the height of normal script. This ornament, together with the unique occurrence of *FINIT,* makes fol. 98a the last and most important of nine major textual divisions in the Exeter Book. Of the six initial capitals for the stanzas of *Deor,* four, including the large *W* of the Weland stanza and the smaller, less elaborate capitals of the Hild, Theodoric, and Eormanric stanzas, are at least modestly decorated; but the capitals of the Beadohild and Deor stanzas are somewhat smaller and noticeably plainer. The initial *L* of *Wulf and Eadwacer,* which follows the last refrain of *Deor* without noticeable extra spacing, is bold and plain, like the *B* of the Beadohild stanza and the capital *S* of the *Deor* stanza, but rather larger. With the riddlic connections of the three poems known, or at least suspected, these letters suggest a riddlic hierarchy of their own.

The plain *B* of *Beadohilde* and the somewhat larger plain *L* of *Wulf and Eadwacer* appear to subordinate the abducted bride's poem to Deor's song much as Beadohild's story ranks below Weland's. In terms of graphic proportion, then, Weland: Beadohild = Deor: Deor's (Wulf's) bride. For Deor's own lament, however, a distinct section of his song, the graphic proportion seems to have been reversed: the *L* of *Wulf and Eadwacer* is conspicuously larger than the *S* of *Deor* 28. If the reversal was intended, it would also follow the major irony of the themes. Not only is the woman a more *leoðcræftig* liar than Deor, but her inadvertent truth also furnishes more important clues of her hidden abduction than any of Deor's heroic fabrications. On the grand scale, the decorative beginnings of *The Soul's Address, Deor,* and *Wulf and Eadwacer* subtly descend in their size and importance: the first two poems have almost equal initial capitals, but *The Soul's Address* outdoes *Deor* with an entire first MS line of block capitals. The *L* of *Wulf and Eadwacer* is smaller than the initial *W* of *Deor,* and it is very plain; but it is also considerably bigger than the initials of the other five *Deor* stanzas.

In case his readers still might not see how the letters work, the scribe has entered one more strange and conspicuous graphic clue. In the left margin of *Deor,* opposite the modestly decorated initials of the heathen stories of Hild, Theodoric, and Eormanric, he has drawn small bold serifed crosses, which imply a further riddle of some sort. Whether they are supposed to match what might be three small crosses in both the initial *H* of *The Soul's Address* and the initial *W* of *Deor* I cannot tell. Nor am I sure how three crosses would fit the three pagan legends, besides marking the three poems of the riddlic sequence. Coincidentally or not, the Hild, Theodoric, and Eormanric Stanzas feature the three major themes of abduction, exile, and sorrow that shape the whole scheme. Or perhaps the scribe's crosses mark the three kinds of poetry—didactic, heroic, and elegiac—of which the unlikely threefold riddle was joined. Stanzas one and two of Deor, on Weland and Beadohild, the scribe did not sign with crosses, even though he had ample room. Like the carefully proportioned initials of these stanzas, the absence of crosses perhaps insinuates the male-female affiliation that also marries *Wulf and Eadwacer* into the riddlic sequence. If I am right about these signs, the Exeter Book scribe might well have smiled as he finished his elaborately interlocked tricks for the mind and eye.

For all these reasons, thematic and graphic, I suggest that the Exeter Book riddles really begin at *The Soul's Address* on fol. 98a. Taken all together, *The Soul's Address, Deor,* and *Wulf and Eadwacer* seem to make up a riddlic pilgrimage of their own, through the *visibilia* of wasted lives in this world to the *invisibilia* of eternal grief in the next. As separate works they seem uninteresting, fragmentary, or obscure; but when they are joined according to their many clues they lead down a remarkable hidden path of contemplative discovery. In my own thinking they comprise Riddle 1, though perhaps their traditional and quite accurate separate names should also be kept as subtitles.[30]

In fairness, and to guard against any smug smiles of my own, I must return to one last faint sign in the MS. This is an unserifed cross, drawn in pencil in a modern hand, to the right of the bold word *behofaþ, The Soul's Address* 1, fol. 98a. Possibly it is one of the less famous pencil marks of the "mighty scholar" George Hickes, made in Queen Anne's time to guide his remarkable copyist to chosen passages of the Exeter Book.[31] Could Hickes, or someone after him, have responded in kind to the scribe's three crosses in the margin of *Deor,* and thus blazed my trail? It is at once humbling and exciting to dog that trail to the end, there to confront the possibility of a silent and long-forgotten predecessor.

NOTES

1. See John F. Adams, "'Wulf and Eadwacer': An Interpretation," *MLN* 73 (1958):5; and Joseph Bosworth, *An Anglo-Saxon Dictionary*, ed. T. Northcote Toller (Oxford: Clarendon, 1898), under *eadwacer* "watcher of property." This dictionary is hereafter cited as "Bosworth-Toller."

2. For a sampling of the diverse opinions on the theme, genre, tone, and number of male figures in the poem, see Adams, "'Wulf and Eadwacer': An Interpretation," pp. 1–5; Gustav Budjuhn, "Leodum is minum—ein ae. Dialog," *Anglia* 40 (1916):256–59; Alain Renoir, "'Wulf and Eadwacer': A Non-interpretation," in *Franciplegius: Medieval and Linguistic Studies in Honor of Francis Peabody Magoun*, ed. Jess B. Bessinger, Jr., and Robert P. Creed (New York: New York University Press, 1965), pp. 147–63; Neil D. Isaacs, *Structural Principles in Old English Poetry* (Knoxville: University of Tennessee Press, 1968), pp. 114–17; A. C. Bouman, *Patterns in Old English and Old Icelandic Literature*, Leidse Germanistische en Anglistische Reeks (Leiden: Universitaire Pers, 1962), 1:95–106; Norman E. Eliason, "On Wulf and Eadwacer," in *Old English Studies in Honour of John C. Pope*, ed. Robert B. Burlin and Edward B. Irving, Jr. (Toronto: University of Toronto Press, 1974), pp. 225–34; Donald K. Fry, "Wulf and Eadwacer: A Wen Charm," *Chaucer Review* 5 (1970):247–63; Emily Doris Grubl, *Studien zu den angelsächsischen Elegien* (Marburg a. d. Lahn: Elwert-Gräfe u. Unzer, 1948), pp. 163–67; 174–75; Charles W. Kennedy, *The Earliest English Poetry* (New York: Oxford University Press, 1943), pp. 48–52.

3. The view of *Wulf and Eadwacer* as an elegy descends mainly from the opinions of Henry Bradley, review of Morley, *English Writers, II*, in *Academy* 33 (1888):197–98; and Levin L. Schücking, *Kleines angelsächsisches Dichterbuch* (Cöthen: Otto Schulze, 1919), pp. 16–19. Identifications of *Wulf and Eadwacer* with various heroic legends or poems stem from Schücking, *Dichterbuch;* W. H. Schofield, "Signy's Lament," *PMLA* 17 (1902):262–95; and Rudolf Imelmann's four books: *Die altenglische Odoaker-Dichtung* (Berlin, 1907); *Zeugnisse zur altenglischen Odoaker-Dichtung* (Berlin, 1907); *Wanderer und Seefahrer im Rahmen der altenglischen Odoaker-Dichtung* (Berlin, 1908); and the best-known, *Forschungen zur altenglischen Poesie* (Berlin: bie der Weidmannschen Buchhandlung, 1920). The possibility that *Wulf and Eadwacer* might be an elegiac set-piece from a heroic poem or cycle first arises in the remarks of Schücking, *Dichterbuch.*

4. Thorpe, ed., *Codex exoniensis, A Collection of Anglo-Saxon Poetry* (London: Society of Antiquaries of London, 1842), p. 527.

5. Schücking, *Dichterbuch*, p. 17. Clifford Davidson, "Erotic 'Women's Songs' in Anglo-Saxon England," *Neophilologus* 59 (1975):459 and n. 42, calls *Wulf and Eadwacer* "one of the summits of Anglo-Saxon poetry" because of the presumed emotional power of its outcries. Imelmann, *Forschungen*, p. 91, attempts to emend l. 13a for the sake of metrical regularity, but Ernst Sieper, *Die altenglische Elegie* (Strassburg: Trübner, 1915), p. 181, argues against emendation. I do not know whether the vocal annoyance I once heard has yet been put into writing.

6. "*Deor* and *Wulf and Eadwacer:* Some Conjectures," *MÆ* 31 (1962):161–75.

7. Bosworth-Toller, *ofergan;* C. W. M. Grein, *Sprachschatz der angelsächsischen Dichter*, unter Mitw. v. F. Holthausen, neu hrsg. v. J. J. Köhler (Heidelberg: Carl Winter's Universitätsbuchhandlung, 1912), *ofer-eode, ofer-gangan.*

8. Motifs of the cock (and hen) also known to the poet of Riddles 42/43 are found in Pliny, *Natural History*, 10:xxv; Stith Thompson (Bloomington: Indiana University Press, 1955–58), B251. 1 2. 1; N543. 2; V211. 7. 1; K2061. 7; E732. 3; Z32. 1. 1; Gertrude Jobes, *Dictionary of Mythology, Folklore, and Symbols*, vol. 1 (New York: Scarecrow Press, 1962), s.v. *cock* and *hen;* Hanns Bachtold-Stäubli, *Handwörterbuch des deutschen Aberglaubens* vol. 3 (Berlin u. Leipzig: de Gruyter, 1930–31), "Hahn" 3, 6, 11, 12, and vol. 4 (1932), "Huhn"; Maria Leach and Jerome Fried, eds., *Funk and Wagnalls Standard Dictionary for Folklore, Mythology, and Legend* (New York:

Funk and Wagnalls, 1972), s.v. *cock;* and Beryl Rowland, *Birds with Human Souls: A Guide to Bird Symbolism* (Knoxville: University of Tennessee Press, 1978), pp. 20–21, 23–24, 25–27.

9. The possible solutions of the runes DNLH in Riddle 75 as *hælend* and of Riddle 76 as "hen" are by W. S. Mackie, ed., *The Exeter Book, Part II, Poems IX–XXXII,* EETS, o. s. 194 (London: EETS, 1934; reprint ed. 1958), p. 242. See also George Philip Krapp and Elliott Van Kirk Dobbie, eds., *The Exeter Book,* Anglo-Saxon Poetic Records 3 (New York: Columbia University Press, 1936), p. 371, n. on Riddles 75 and 76. This latter edition is hereafter cited as *ASPR 3.*

10. The OED, s.v. *Purple,* cites this meaning beginning in the 1590s. Perhaps because OE *wurma* "purple" (dye made from a snail, etc: see esp. Grein, *Sprachschatz*) did not survive, this OE instance of *purple* meaning "blood" has escaped general notice.

11. Grubl, *Elegien,* pp. 163–67; Ruth P. M. Lehmann, "The Metrics and Structure of 'Wulf and Eadwacer,'" *PQ* 48 (1969):151–65, esp. p. 163. Less successful attempts to identify *Wulf and Eadwacer* with specific Norse poems have been made by Imelmann and also by Bouman, *Patterns,* pp. 95–106.

12. *ASPR* 3, p. 320, reviews the various emendations of MS *earne* in older scholarship. Many scholars, including Martin Lehnert, ed., *Poetry and Prose of the Anglo-Saxons* (Berlin: Deutscher Verlag der Wissenschaften, 1955), 1:24, and Lehmann, "Metrics and Structure," pp. 162, 164, emend to or accept *ear[m]ne.* Possibly the poet had in mind a gnomic idea: *Wulf sceal in bearwe, earm anhaga* (Cotton *Gnomes* 18). See also discussion and n. 26, below.

13. Bosworth-Toller gives *mæring* as "a plant name," but notes that Oswald Cockayne, ed., *Leechdoms, Wortcunning, and Starcraft of Early England,* Rolls Series, 3 vols. (London: Longman, Green, Longman, Roberts, and Green, 1864–66), 3:2, 21, suggests "sweet basil" from context.

14. See T. Northcote Toller, *Supplement to An Anglo-Saxon Dictionary* (Oxford: Clarendon, 1921), s.v. *Mæðhild.* The widely various readings and emendations of MS *mæð hilde* may be traced in Grein, *Sprachschatz,* under *mæð,* and also in *Bibliothek der angelsächsischen Poesie* (Göttingen: Georg H. Wigand, 1857), 1:250; Mackie, *The Exeter Book, Part II,* pp. 82–83; Sieper, *Elegie,* pp. 125, 156–57; Kemp Malone, "On *Deor* 14–17," in *Studies in Heroic Legend and in Current Speech by Kemp Malone,* ed. Stefan Einarsson and Norman E. Eliason (Copenhagen: Rosenkilde & Bagger, 1959), pp. 142–58; Malone, ed., *Deor,* Methuen's Old English Library A2 (London: Methuen, 1933), pp. 8–9 and 37 n. 1; Malone, "An Anglo-Latin Version of the Hjaðningavíg," *Speculum* 39 (1964):35–44; Malone, "The Tale of Geat and Maeðhild," *ES* 19 (1937):193–99; Malone, "Maeðhild," *ELH* 3 (1936):253–56; F. Norman, "Deor: A Criticism and an Interpretation," *MLR* 22 (1937):374–81; Norman, "Deor and Modern Scandinavian Ballads," *London Mediaeval Studies* 1, no. 2 (1937–39):165–78; Thorpe, ed., *Codex exoniensis,* p. 378; R. K. Gordon, trans., *Anglo-Saxon Poetry,* rev. ed., Everyman's Library 794 (New York: Dutton, 1954), p. 71; R. W. Chambers, *Widsith: A Study in Old English Heroic Legend* (Cambridge: Cambridge University Press, 1912), pp. 21 ff; R. M. Wilson, *The Lost Literature of Medieval England* (London: Methuen, 1952), p. 25; and in numerous other places.

15. See Chambers, *Widsith,* pp. 101, 104; Malone, "An Anglo-Latin Version of Hjaðningavíg," pp. 36–38.

16. Felix Liebermann, *Die Gesetze der Angelsachsen* (Berlin: Savigny-Stiftung, 1906; reprint ed. 1960) 2:80–81, under *freo;* and (1903; reprint ed. 1960), 1:128 ("Ælfred und Guthrum" 5). Sieper, *Elegie,* pp. 157–58, follows older scholarship in reading *frige* of *Deor* 15 as "Freien," *homines liberi, viri ingenui, proceres*—i.e., men of some kind rather than "loves, affections," etc. The legal meaning of *frige* then perfectly fits Deor's riddlic touch.

17. Malone, "On *Deor* 14–17," pp. 146–47, rightly finds no evidence for Grein's and Mackie's assumption of a neuter OE noun corresponding to ON *meiða.* But Bosworth-Toller and Toller, *Supplement,* give good OE and MHG authority for a neuter noun *mæð* "mowing, hay-harvest."

18. On the peculiar grammar of *Deor* 16 the best brief review is still *ASPR* 3:319n.

19. Bosworth-Toller; Grein, *Sprachschatz;* P. Holthausen, *Altenglisches etymologisches Wörterbuch* (Heidelberg: Carl Winter's Universitätsbuchhandlung, 1934); J. R. Clark Hall, *A Concise Anglo-Saxon Dictionary,* 4th ed. with Supp. by Herbert D. Meritt (Cambridge: Cambridge University Press, 1931), all s.v. *lac.* The difficulties that l. 1 (and the poem as a whole) has presented in scholarship may be deduced from Imelmann, *Forschungen,* pp. 100–105; Lehmann, "Metrics and Structure," p. 157; and from comparison of several full translations: by Henry Bradley in Kennedy, *The Earliest English Poetry,* p. 49; Malone, "Two English *Frauenlieder,*" in *Studies in Old English Literature in Honor of Arthur G. Brodeur,* ed. Stanley B. Greenfield (Eugene: University of Oregon Press, 1963), p. 108 (prose); Malone, *Ten Old English Poems Put into Modern English Alliterative Verse* (Baltimore, Md.: Johns Hopkins, 1941), p. 21 (poetic); Mackie, ed., *The Exeter Book, Part II,* p. 87; Adams, "'Wulf and Eadwacer': An Interpretation," p. 5; Burton Raffel, *Poems from the Old English,* 2d ed. (Lincoln: University of Nebraska Press, 1964), p. 64; Bouman, *Patterns,* p. 105; Gordon, *Anglo-Saxon Poetry,* rev. ed., p. 81; Sieper, *Elegie,* pp. 179–82 *passim* and p. 275; Lehmann, "Metrics and Structure," 164.

20. On *apecgan,* see the various renderings in the translations (n. 19, above); Imelmann, *Forschungen,* pp. 82–85; Schofield, "Signy's Lament," p. 266; Lehmann, "Metrics and Structure," p. 158. The meaning of *apecgan,* however, seems best deduced from the various dictionary entries for *(a-)pecgan, picgan, gepecgan, ofpecgan, gepywan, gepewan,* etc.

21. For the type of (rare) versification perhaps involved in *Wulf and Eadwacer* 9b, see, for example, A. J. Bliss, *An Introduction to Old English Metre* (Oxford: Basil Blackwell, 1962), pp. 15–16, 30. On the single occurrence of OE *docgena,* gen. pl. of *docga,* see Herbert D. Meritt, *Fact and Lore about Old English Words,* Stanford University Publications in Language and Literature 13 (Stanford: Stanford University Press, 1954), p. 123, par. 4. For the history of (unconvincing) emendation of MS *dogode* to *hogode* see Imelmann, *Forschungen,* p. 86; and Bosworth-Toller, reversed by Toller, *Supplement,* and Alstair Campbell, *Addenda and Corrigenda to An Anglo-Saxon Dictionary* (Oxford: Clarendon Press, 1972). The MED has *dogged, doggedli, doggedlice,* all possible evidence of an unrecorded verb *dogge(n),* from OE **do(c)gian.* For early sixteenth-century citations of "to dog" as "to follow or pursue" (usually with stealth or malicious intent), see the OED, s.v. *Dog v.*

22. Max Förster, *Keltisches Wortgut im Englischen* (Halle: Max Niemeyer, 1921), p. 18 (ae *hogg* oder **hocg*) documents ME variants *hogge, hoge,* and suggests that *dog,* like *hog,* was originally a Celtic loanword. See also Thomas Wright, *Old English Vocabularies,* ed. Richard Wülcker, 2 vols. (London: Trübner, 1883–84), 1:698, 36–37; 1:758, 18–19; 1:611, 35 for ME spellings *hoge, hoggeshere.*

23. Johannes Hoops, *Reallexikon der germanischen Altertumskunde* (Strassburg: Trübner, 1911–19), 3:460 ff. ("Raubehe"), finds only elopements, and no forcible rapes, as Germanic literary themes.

24. Germanic sources themselves do not entirely sustain Tacitus's (or some modern scholars') enthusiastic description of the dignity and respect given to Germanic women. Cf. the laws of Æthelberht of Kent, which provide monetary compensations and fines for injuries done to women by beating, seduction, and possibly even rape, but do not expressly forbid such treatment. See Liebermann, *Gesetze,* 2:ii, "Eheschliessung," for review of women's elaborately defined (but also thereby restricted) freedoms in the English marriage codes. Two other important studies on the question of Germanic women's status are Gerda Merschberger, *Die Rechtsstellung der germanischen Frau,* Mannus-Bücherei, vol. 57 (Leipzig: Curt Rabitzsch, 1937) and Reinhold Bruder, *Die germanische Frau im Lichte der Runeninschriften und der antiken Historiographie,* Quellen und Forschungen zur Sprach- und Kulturgeschichte der germanischen Völker, vol. 57 (Berlin: de Gruyter, 1974). For extreme modern acceptance of Tacitus's view of respected Germanic women and their "companionable" marriages, see Hilda Ellis Davidson, *Gods and Myths of Northern Europe* (Harmondsworth: Penguin Books, 1964), p. 10; but for equally overstated opposition to Tacitus's view see John Thrupp, *The Anglo-*

Saxon Home: A History of the Domestic Institutions and Customs of England, from the fifth to the eleventh century (London: Longman, Green, Longman, and Roberts, 1862), p. 21.

25. On the legal meaning of *folgað*, see R. F. Leslie, ed., *Three Old English Elegies: The Wife's Lament, The Husband's Message, The Ruin* (Manchester: Manchester University Press, 1961), p. 7; and Liebermann, *Gesetze*, II, ii, 425 (*Gefolge* 9b); 1:165 (*II Æthelstan* 25, 1); 3:107 n. 3. On *londryht*, see Murray L. Markland, "*Deor: þæs ofereode, þisses swa mæg*," *AN & Q* 11, no. 3 (1972):35; Grein, *Sprachschatz*; and Liebermann, *Gesetze*, II, i, 131. By picking legal words, Deor is perhaps grasping for a legal basis for his complaint.

26. Adams, "'Wulf and Eadwacer': An Interpretation," p. 5, takes *earne hwelp* as "eaglet," without explanation and with no apparent concern for the mixed metaphor in the phrase "eagle's whelp." But another awkward pun of the type *earne, ear[m]ne* might be lurking in Riddle 50, which hides the answer "pen and fingers" amid imagery of birds, breezes, and waves: possibly, then, MS *fleotgan*, l. 4b, an otherwise unknown word, is a hybrid of *fleogan* and *fleotan*. If, as I have already suggested, there is concealed sarcasm in the rhetorical contrast of *eadwacer* and *ear[m]ne*, possibly the play is on the (legal) alliterative *earm ond eadig*, L. *dives et pauper:* see Liebermann, *Gesetze*, II, i, 57 (*eadig* 3). See also n. 12, above, for a possible gnomic reference for *ear[m]ne*.

27. Bosworth-Toller, under *wearg*. Grein, *Sprachschatz*, under *wearg, wearh, werg*, also gives 1. *Wolf;* 2. *geächteter friedloser Verbrecher*.

28. I am now preparing studies on previously unknown East Anglian material among the Exeter Book riddles, including concealed narratives of St. Edmund and St. Guthlac.

29. Craig Williamson, ed., *The Old English Riddles of the Exeter Book* (Chapel Hill: University of North Carolina Press, 1977), p. 276, thinks (apparently along with most other editors) that Riddles 42/43 and 46/47 were joined by "a similar [scribal] mistake." For reasons advanced here and in other studies now in circulation, I think both pairs of texts were deliberately rather than mistakenly joined.

30. I am now following this compromise as I prepare a book-length edition and commentary of this and one other riddlic sequence. The study is provisionally titled *Two Long Allegorical Riddles of the Old English Exeter Book*.

31. R. W. Chambers, "Modern Study of the Poetry of the Exeter Book," in Chambers, Max Förster, and Robin Flower, eds., *The Exeter Book of Old English Poetry* (London: Dean and Chapter of Exeter Cathedral, 1933), p. 34. This is the MS photofacsimile edition of the Exeter Book. The words *mighty scholar* are Chambers's. Chambers also discusses and lists the eight runic passages that Hickes is known to have marked in pencil for his copyist: see p. 34 and n. 9. One of the copied passages, still preserved in Exeter Cathedral Library, is an astonishingly faithful counterfeit of the original.

Contributors

JAMES E. ANDERSON is currently on the faculty of Vanderbilt University. He has published essays on *The Husband's Message* and *The Wife's Lament,* and he is completing a study of The Exeter Book that incorporates the material on *Deor, Wulf and Eadwacer,* and *The Soul's Address* included in this volume.

MARTIN GREEN is a professor of English at Fairleigh Dickinson University (Florham-Madison Campus) and editor-in-chief of *The Literary Review,* a quarterly of fiction, poetry, and criticism. His papers on Old English poetry have appeared in *JEGP* and *PLL,* and he has written essays and reviews on modern literature in a number of periodicals.

JOSEPH HARRIS is a professor of English at Cornell University and he has taught previously at Harvard and Stanford. His essays on Old English and Old Norse have appeared in *Scandinavian Studies, NM, PQ, Harvard English Studies,* and *Archiv für nordisk Filologi,* and he is a contributor to *The Dictionary of the Middle Ages* (ACLS), the Festschrift for Albert Lord (Slavica Press/University of Ohio), and *The Vikings,* ed. Robert Farrell (Phillimore). In 1971 he won the Elliott Prize of the Medieval Academy of America.

IDA MASTERS HOLLOWELL has published essays on Old English prose style, Old English prosody, and the Old English wisdom tradition in *JEGP, PQ, SP, ES* and *Neophilologus.* She is at present an associate professor of English at the University of Arkansas at Little Rock.

WILLIAM C. JOHNSON, Jr., is an associate professor of English at Lewis-Clark State College (Idaho) where he teaches writing and linguistics. He has published in *PQ* and *Chaucer Review* and has completed a book-length study of *Beowulf.*

ROY F. LESLIE, a professor of English at the University of Victoria (British Columbia), is the editor of *Three Old English Elegies* and *The Wanderer* (Manchester University Press). Along with G. L. Brook, he has also edited La3amon's *Brut*. His other publications include articles on Old English style, *Seasons for Fasting*, and Riddle 60.

JANEMARIE LUECKE is a professor of English at Oklahoma State University and a Benedictine nun of Red Plains Priory, Oklahoma City. She is the author of *Measuring Old English Rhythm*, articles on literary criticism, prosody, and feminist theory, and a volume of poems. She is currently at work on a book on the prosody of free verse and doing research on Anglo-Saxon nuns.

MARIE NELSON is an associate professor of English at the University of Florida. She has published essays on Old and Middle English poetry and on modern Arthurian fiction in *Speculum, Neophilologus, NM, Language and Style,* and *Mythlore.* She has served as secretary-treasurer of the Southeast Medieval Association.

MARIJANE OSBORN studied Old English at Stanford and Oxford and has taught on both sides of the Atlantic. She is currently on the faculty of the University of California at Davis. She has been a Senior Fulbright Fellow in Iceland and a Fellow of the Institute for Advanced Studies in the Humanities at Edinburgh University. Her publications include essays on the Old English elegies and two books, *Beowulf: A Verse Translation with Treasures from the Ancient North* and *Rune Games* (with Stella Longland).

BURTON RAFFEL studied medieval language and literature with Morton Bloomfield and F. L. Utley. *Poems from the Old English,* his first book in the field, appeared in 1960, followed by his translations of *Beowulf* (1963) and *Sir Gawain and the Green Knight* (1970). His most recent translation is *The Essential Horace.* Mr. Raffel writes and reviews widely on both Old and Middle English and he is currently a professor of English at the University of Denver.

ALAIN RENOIR is a professor of English at the University of California, Berkeley, where he teaches medieval English and the history of the English language. He has published *The Poetry of John Lydgate*, the Lydgate section of the *Manual of Writings in Middle English* (in cooperation with C. David Benson), and various essays on medieval literature.

RAYMOND P. TRIPP, Jr., a professor of English at the University of Denver, has written books on Chaucer, Thoreau's *Walden*, and structural linguistics, and articles on various literary topics ranging from medieval literature to pedagogical problems.

Elegy Scholarship 1973–82:
A Select Bibliography

This bibliography contains a list of major studies done since the compilation of Greenfield and Robinson's *Bibliography of Publications on Old English to the end of 1972* (See below, section 1). Entries for 1982 are based on a selective check of major journals publishing OE studies.

M.G.

I. BIBLIOGRAPHY TO 1972

Beale, Walter A. *Old and Middle English Poetry to 1500: A Guide to Information Services.* Detroit: Gale Research, 1976. [Lists basic items]

Greenfield, Stanley B. and Fred C. Robinson. *A Bibliography of Publications on Old English Literature to the end of 1972.* Toronto: University of Toronto Press, 1980.

Knapp, William Bruce. "Bibliography of the Criticism of the Old English Elegies." *Comitatus* 2 (1971):71–90. [Bibliography through mid-1970.]

II. EDITIONS

Thorpe, Benjamin, ed. *Codex Exoniensis: A Collection of Anglo-Saxon Poetry.* London: Society of Antiquaries, 1842; reprinted New York: AMS Press, 1975.

III. GENERAL STUDIES

Anderson, James, E. "Strange Sad Voices: The Portraits of Germanic Women in the Old English Exeter Book." *DAI* 39 (1979):6752A.

Blake, Norman F. *The English Language in Medieval Literature.* London: J. M. Dent; Totowa, N.J.: Rowman and Littlefield, 1977. [Contains discussion of *Wanderer* and *Seafarer*]

Calder, Daniel G., ed. *Old English Poetry: Essays on Style*. Berkeley and Los Angeles: University of California Press, 1979.

———— and Michael J. B. Allen, eds. *Sources and Analogues of Old English Poetry: The Major Latin Sources in Translation*. Cambridge: D. S. Brewer; Totowa, N.J.: Rowman and Littlefield, 1976.

Conner, Patrick Wayne. "A Contextual Study of the Old English *Exeter Book*." *DAI* 36 (1975):3647A.

Cunningham, J. S. " 'Where Are They?': The After-Life of a Figure of Speech." *Proceedings of the British Academy* 65 (1979):369–94.

Goldman, Stephen A. "The Use of Christian Belief in Old English Poems of Exile." *Res Publica Litterarum: Studies in Classical Tradition* 2 (1979):69–80.

Grant, Raymond J. S. "*Beowulf* and the World of Heroic Elegy." *Leeds Studies in English* 8 (1975): 45–75.

Grose, M. W. and Deirdre McKenna. *Old English Literature*. Totowa, N.J.: Rowman and Littlefield, 1973.

Holoka, James P. "The Oral Formula and the Anglo-Saxon Elegy: Some Misgivings." *Neophilologus* 60 (1976):570–76.

Hume, Kathryn. The Concept of the Hall in Old English Poetry." *Anglo-Saxon England* 3 (1974):63–74.

————. "The 'Ruin Motif' in OE Poetry." *Anglia* 94 (1976):339–60.

Jensen, Emily R. "Narrative Voice in OE Lyric Poetry." *DAI* 33 (1973):3587A. [Discusses *Wand., Seaf., WL, WE.*]

Lally, Tim D. P. "Synchronic vs. Diachronic: Popular Culture Studies and the OE Elegy." In *5000 Years of Popular Culture: Popular Culture Before Printing*, edited by Fred E. H. Schroeder. Bowling Green, Ohio: Popular Culture Press, 1980.

Raw, Barbara C. *The Art and Background of Old English Poetry*. London: Edward Arnold, 1978.

Stanley, E. G. *The Search for Anglo-Saxon Paganism*. Cambridge: D. S. Brewer; Totowa, N.J.: Rowman and Littlefield, 1974.

Tripp, Raymond P., Jr. "The Effect of the Occult and the Supernatural on the Way We Read OE Poetry." In *Literature and the Occult: Essays in Comparative Literature*, edited by Luanne Frank. Arlington, Tex.: University of Texas at Arlington, 1977.

Webb, Suzanne S. "Imagery Patterns and Pagan Substructures: An Exploration of Structural Motifs in Five OE Elegies." *DAI* 33 (1973):3606A [*HM, WE, WL, Deor, Ruin*]

Wilson, James H. *Christian Theology and OE Poetry*. The Hague: Mouton, 1974.

IV. INDIVIDUAL POEMS

A. *Deor*

Boren, James L. "The Design of the OE *Deor*." In *Anglo-Saxon Poetry: Essays in Appreciation for John C. McGaillard,* edited by Lewis Nicholson and Dolores Warwick Frese. Notre Dame, Ind.: University of Notre Dame, 1976. Pp. 264–76. [Hereafter cited as *ASP*.]

Condren, Edward I. "'Deor's' Artistic Triumph." *Studies in Philology* 78 (1981):62–76.

Kiernan, Kevin. "*Deor:* The Consolation of an Anglo-Saxon Boethius." *Neuphilologische Mitteilungen* 79 (1978):333–40.

———. "A Solution to the Mæthhild-Geat Crux in *Deor*." *English Studies* 56 (1975):97–99.

Malone, Kemp. "The Rhythm of *Deor*." In *Old English Studies in Honor of John C. Pope,* edited by Robert B. Burlin and Edward B. Irving, Jr. Toronto: University of Toronto, 1974. [Hereafter cited as Pope Studies.]

Mandel, Jerome. "Exemplum and Refrain: The Meaning of *Deor*." *Yearbook of English Studies* 7 (1977):1–9.

Rubin, Gary I. "A Rhetorical Analysis of *Deor, The Ruin,* and *The Wanderer*." *DAI* 35 (1975):6680A.

Tuggle, Thomas. "The Structure of *Deor*." *Studies in Philology* 74 (1977):229–42.

B. *Husband's Message*

Anderson, Earl R. "*The Husband's Message:* Persuasion and the Problem of *Genyre*." *English Studies* 56 (1975):289–94.

———. "Voices in *The Husband's Message*." *NM* 74 (1973):238–46.

Anderson, James E. "Die Deutungmöglichkeiten des altenglischen Gedichtes *The Husband's Message*." *NM* 75 (1974):402–7.

Goldsmith, Margaret E. "The Enigma of *The Husband's Message*." *ASP*. Pp. 242–63.

Orton, Peter. "The Speaker in *The Husband's Message*." *Leeds Studies in English* 12 (1981):43–56.

Renoir, Alain. "The Least Elegiac of the Elegies: A Contextual Glance at *The Husband's Message*." *Studia Neophilologica* 53 (1981):69–76.

Thundyil, Zacharias. "The Sanskrit *Meghaduta* and the OE *Husband's Message*." *Michigan Academician* 8 (1976):457–67.

C. *Resignation*

Berkhout, Carl T. "The Speaker in *Resignation:* A Biblical Note." *Notes and Queries* 21 (1974):122–23.

Bestul, Thomas H. "The Old English *Resignation* and the Benedictine Reform." *NM* 78 (1977):18–23.

Bliss, Alan and Allen J. Frantzen. "The Integrity of *Resignation*." *Review of English Studies* 27 (1976):387–402.

D. *The Ruin*

Johnson, William C., Jr. "*The Ruin* as Body-City Riddle." *Philological Quarterly* 59 (1980):397–411.

Lee, Anne T. "*The Ruin:* Bath or Babylon." *NM* 74 (1973):443–55.

Marsteller, Daniel F. "An OE Poem: *The Ruin:* A Study of Exegesis and a Reappraisal." *Bulletin of the West Virginia College English Teachers* 5 (1979):1–11.

Rubin, Gary I. "MS Integrity, Lines 3a–4b of *The Ruin*." *Neophilologus* 63 (1979):277–97.

Talentino, Arnold. "Moral Irony in *The Ruin*." *Papers on Language and Literature* 14 (1978):3–10.

Wentersdorf, Karl P. "Observations on *The Ruin*." *Medium Ævum* 46 (1977):171–80.

E. *The Seafarer*

Arngart, O. "*The Seafarer:* A Postscript." *English Studies* 60 (1979):247–53.

Bosse, Roberta Bux. "Aural Aesthetic and the Unity of *The Seafarer*." *PLL* 9 (1973):3–14.

Campbell, A. P. "*The Seafarer:* Wanderlust and Our Heavenly Home." *Revue de la Université de Ottawa* 43 (1973):235–47.

Davenport, W. A. "The Modern Reader and the OE *Seafarer*." *PLL* 10 (1974):227–40.

Green, Brian K. "*Spes Viva:* Structure and Meaning in *The Seafarer*." In *An English Miscellany Presented to W. S. Mackie,* edited by Brian S. Lee. Cape Town: Oxford University Press, 1977. Pp. 28–45.

Greenfield, Stanley B. "*Sylf,* Seasons, Structure, and Genre in *The Seafarer*." *ASE* 9 (1981):199–211.

Horgan, A. D. "The Structure of *The Seafarer*." *Review of English Studies* 30 (1979):41–49.

Hultin, Neil. "The External Soul in *The Seafarer* and *The Wanderer*." *Folklore* 88 (1977):39–45.

Mandel, Jerome. "*The Seafarer*." *NM* 77 (1976):538–51.

Moore, Bruce. "Author Unknown: *The Seafarer* 11.1–8a." *Explicator* 35 (1976):11–12.

Orton, Peter R. "*The Seafarer* 58–64a." *Neophilologus* 66 (1982):450–59.

Osborn, Marijane. "Venturing upon Deep Waters in *The Seafarer*." *NM* 79 (1978):1–6.

Pope, John C. "Second Thoughts on the Interpretation of *The Seafarer*." *ASE* 3 (1974):75–86.

Shields, John C. "*The Seafarer* as a *Meditatio*." *Studia Mystica* 3 (1980):29–41.

F. *The Wanderer*

Brown, George Hardin. "An Iconographic Explanation of *The Wanderer*, Lines 81b–82a." *Viator* 9 (1978):31–38.

Clark, Susan L. and Julian N. Wasserman. "The Imagery of *The Wanderer*." *Neophilologus* 63 (1979):291–96.

Cornell, Muriel Anne. "Paths of Exile: A Stylistic Analysis of *The Wanderer* and *The Seafarer*." *DAI* 36 (1976):7434A.

Frankis, P. J. "The Thematic Significance of *enta geweorc* and Related Imagery in *The Wanderer*." *ASE* 2 (1973):253–69.

Green, Brian K. "The Twilight Kingdom: Structure and Meaning in *The Wanderer*." *Neophilologus* 60 (1976):442–51.

Green, Martin. "Man, Time, and Apocalypse in *The Wanderer, The Seafarer*, and *Beowulf*." *JEGP* 74 (1975):502–18.

Howlett, D. R. "The Structure of *The Wanderer* and *The Seafarer*." *Studia Neophilologica* 47 (1975):313–17.

Kintgen, Eugene R. "Wordplay in *The Wanderer*." *Neophilologus* 59 (1975):119–27.

Klein, William. "Purpose and the 'Poetics' of *The Wanderer* and *The Seafarer*." *ASP*. Pp. 208–23.

Lally, Tim D. P. "The Emotive Diction and Structure of the OE *Wanderer*." *DAI* 41 (1981):4043A.

Malmberg, Lars. "Poetic Originality in *The Wanderer* and *The Seafarer*." *NM* 74 (1973):220–23.

Millns, Tony. "*The Wanderer* 98: *Weal Wundrum Heah, Wyrmlicum Fah*." *Review of English Studies* 28 (1977):431–38.

Mullen, Karen. "*The Wanderer:* Considered Again." *Neophilologus* 58 (1974):74–81.

Osborn, Marijane. "Classical Meditation in *The Wanderer.*" *Comparison* [University of Warwick] 1 (1975):67–101.

———. "Toward the Contemplative in *The Wanderer.*" *Studia Mystica* 1 (1978):53–69. [Revised version of previous item.]

———. "The Vanishing Seabirds in *The Wanderer.*" *Folklore* 85 (1974):122–27.

Ray, T. J. "*The Wanderer* 78–84." *South Central Bulletin* 38 (1978):157–59.

Spolsky, Ellen. "Semantic Structure of *The Wanderer.*" *Journal of Literary Semantics* 2 (1974):101–19.

Wentersdorf, Karl P. "*The Wanderer:* Notes on Some Semantic Problems." *Neophilologus* 59 (1975):287–92.

Woolf, Rosemary. "*The Wanderer, The Seafarer,* and the Genre of *Planctus.*" *ASP.* Pp. 192–207.

G. *The Wife's Lament*

Ellis, Deborah. "*The Wife's Lament* in the Context of Early English Literature: The Paralysis of Desertion." *Journal of Women's Studies in Literature* 1 (1979):220–32.

Harris, Joseph. "A Note on *eorðscræf/ eorðsele* and Current Interpretations of *The Wife's Lament.*" *English Studies* 58 (1977):204–8.

Howlett, D. R. "*The Wife's Lament* and *The Husband's Message.*" *NM* 79 (1978):7–11.

Renoir, Alain. "Christian Inversion in *The Wife's Lament.*" *Studia Neophilologica* 49 (1977):19–24.

———. "A Reading Context for *The Wife's Lament.*" *ASP.* Pp. 224–41.

———. "A Reading of *The Wife's Lament.*" *English Studies* 58 (1977):4–19.

Straus, Barrie Ruth. "Women's Words as Weapons: Speech as Action in *The Wife's Lament.*" *Texas Studies in Language and Literature* 23 (1981):268–85.

Wentersdorf, Karl P. "The Situation of the Narrator in the OE *Wife's Lament.*" *Speculum* 56 (1981):492–516.

H. *Wulf and Eadwacer*

Baker, Peter S. "The Ambiguity of '*Wulf and Eadwacer.*'" *Studies in Philology* 78 (1981):39–51.

Davidson, Arnold E. "Interpreting *Wulf and Eadwacer.*" *Annuale Medievale* 16 (1975):24–32.

Eliason, Norman E. "On *Wulf and Eadwacer.*" Pope Studies. Pp. 225–34.

Fanagan, John M. "*Wulf and Eadwacer:* A Solution to the Critics' Riddle." *Neophilologus* 60 (1976):130–37.

Jensen, Emily. "Narrative Voice in the Old English *Wulf and Eadwacer.*" *Chaucer Review* 13 (1979):373–83.

Mattox, Wesley S. "Encirclement and Sacrifice in *Wulf and Eadwacer.*" *Annuale Medievale* 16 (1975):33–40.

Spanier, James B. "The Marriage Concept in *Wulf and Eadwacer.*" *Neophilologus* 62 (1978):143–44.